PILGRIM OF LOVE

PILGRIM OF LOVE

The Life and Teachings of Swami Kripalu

COMPILED AND EDITED
BY
ATMA JO ANN LEVITT

MONKFISH BOOK PUBLISHING COMPANY
RHINEBECK, NEW YORK

Library of Congress Cataloging-in-Publication Data

Levitt, Atma Jo Ann.
 Pilgrim of Love : the life and teachings of Swami Kripalu/compiled and edited by
Atma Jo Ann Levitt.
     p. cm.
 Includes bibliographical references.
 ISBN 0-9749359-3-X
1. Kripalvanandji, Swami, 1913-1981. 2. Yogis--India--Biography. 3. Religious life--
Hinduism. 4. Ku~n~linŒi. I.Kripalvanandji, Swami, 1913-1981. II. Title.
 BL 1175.K68L38 2004
 294.5'092-dc22
                            2004008764
Portions from "Infinite Grace: The Story of my Spiritual Lineage" by Swami
Rajarshi Muni have been reprinted with kind permission from LIFE MISSION
Organization, RBG Complex, Vadodara-390018, Gujarat, India.

Swami Kripalu's speeches, darshan, and biographical materials provided through
Kripalu Center archives, Lenox, MA.

Closing Bhajan Prayer: "Guru Mara" and "Hare Ekvara Nirakho..." lyrics available
courtesy of Satyam Shivam Sundaram, Kripalu Muni Mandal, Malav, 389310, India.

Book and cover design by Georgia Dent

Bulk Purchase discounts for educational or promotional purposes are available.
Contact the publisher for more information.

First Edition

First Impression

10 9 8 7 6 5 4 3 2 1

Monkfish Book Publishing Company
27 Lamoree Road
Rhinebeck, New York 12572

To pilgrims of every path,
and especially those willing to be fools for love.

CONTENTS

PHOTO CREDITS

Swami Kripalu (Bapuji) in India

PREFACE

The bulk of this work is a compilation of talks given by Swami Kripalu throughout North America. Bapuji, or "dear father," as we lovingly called him, taught at the Kripalu Ashrams in Pennsylvania while visiting the United States between 1977 and 1981. Along with speeches in North America, this work also includes excerpts from speeches he gave in India for visiting residents and disciples, plus portions of his letters to Yogi Amrit Desai, Dinesh Majmundar, and other close disciples. In addition to Bapuji's self-narrated life stories and discourses on yogic principles, this work contains commentary from disciples who studied with him, reflecting a different aspect of his achievements and influence.

For more than thirty years Bapuji practiced intensive yoga sadhana or spiritual practice. Part of that practice included a commitment to silence. Although he may not have spoken, he generally wrote his speeches on a slate or sheath of papers, which were then translated from his native Gujarati into English by Yogi Amrit Desai, Swami Vinit Muni or other assistants. Since he broke his customary silence for the first few months of his stay in the U.S., we were fortunate to hear him speak at first and then receive the translations. Later he remained in silence except during major celebrations. Some of this text's inconsistencies may be due to the varied or incomplete translations that we received and the difficulty conveying certain yogic concepts cross-culturally.

Although I've tried to make Bapuji's prose more accessible through light editing, I've stayed close to the original translations wherever possible. Since the Indian style of speechmaking may ring formal to our western ears and since Bapuji spent so much time in silence, there are times when his language takes on a serious, ponderous tone. But that's not always the case and certainly, he—more than anyone—knew when comic relief was due.

Throughout the discourses I've chosen not to change his predominant use of male pronouns in favor of inclusive language. It was not a convention of his time. Keep in mind that Bapuji saw us all—male and female—as seekers and in his life and practice as a swami he largely had transcended gender issues. Thus we can allow "he" and "him" to translate as "we" and "us."

Above all, Bapuji refers to himself as a pilgrim on the path of love. If we were to follow him on this path, he would entreat us to study the tenets of eternal religion (sanatana dharma) so that in our lives we may experience the whole world as one family (vasudhaiva kutumbakam).

ACKNOWLEDGMENTS

ALTHOUGH BAPUJI was a master of kundalini yoga who spent long periods in silence, when he did speak he provided numerous details of his life's journey. In truth I feel more like a quilt-maker, stitching together his anecdotes, as opposed to a biographer.

I want to thank Yoganand Michael Carroll for Chapter Sixteen and for his help in creating a context through which we can experience Bapuji's sadhana directly. For an in-depth description of Yoganand's courses, which include advanced yoga practices, please refer to the Kripalu Program Guide. I thank Charles Hirsch, who's been my close consultant and quilter in conceiving this work. His practiced eye and his gift for words have added color, texture, and depth to this endeavor. For faith in its conception I thank Monkfish editors Paul Cohen and Georgia Dent.

I'm indebted to the contributions of Kripalu Center and its vast archival material, and the teachings of Yogi Amrit Desai and Yogeshwar Muni, who knew him intimately. I'd also like to thank Sant Rajarshi Muni for his inspiration in furthering sanatana dharma in India. He was the first to bring Bapuji's stories to the light.

I'm also indebted to Bapuji's nephew, Shri Dinesh Majmundar, for contributing the Foreword to this book. Dinesh has made it his lifetime mission to preserve and propagate Bapuji's vast musical knowledge and repertoire. Dinesh is a renowned musician, scholar, and former Dean of Music at the Kala Kendra College, now known as the Rama Manubhai College of Music and Dance, in Vallabh Vidyanagar, Gujarat State, India.

I'd also like to acknowledge Bhavani Lorraine Nelson, Adam Mastoon, Sanat Shivdas, Mark Swirsky, Lata Olivia Margaret Woodford, Tom Gillette, and Paul Protzman for help with various stages of production and various incarnations of this work.

For their role in providing inspiration and support, I thank Stephen Cope, Marjory Levitt, Joel Levitt, Ma Indukanta Udasin, Saraladevi Liza Dousson, Yogacharya Yogindradev, Sandip Dennis Konchak, Navin John Panzer, Elizabeth Law, Carol Emanuel, Govinda Ron Dyer, Piyush Stuart Sovatsky, Modini Lila Ivey, Suresh and Subodh Desai, Devanand Christopher Baxter, Vidya Carolyn Dell'uomo, Rambha Suzanne DeWees, and Yogindra Richard Cleaver. Their contributions and support were like adding golden threads to the quilt.

Most of all I'm indebted to the vast Kripalu network stretching from one end of this earth to the other. Many knew Bapuji, and I wish there were room for everyone's story. Although the Kripalu network is invisible in many ways, it continues to spread the light and liveliness of Bapuji's path of love.

FOREWORD

FLYING KITES was one of Bapuji's favorite pastimes when he was young. Early on he was also a great lover of detective stories. In fact, he wrote his own detective novel at the age of seventeen. Later in life he was delighted when two CID agents, India's equivalent to the FBI, came to pay him a visit.

There are many things people don't know about Bapuji. As his nephew and disciple, I was fortunate to know him through the years and to see the many sides of my uncle. For example, most people knew he loved cows dearly and devoted his attention to them. What they may not have known, however, is that he gave each cow a different name, such as Ganga or Saraswati, and when he called that particular cow by name, she would come to him.

In his early years Bapuji worked at many different types of jobs. He was at one time or another an accountant, a composer, a tollbooth operator, a machinist, a bicycle repairman, an actor, a playwright and manager of a drama company, a lecturer, music teacher, and of course a *yogacharya*, or master teacher of yoga.

It would take an average person three or four lifetimes to produce what Bapuji did in one lifetime alone.

Interestingly, Bapuji was a great matchmaker! Who would have thought this swami whose life was dedicated to yoga would be finding husbands for different women, but that was important to him. I myself begged Bapuji to let me study with him and become a monk but he refused. Instead he found me a wife and got me married, saying, "Someone in our family must carry on the musical tradition. You're the one with talent."

Although he was my uncle, more importantly he was my guru, and our tradition is to follow whatever the guru asks of you. So I was appointed guardian of music. From 1935 to 1940 Bapuji ran a music school in Maninagar, a suburb of Ahmedabad, and wrote his definitive three volume work on music, which earned him the title of *Sangeetacharya*, Master of Music. In all he published more than fifty articles on music. His research was considered revolutionary in the world of Indian music.

Many people wonder if Bapuji was ever engaged or married. It so happens that while he was in Ahmedabad, he did get engaged to a lovely woman named Jyoti. However, as time drew near for their wedding, there was some bickering back and forth between her family and his, and conflicts arose over the dowry and marriage arrangements. At the same time he questioned himself, "Am I choosing the right direction?"

In 1941 he fled to Bombay, severing contact with his family as well as that of Jyotibhen. For six months he lived in complete oblivion. Then he left Bombay to travel through the state of Gujarat. Years after he had assumed the robes of the swami, Jyoti appeared in town for one of his darshans and received his blessing, while her mother and family wept. Later, remembering her with fondness, he dedicated his principal work of music to her, entitling it *Raga Jyoti*.

I was so happy to be close to Bapuji and to hear whatever were his musings of the moment. In Ahmedabad I had a chance to study yoga *asana* and *pranayama*, or yogic breathing, directly with him. He was very rigorous and made us learn 220 different types of pranayama. When I balked and asked him how I could possibly put so many different pranayams to use, he replied, "Save them for your next lifetime."

Bapuji told me all the stories of his early years with his guru. He also revealed that earlier he had joined Gandhi's ashram in Ahmedabad and for a period worked with the freedom fighters. Bapuji was sent by Gandhi to help calm tensions in a local village but failed in his mission. When Gandhi arrived at the village and questioned him, evidently Bapuji was said to reply, "Gandhiji, I'm sorry but I'm not a Gandhiji. I cannot tolerate the fighting and violence here." So he was willingly "fired" from his position. From there he traveled south, visiting Pondicherry in search of a guru. He was eighteen at the time.

In his early years he played the tamboura and harmonium so skillfully he could have been a concertmaster. He also did extensive research and wrote about ancient Indian music. After he became a sannyasi, however, he no longer focused on music until his kundalini was awakened. When in 1950 he experienced *anahat nad*, or the emergence of divine inner sounds, his love for music was rekindled. In his research over the next four years, he realized the deep connection between anahat nad and classical music.

Bapuji was so prolific that it is a great pity the world does not have access to more of his work in translation and to the remarkable spirit of his teachings in general. His enormous output of *bhajans* (spiritual songs) alone would serve as great sources of strength, for they give instruction in how to live, how to attune to God and overcome obstacles in sadhana.

Besides his signature work on yoga entitled, *Asana and Mudra*, and the *Science of Meditation*, Bapuji wrote an astounding number of books on the various disciplines of yoga. Unfortunately for the American public, many of his commentaries on scripture have not been translated into English and his final three volumes, *Pilgrimage of Love*, are out of print. For that reason this book fills a significant gap in relaying the essence of his life and teachings.

I too have dedicated my life to preserving Bapuji's heritage, only in the realm of music. Despite assiduous work, there are things that are irretrievably lost. For example, even though I begged Sucharit Muni to preserve the master spool of Bapuji's *dhuns* (repetitive chants) and bhajans recorded during the opening of the Kayavarohan Temple in 1974, somehow it got lost.

In his later years Bapuji seemed resigned to the slights and differences of opinion among his disciples and focused his attention solely on his sadhana. When that became impossible, he traveled to America, where he could distance himself from such conflict. From a brief three-month stay, he extended his time to more than four years in America. Clearly he saw the possibilities for doing sadhana unhindered. He later told me how beautiful the ashram was and how well he was treated by Amrit and Urmila Desai. During that period he interacted a great deal with the ashram residents, clarifying many aspects of yogic practice for them in his speeches and his writings. Most importantly, during that time he finally attained the highest stage of sadhana he'd been longing to complete for so many years.

I received word that he had returned from America in the fall of 1981. When I learned that his health had deteriorated, I rushed my family to Bombay to see him. On December 24th, we arrived at the home where he was staying. There were many people milling about, concerned about his condition. I asked them to tell him Dinesh had arrived and was immediately ushered in.

Bapuji was lying in bed, and he said to me, "Dinesh, I've worshipped God all my life and if he wishes me to surrender this eternal body to him, let him take it. I can't go on much longer like this."

It was his wish to go from there to Ahmedabad and remain in silence. I pleaded with him to let me accompany him and serve him in Ahmedabad but he said, "No, Dinesh, not now."

On the 25th of December I visited him again, and he was still lucid, commenting on events in his life. He said, "This current state of yoga I'm in will subside within fifteen days."

When I learned that his condition had worsened yet again, I visited him in Ahmedabad. It was the 28th of December, and as soon as I saw Bapuji lying in his bed, I broke down and started weeping uncontrollably. I knew his time had come, yet it was hard for me to let him go. He was my most beloved guru and uncle — the source of my life. It was clear to me as I sat meditating by his bed, however, that Bapuji had intentionally turned his soul over to God.

On December 29th Bapuji achieved his final Mahasamadhi and in his sweet state of repose was buried in the manner appropriate to a saint, upright and seated.

For sixteen days following the Mahasamadhi there were ceremonies dedicated to him and a temporary altar was built in the town of Malav that would later become the site of Bapuji's memorial shrine.

Offered by his humble servant,
nephew, and devotee,
Dinesh Majmundar
Baroda, India
1/10/04

Bapaji's nephew:
Dineshchandra Pannalal Majmundar
"Sangeetacharyaratna"

INTRODUCTION

I FIRST LAID EYES on Bapuji in May of 1977. I had been living at Kripalu Ashram in Pennsylvania studying with Yogi Amrit Desai for four years. During that time I stared at a somber picture of Swami Kripalu in the meditation room. I somehow expected him to emerge dour and unsmiling, oblivious to his surroundings. On the contrary, when he arrived I was surprised to find him animated and jolly. The light in his eyes and the energy in his face glowed with excitement. With a smile or the wink of his eye he seemed to make fun of life around him.

How easily he made contact with us, despite the fact that he spoke no English and we spoke no Gujarati. We called him Bapuji, or dear father, though in truth he seemed more like a grandfather to us, who at the time were young adults.

Some twenty-five years have passed since then. Grateful to Yogi Amrit Desai for laying the groundwork, presenting the yogic teachings and finally the master teacher himself — Bapuji — many of us continued experimenting with a yogic lifestyle in Pennsylvania and later in Massachusetts. Today many remain close to Kripalu Center's orbit or have taken up the demands of a more internalized *sahaj* (spontaneous) yoga practice. Others distanced themselves or chose separate paths when evidence of Yogi Desai's abuse of power and sexual exploits surfaced in the nineties. At the same time, the excesses of other prominent spiritual leaders came to light. Having lived through that turmoil, those failings ultimately provided me a deeper understanding not only of human nature, but also of the great difficulty in pursuing a spiritual path with unshakeable virtue. To embody the principles one teaches without compromising, selling out, or giving in is evidently a rare gift. For me, there was total congruence in the experience of Bapuji. His teachings were impeccable because his committment to sadhana was impeccable. Through the years I've discovered the true impact of his visit to America and especially his role in my life. What extraordinary grace to have been in Bapuji's presence, bopped lovingly on the head while bowing (perhaps he rearranged something?) only to wake up years later to the startling realization that he was the true guru and that to him alone I owed my allegiance.

Many of us still practice on yoga mats, zafus, or meditation cushions, longing to transcend ordinary states and experience a deeper level of integration, wisdom, and freedom. Though we may not be ready to forsake everything for a life of *sadhana*, or spiritual practice, we have in his example an embodiment of what is possible. In his life and teachings Bapuji models a synthesis of both human and sublime qualities. My hope is that *Pilgrim of Love* may convey the experience not only of a spiritual seeker, but also of a true master, intent upon liberation.

As Bapuji himself said in one of his early talks, "The life of a great master cannot be described in words. It's like drawing the map of the world on a tiny piece of paper. There's a special character to a great master. He continuously takes on challenges. You might say the difficulties of living defeat him thousands of times, and yet, in the end, he defeats them all. That's why the world bows at his feet. Very few people understand why it's important to have the darshan of a great master. By having his darshan, our intellect becomes purified and pure light enters our being."

Although Bapuji was referring to the life of Buddha in this passage, these words apply no less accurately to his own life. Thus we're fortunate that we can learn about him. To study Bapuji is to attain his *darshan*, (the divine light that emanates from the guru's presence) which then surrounds and amplifies our own divine light.

Bapuji was born in the small town of Dabhoi in the western state of Gujarat, India in 1913. For years his father held a position as secretary in the Department of Revenue for the Baroda State government and his mother helped raise the two boys and four girls, plus stepchildren. Of all the children, Bapuji was the most studious and the most intent on worshipping saints and deities. A story is told that he would observe the practice of *puja* (a worship ceremony) by pouring water over the tiny figures on the altar in his home. However, he used such quantities of water that it poured out onto the streets. Passersby on their way to work exclaimed at how much water there was in the streets after such a long absence of rain!

His brother looked up to him and often reflected back his saintly qualities while his sisters (especially the older ones) made fun of his endless appetite. Above all, his father, himself a great devotee, sensed the spiritual proclivities of his younger son.

Bapuji became a master of kundalini yoga. For thirty years he spent eight to ten hours of each day in depth sadhana or intense spiritual practice. He spent twelve years in total silence and many more speaking only during important events or celebrations. Who would have guessed that this scholarly fellow, at once a playwright, poet, musician, and actor, would turn into a master of kundalini yoga? Without a formal yoga teacher or mentor, Bapuji essentially forged his own path of yoga, once he had met his distinguished guru, Swami Pranavanandji. Their time together lasted only 1¼ years.

From there all things became possible, including his miraculous travel to the United States. I remember sitting on the floor of the meditation room in his home in Summit Station, PA. We dressed in white as was customary for darshan. Crowded together, we strained to hear a few words or decipher the writings Bapuji wrote on his small chalkboard and handed Yogi Amrit Desai to translate. He had been teaching us about the purity of practice, particularly *brahmacharya* (celibacy). That day my mind was preoccupied and my energy scattered. Although we sat together in meditation, my thoughts kept darting around. Finally, exasperated, I opened my eyes and gazed around the room. I saw Amrit sitting to Bapuji's right. Bapuji was in the center dressed in his red-orange robe, wearing a pale tangerine knit cap to keep his bald head warm. To his left sat Swami Vinit Muniji, one of Bapuji's initiated disciples from India who had accompanied him to this country.

As I studied Vinit Muni for a moment, the thought began to coalesce in my addled brain: "What would it be like to sleep with him?" Then as I gazed at him further, I thought to myself, "Do swamis get a hankering for sex?" No sooner had that thought emerged than Bapuji's eyes popped open and he gazed directly at me. He waved his index finger back and forth, while his eyes became big and round. It was as if he had caught me in the virtual act of sex itself. As he smiled and raised his eyebrows, I got his message. Watching him close his eyes, I followed suit.

He had an uncanny ability to read my mind under any circumstance. One Sunday I was leading chanting in the meditation room before his arrival. Many of us disciples would fall over one another in order to lead chanting because we could sit up close to him afterward. On that particular Sunday I was feeling disconnected. I felt that spiritual practice was stupid; God didn't respond, and what difference did it make because I couldn't see God anyway.

Bapuji came in, and even before people came filing up front, he immediately wrote a message on his slate for Amrit to translate.

The message was bold and clear: "God is everywhere. God is behind you and in front of you. God is watching over your left shoulder. He's always taking care of you. Anywhere you turn, you find God."

Thus it's my hope that anywhere you turn in these teachings of Bapuji's, you will find God. In one of his last speeches he reflects that great masters do not write autobiographies but rather God-biographies. Although Bapuji was frequently asked to compile his autobiography, he balked, saying, "The author of an autobiography should be world-renowned, exceptionally influential, charismatic, and pure in character. Not a drop of ego should be in an autobiography, otherwise it will turn out to be mere self-aggrandizement."

By such admission Bapuji was certainly qualified to write his autobiography. However, it's left to me to deliver his life story. Fortunately he did cut the biographer a little slack, for which I'm relieved. He said that biographers should know and love their subjects well. My love for Bapuji is unbounded. But despite all my years of study (eighteen of them within Kripalu Ashram), getting to know Bapuji's teachings continues to be a work in progress.

Reading his story verges on the supernatural, both in the description of his guru and his subsequent path of sadhana. However, at Bapuji's own urgings as a man of science, we should never take things on face value but question and believe only on the basis of sound empirical evidence. In other words we must engage in spiritual practice in order to test his hypotheses so we can transform them into firm beliefs of our own.

More important than his legacy of speeches, songs, or special yoga sequences, however, is the way of life Bapuji bequeathed us, which in essence embodies the posture of enlightenment. Getting to know a saint, as he tells us, is the means to know God.

PILGRIM OF LOVE

Bapuju teaching in America

PART ONE

BAPUJI'S LIFE IN HIS OWN WORDS

Om shri ganeshay namaha.
I bow to Ganesh and honor him.
The Ganesha Mantra blesses new beginnings
and helps remove all obstacles.

Bapuji as a young boy

CHAPTER ONE

My Early Life

For many years there's been an error calculating the date of my birth. Before I became a swami, my birthday was celebrated according to the Indian calendar on January 15. Invariably my family prepared a big feast and afterward I waltzed around in my brand new birthday clothes. By nightfall the party was over and the next day I went back to my normal routine. In truth it was a simple celebration compared to the huge festivals disciples prepare for me nowadays.

However, a disciple of mine who's an astrologer dug up an old Indian almanac from 1913, the year I was born. He discovered that the day I was born fell on Makar Sakranti (which celebrates the passage of the sun into Capricorn). This was not the fifteenth but the thirteenth of January. When I got this news I laughed out loud. All these years we've been celebrating someone else's birthday!

When my disciple asked me where he could possibly find my horoscope. I said to him, "I have no idea where it is. We've never set eyes on each other." In India as soon as a child is born, a horoscope is prepared. This chart is treasured and preserved throughout the person's entire life. Naturally one was drawn up at my birth; but when I was one or two years old, for some reason (either it felt hurt or uncared for) it renounced my home. Thus my horoscope became a renunciate long before I did. Now even archeologists have no luck digging up my chart.

For that reason I have not paid close attention to astrology, although I have great respect for its workings. The astrological scriptures teach that key planets revolve around the sun affecting human lives. But when I looked closer I saw that these planetary bodies seemed to revolve around human beings rather than the sun. All these planets work like an administrative committee. Some get along and others don't. People have charts drawn up to find out how the planets are behaving and whether they've separated or reconciled. When a planet gazes hatefully upon his neighbor, it creates a huge amount of havoc below, and the poor fellow whose life is influenced may never know what hit him. I feel very fortunate that since I have no horoscope, I only have to suffer once—when my experiences come—whereas those who know their planets suffer beforehand and again when the mischief arrives!

Not only was the date of my birth messed up, but my age was also miscalculated by a whole year, and this mess continued throughout my life. Although I said I was entering my sixty-seventh year during my last birthday festival, that was a mistake. It was actually my sixty-eighth year. So this year I have lived sixty-nine years and am entering my seventieth year.

I was given the name Haridas Majmundar, but because of my studious nature I was also called Saraswati Chandra, the name of a great scholar and saint. In addition, many friends called me Kaviraj (royal poet) once I became involved with drama and poetry writing, and I was also called Narayan (a loving term for Krishna). When I was initiated as a swami I received the name Kripalvanandaji, meaning "the bliss of God's grace." That name was shortened to Kripalu. Then disciples called me Guruji, (dear Guru) which soon got translated to Bapuji, or dear father. Thus you have a good number of choices in how to address me, and I usually respond no matter what I'm called.

The Greater Treasure

From childhood I was surrounded by love. As a result I have one great limitation: I cannot survive a single moment without love. I'm not skillful at pretending, playing games, or deceiving anyone about love.

My father's name was Jamnadas Majmundar and my mother's name was Mangalabahen. I was born in Daboi, in the state of Gujarat. I had four sisters, a brother, and two stepsisters. In my family we rarely quarreled but lovingly lived together. We couldn't bear any separation. Even if someone picked a fight, it never lasted more than a day or two. Then our family atmosphere resumed its loving nature.

Although on rare occasions I might succumb to an urge and do something others disliked, I would immediately realize my mistake and apologize. Even after becoming a swami and the guru of thousands of disciples, I still behave in a way that keeps others happy. Just as parents become tolerant of the din and clatter of several small children, I've learned to be tolerant of thousands of disciples.

In childhood I loved chanting mantras and meditating. I often performed special pujas or ceremonies to the images of Krishna we had in our home. Through my mother and father I had a basic religious training and, by the strength of that alone, was attracted to live a life in pursuit of God.

When my father died I was only seven years old, but he gave me blessings at the time of his death that have come true after all these years. After he died we discovered that he had accumulated a lot of debt which caused my family great suffering. Unhappy with our poverty, I would imagine being rich and felt certain that if only my father had had enough money, I would have been able to get a better education and progress in life. But that dissatisfaction is long gone.

My father was a great devotee of the Lord. After becoming a swami and doing years of sadhana, or spiritual practice, I discovered that my father left me a greater treasure — that of devotion, or bhakti. The seed of bhakti that he planted within me has come into full bloom in my life.

That's why I have been able to do yoga sadhana for such a long time. Even after coming to a prosperous country like America, I had no desire to tour or see the sights. I was simply in love with sadhana and there were no other attractions that claimed my attention. I believe this love for sadhana is a legacy from my parents and particularly from my father.

I remember very clearly the day he died. It just so happened that no one was home except my mother, my father, and me. My father was lying in a bed on the floor and my mother was sitting next to the door. Knowing that he didn't have much time left, he hugged me close to his frail body.

As if speaking his last words, all of a sudden he said, "As far as wealth is concerned, I'm not leaving you anything. And since there are a lot of debts, you will suffer and so will the family. I'm helpless. Worst of all, there's nothing I can do about it." Evidently that caused him great pain, for he began sobbing. Seeing him cry, my mother started crying. Then I too began to cry. After a few moments, he steadied himself, however, and said to me, "Nonetheless the God whom I've prayed to day after day is omnipotent. He will protect you."

Then, looking at my mother he said, "There is one thing I would like to tell you. This child will bring good fortune to our family." I feel certain that that helped shape my life. Perhaps I'm sitting in front of so many devotees because of that blessing.

By the age of seven, however, I could not bear the pain of our circumstance. At that time I firmly decided to give my life to God and to find a way to make my family happy. Because of our financial condition, I had to drop out of school and soon after that we were evicted from our home. Nevertheless, I continued studying in a very scientific manner and even now consider myself a student.

My Love of Study

Two tendencies have turned my life's direction toward music, literature, and yoga: the devotion I inherited from my father and the musical influence of my older brother. Oddly enough, I have felt excruciating pain whenever I had to be sidetracked from my pursuit of music, literature, or yoga.

Not only did I excel in my studies in my early years, but I also learned what it takes to be a good student. If you want to see your reflection in a mirror, you have to keep the mirror steady. If you keep moving it back and forth, you'll miss your image. To properly study a subject, hold the mirror steady. That is, observe everything with a steady mind and dwell deeply on your subject.

When I was eight years old, I visited a neighbor's home and learned that he had a harmonium stored in the closet. That excited me. When my friends left, I took down the harmonium and attempted to play it. But I was pumping air and couldn't get it to work. Gathering it was broken, I went downstairs and announced to the owner that his harmonium didn't work.

"How do you know it's broken?" he asked me.

"I tried to play it, but nothing happened."

Immediately he went upstairs and took out the harmonium. As he pumped the bellows, it began to make sounds. "I didn't know this is how to play it," I said.

"It's a good thing you didn't know," he replied. "If you had, you would have broken it."

Not long after, my brother taught me the essentials of harmonium playing, and I began developing a lifelong fondness for music.

Even though my school life was short-lived, my love of study was lifelong. Essentially I taught myself to read. At the age of ten I became attracted to books of all types, and every day without fail I read a book of 200 or 300 pages. You could say I was addicted to reading.

The public library opened promptly at 8:00 AM each morning, and each morning I was there before eight waiting to enter. Making friends with the janitor, I helped him with his work so that he would not become annoyed with my being there so often. I also made myself useful to the librarian, who was familiar with my thirst for reading. Although there was a ten-day limit on books, invariably I returned mine the next day. After checking one out, I would immediately begin reading while walking down the stairs. On my way home from the library, I read the book while passing the market and shops along the street, often bumping into people as I walked.

I did not stop reading even to eat. During meals my lap contained one text or another. If I couldn't finish a particular book during the day, I would stay up all night to finish it. Whenever my mother or brother caught me up late reading, they would scold me, turn off my lamp, and tell me to go to sleep.

As early as age thirteen, I turned this love of knowledge into a love of writing and began writing articles and stories. By the time I was seventeen, I had several articles accepted by respectable publications.

As I grew up, I read from every genre, including poems, dramas, short stories, and finally long novels. I also read in other languages such as Hindi, and later Sanskrit, and would reflect a bit after each reading. My mind was very scientific and wanted to understand how each piece was composed. In the field of literature you could say I was a runner, but by the time I studied scripture I had slowed down to a halt. I would read just one sutra or paragraph and then contemplate it deeply. Just as it takes time to digest a large meal, deep reflection is necessary to digest the scriptures.

Krishnalal, Bapuji's brother

CHAPTER TWO

MY FAMILY

In my family we grew up listening to scriptures and envisioning the battlefields of the *Mahabharata*, India's great epic story, and the woes of poor Ram who lost his wife in the *Ramayana*, an epic story of Ram's life. We listened to Sri Krishna describing how a yogi should serve God in the Gita and then took advice from Sri Ram on the meaning of dharma and true service in the *Ramayana*.

My Last Incarnation

There were two brothers in our family. I was younger, and my brother Krishnalal was seven years older. I used to call him Shri Pagal Maharaj, or Crazy King. We were more like friends than brothers. He was very openhearted. He used to brag about my saintliness and would insist that I was the good soul Lakshman (from the *Ramayana*). Then I would fight with him, insisting, "No, you're Ram, but I'm not Lakshman."

A memory of him remains clear to this day. I must have been about twenty at the time. After finishing my morning practices at 7 a.m., I left home to teach music in the local school. Shri Pagal Maharaj, also a musician, had fostered my love of music. He was of a saintly nature and opposed my being overly active all day long.

One morning my brother had just awakened and was brushing his teeth. I had been up since four o'clock in the morning doing my morning practices. As I passed him on my way to work, he called out, "Brother!" and I turned to look at him. He knew I was very particular about time. "Why is he stopping me now?" I thought to myself, "I'll be late."

Oblivious to the time, he asked me, "Do you know who you were in your last incarnation?"

I was surprised. What kind of question is that? Loving my brother, however, I said, "No, I don't know who. Do you?"

"Yes, I know," he said.

"Well, tell me, then."

"In your last incarnation you were a donkey," he replied.

"How do you know that?" By now I was grinning.

"Because you work like a donkey all day long. You get up at four o'clock in the morning and work, work, work. You come home late, fall asleep by nine and again you wake up early and sing auuuuuuu every morning. The donkey is braying and you are singing — what is the difference?"

He probably didn't like my singing because he slept in each morning. But all he said was, "You can go now." As I walked out, I felt as if I was growing two long ears, a tail, and a long face.

My Mother and Sisters

From earliest childhood I'd go to my mother all day long with only one request, "Please give me something to eat." Hunger stalked me voraciously and the fire of my appetite never subsided. Whenever I ate more than normal, however, mother would raise her rolling pin in the air and say, "Look how much you're eating! That's enough." Even after playing outside, I'd soon run back inside for another snack.

My mother did not appreciate this behavior and responded, "All day eating?"

"I'm always hungry," I replied.

"Just one more slice of bread," I'd say. Sometimes she took pity on me and served me an extra slice of bread. At other times she hit me for eating too much.

As I was born into a Vaishnava family, religious rituals were very important and fasting was counted as an important practice. Parents often inspired children as young as five or six to go on fasts. However, most of the time this yogi escaped such trials. One day without my knowing it, however, my mother announced to my sisters, "Saraswatichandra has never fasted. I am determined to have him fast on the day of Bhima Ekadashi." Bhima, the elder brother of Arjuna, was large-bellied and rumored to have an appetite as big as his belly. The day of Bhima Ekadashi must have been named after him because he fasted only once a month. I too was to be honored by fasting on that day. My sister Indumati who was two years older often teased me and called me Bhima or Bhimado because of my appetite. When my mother proclaimed that I should fast, Indumati agreed but then advised my mother, "If you want him to fast, you'll have to lock him up."

Unbeknownst to me, the dreadful day dawned, and after I had washed and brushed my teeth, my mother said, "Come upstairs."

"What do you want?" I asked.

"Would I ask you to come up without a reason?" she replied. So I followed her to my study on the second floor. The moment I entered, she locked the door behind me and announced, "Today is the auspicious Day of Bhima Ekadashi, and you must observe the fast. I will call you when it's time for fruit."

This unexpected attack astonished me. Yet I replied as casually as I could, "Why do I need fruit? I'll just fast on water." She said, "That's fine." As soon as mother went downstairs, hunger came upstairs. I knew I couldn't fast. Yet the family was resolved.

Our entire household did *japa* (the reciting of mantra or sacred prayers) daily, including me. But there is a big difference between japa and fasting. Doing japa means sitting on the floor and fasting means climbing the walls. After walking back and forth, I said to myself, "Not to worry. I'll find a way to sneak some food even if I have to fight an entire army that wants me to fast."

My room opened onto a courtyard. There was a small balcony off my study from which I could make my way down to the courtyard. I used a dhoti or large cloth hanging on the line as a rope and swung down, carefully peering through a window to make sure no one was around. Mother had gone out to do some chores. My sisters were visiting friends. Only my aunt sat in the front room immersed in her morning prayers.

My mission was to find food stored in the pantry. Although mother never left food out because of the cat (actually there were two cats in the house, including me), I was able to grab a bag of rice flakes from the cupboard and make my way back up the balcony to hide in my room.

Then I told Bhima Ekadashi to leave my room and go circle the house while I sat down to eat. Peering at the little bundle of rice flakes, I said to it, "By this evening, you'll be gone." Then at lunchtime mother came upstairs and knocked on my door, saying, "Son, I have some fruit for you."

After quietly chewing what I had in my mouth, I said, "Thanks but I'm not hungry." Then mother said, "That's fine. Just knock on the door if you get hungry later on."

A little later my younger sister Kundanbala came upstairs. Usually I did whatever she asked. She cried, "Please brother eat a little fruit. You know you can't stand hunger. " But I comforted her saying, "Today I have decided to fast. Even you fast every eleven days and you're younger than I am."

Reluctantly she went back downstairs and said, "If brother doesn't take any food, I won't eat, either." Needless to say I went back to my chewing. To eat two pounds of rice flakes in twelve hours isn't an easy job for a ten-year-old boy. If a weak older person tried it, you'd have to pry open his jaws the next day.

Meanwhile my older sister Indumati, who knew me well, was astonished when she heard I wasn't hungry. She too came to my door and said, "Open up. I have some fruit for you."

Again I replied, "I'm not hungry."

When I came out the next morning, my mother and aunt complimented me and promised me a good lunch to make up for yesterday's fasting. Indumati did not like to hear me praised, though. The wheels were turning as she quietly searched for some explanation.

About two weeks later my older brother came home from work very hungry and asked my mother for a snack. Unable to find the rice flakes in the pantry, my mother asked Indumati for help locating them. My sister searched a while and found nothing. Then she came straight upstairs and grabbed hold of my ear. "Where is that bundle of rice flakes?" Indumati demanded.

"It was my meal on Bhima Ekadashi," I admitted. She yelled and slapped me. With the noise, everyone came running. "What's going on?"

"I knew he didn't fast on Bhima Ekadashi," Indumati said.

Astonished, my mother said, "But I locked him in his room."

"Well, mother, you don't really know this Bhimado here," Indumati replied and repeated the whole story to her.

My Sister Indumati

Six years after I took *sannyas*, or my swami initiation, my family saw me again for the first time. Their hearts were overwhelmed both with joy and grief. At that time I lived in Halol, and I was giving lectures on the *Bhagavad Gita*. People came from nearby towns as well.

One day the organizers thought they would surprise me by inviting some of my relatives to attend. So they extended a special invitation to my family. It was the last day of the lectures, so it was very crowded in the hall. My sister Indumati came with my mother. When she saw that numerous villagers loved me and were taking care of me, her heart was struck with intolerable pain and she began crying.

After the lecture we had a moment together. She said to me, "I suppose after all this time you've forgotten me. Now you have many mothers and many sisters so this poor sister is pushed out of your heart. There's no room left."

"My sister," I said, "You're making a big mistake."

"Mistake?"

I said, " Not only in this village, but in all the villages I've visited, I see your face. I see one sister among countless sisters. Let me give you an example. Suppose I have an apothecary's scale with two pans. One has weights in it; the other holds the thing to be weighed. If you look again, you'll find that one pan always contains the same weight. Only the other side keeps changing. There's a weight known as "sister" that stays in this pan. That is you. You are the first balance of my heart. In the other pan sisters may keep changing, but their love will always be measured in reference to this original sister."

Her face lit up and her eyes were flooded with tears, "Really?"

"Yes, dear sister. You must realize that I've never forgotten you. You remain with me every moment."

My Brother Krishnalal

There was tremendous love among my brother and sisters as well as among the many children who lived on my block. After leaving home and becoming a swami, in a sense I was still a worldly man because I was surrounded with so much love. Love is not excluded from any path, whether you are sannyasi or worldly.

My older brother left home as soon as I became a swami. Before that we were always together. Sometimes we quarreled but this only happened when we were discussing spiritual principles. We never fought over land, money, or material things. I was happy for my brother to have whatever he liked, and in the same way he was happy to see me have the things I liked.

However, one time we had a big disagreement. My brother was the worshipper of Lord Vishnu. One day I saw a package of cigarettes lying on his altar and I asked him, "Why do you have cigarettes in front of God?"

He answered, "God has not helped me get rid of my bad habit, and I cannot do it on my own, so I offer these to Him and then I accept them back from Him."

"Can't you see you're breaking the rules of scripture?"

He got mad and said, "I don't care for scriptures written by someone else. I believe in the religion of love and in what my heart says, that's all."

I said, "Can you trust that your inner voice is pure? Perhaps there is a difference between a saint and a —?"

Even more angrily, he said, "Your God may not smoke, but my God does, and he drinks as well. Your God may become impure very quickly, but my God does not. Since he's the one who purifies everyone else, he's not so easily polluted."

"Whoever offers God cigarette smoke instead of the smoke of incense is not a devotee but an addict. I may be younger than you, but I've studied the scriptures well. You're only reinforcing the weakness of your mind by offering cigarettes to God. Whoever's a slave to his mind can never be a true devotee."

Immediately I picked up my begging bowl and walked away. My older brother sat quietly. After walking a mile or so, my excitement subsided. Insulting my older brother felt terrible.

That conversation took place when I was forty, and my brother was forty-seven years old. A year later we met again in Dakor. Immediately he bowed, held my feet and cried saying, "Please forgive me for that day."

"I was wrong myself, please forgive me," I replied.

We both cried openly. After quieting down, he said, "Whatever we did, it was not us doing it, but someone making us do it. Don't you feel that way?"

I smiled, and said yes, explaining, "People who follow the path of *jnana* yoga (yoga of knowledge) call it *prakriti*—it's nature—that makes you do those things. But devotees call it the will of God."

My Rebellion

Every new generation rebels against the last one, trying to replace old customs with new ones. It was no different in my town. Although I was born into a Brahmin family and it's traditional for men to wear *dhotis* (long wrap-around cloths) instead of pants, I decided to change that. I found the dhotis impractical and decided to wear a pair of pajama-like pants I kept hidden in a drawer. One particular morning I came downstairs with my pants on.

My entire family reacted. "Take off those pants," they told me. "We are Brahmins and do not wear the clothes of other classes." I began to question this. Why can't a Brahmin wear either of them? After all, a dhoti is a loose unsewn garment and a pajama is a sewn garment. That's the only difference.

Refusing to succumb to anyone's opposition, I wore them anyway. News of my "rebellion" swept through the neighborhood and soon the elders gathered. Talking among themselves, finally they stated, "We must stop this young man from wearing pajamas. We cannot allow such corruption to spread any further."

Evidently several of the elders disagreed, "We should not impose our thoughts on young people. They should be persuaded to reconsider their actions only through love." Another wise man added, "How is Brahmin dharma harmed by wearing pajamas? Are you a Brahmin merely because you wear certain clothes?" After much consideration others began to agree with him. "This is a result of changing times. Let him wear pants." But others countered, "If we let him wear such garments, others will follow his example. Soon all young people will dress like this."

After much talk they were unable to agree on any course of action, so I continued wearing pajamas. As predicted, my friends began to imitate me. They too encountered conflict in their homes, but in the end the young people won.

Today girls and women have also joined the ranks of pants-wearers and restrictions on clothing are rare or nonexistent.

After so many years as a swami, I can now see the wisdom in wearing certain clothes. The clothing you wear influences your actions. Even more importantly, it influences the impressions in your mind about your path and your purpose in life. So now I'm having a second clothing rebellion to upstage the original one from my youth.

The Dharma of Love

Since the Brahmin caste in India was predominantly ascetic, scholarly, and self-disciplined, it was considered to be the superior caste. Although anyone could eat food prepared by Brahmins, Brahmins were not permitted to eat food prepared by others. Thus their spiritual focus extended to the kinds of foods they ate and the inclination toward a more *sattvic* (pure) diet.

At that time there were both Hindu and Muslim hotels in Gujarat. Only Hindus entered Hindu hotels, likewise only Muslims entered Muslim hotels. Today of course these restrictions have been dropped and you can enter any hotel you like.

In my literary circle there were more Muslims than Hindus. We met on a regular basis to discuss literature and departed after tea and snacks were served. There was great love among us as we feasted upon the aspects of literature, but when it was time to feast upon real food we had to go our separate ways. Thus my Muslim friends went to their hotel and my Hindu friends and I to our hotel.

Needless to say this was very aggravating and we often complained among ourselves, "How can we follow religious practices that separate human beings and create a wall between us? The supreme dharma is the dharma of love. The whole world should accept this."

One day I made a suggestion, "There are ten of us: three Hindus and the rest Muslims. Although we usually separate for refreshments, today I'll have food brought from the Hindu hotel and we'll eat together. After all, courage is an integral part of love."

In those times it was also considered improper even to stand next to a Muslim, let alone eat with him. So this was considered a big offense. My friends didn't like my proposition. One of them said lovingly, "It's not such a good idea to deliberately provoke conflict. If anyone sees you eating food at the Muslim hotel, even if it has been prepared elsewhere, they will believe you're eating Muslim food and consider you in violation of your caste's restrictions."

"Friends, I appreciate your love and concern, but I want to carry out this experiment in earnest," I responded. Reluctantly they consented.

So one day I went ahead with my experiment and had food brought from the hotel. Needless to say, the townspeople soon found out about it. One elderly person scolded me, twisting my ear, "You rascal. Why did you do that? Don't think that's an act of courage; it's the work of a fool."

"Why is there such opposition?" I asked. "The scriptures say that Brahmins are gods on earth and the abodes of purity, in fact powerful enough to purify the whole world. Do you think one Muslim hotel can make me impure?"

He gave me a rap on the head, "You fool. You may read scriptures, write essays, and consider yourself a great scholar, but you have no experience. The glorious Brahmins you refer to are great yogis and saints. You're not worthy to kiss the dust of their feet."

"I'm a Hindu," I declared. "I don't need to become a Muslim. But why can't I sit with them?"

"Who's keeping you from sitting with them? We only ask that you not go to their hotel."

Since this incident seriously disturbed the community, eventually I had to take an oath not to do it again. Thus I was rendered helpless. Still I felt unhappy about following restrictions that didn't serve a useful purpose.

The Price of One Slap

From early on I was accustomed to witnessing and taking stock of my life. One event helped me to grow immeasurably. It happened many years ago when I had a music school in Ahmedabad. At that time my sister's son Radnikant lived with me and came to the school. He was eight years old. Although he was not enrolled and often sat in the corner, I could see that he enjoyed the music.

One day I had been out and returned home. At that time I heard someone playing and singing a song that I had taught the third grade. It was a difficult song to master. At first I didn't recognize the singer, but as soon as I entered the house I realized it was Radnikant. Immediately I picked him up and hugged him. "You sing so well that I want you to attend my classes regularly," I told him, and he seemed pleased.

From then on I started singling him out for attention. I always checked on his work and worried if he was absent. Even though he hadn't learned everything in the lower grades, he was still a singer of the highest order. However, one day when I was teaching a very difficult lesson, Radnikant got up and left. I hadn't realized he was gone but when class was over, I looked for him and couldn't find him.

Asking the students when he had left, I got no answer. Then I got angry. After all, this was a very important lesson, and he shouldn't have missed it. Finally he came back in. I called out, "Radnikant, why did you run away?" and I slapped him across the face. He burst out crying.

A short while later I felt badly that I had punished him. How could I do such a thing? I loved him so much. My mind was very disturbed. After all, I had never punished a child in that way. In fact I prided myself on the way I worked so patiently and so lovingly with children of all ages.

I regained my balance after an hour or so, and I called for him. "Radnikant, I'm sorry that I punished you. I got angry because you missed the class. But I will never do that again. I promise you." To keep my promise I took him into the city the next day and bought him all the toys he wanted. I spent fifty rupees on Radnikant—a huge amount in those days, but that was the price of one slap.

One Heartbreak after Another

One day my brother came to see me at my ashram in Odi. He was my closest loved one and well-wisher. As we talked, he reminded me of some things that had happened in our past and finally said, "Narayan, there's one trait of yours I really can't stand." I told him to explain it to me without hesitation. Then a very serious look came over his face and tears flowed from his eyes. Finally he pulled himself together and said, "Throughout your life I've observed that you tend to place your trust in people immediately, whether you know them or not. You don't care if they're worthy of it. That has brought you one heartbreak after another all your life, yet you refuse to give up that habit."

After listening very carefully, I responded, "What you say is true, for you know me better than anyone else. In fact, your life has shaped mine. Although it's true that I've suffered by trusting others, in spite of that, I adore this quality with my whole heart. How can your love grow when you doubt someone's love from the beginning? It's only fair to decide about a loved one after getting to know him; to judge him without experience isn't fair."

Shri Pagal Maharaj listened with his eyes closed. He then replied, "I only wish you the best. I'm well aware of your habit of contemplation, but in the past I was concerned that you'd get hurt placing your trust in others. However, your explanation has eased my mind. God's grace is with you and he'll always protect you. I give you my heartfelt blessings."

Bombay train station

CHAPTER THREE

MY PURPOSELESS EXISTENCE

Krishna govind gopijana valabha namah
I surrender to Krishna in his many forms.

(Krishna Mantra)

No matter how expert an artist is nor how great a picture he paints of the sun, no light shines from it because it's not real. In the same way, no matter how well I describe my guru, I can never project his true light.

When I was nineteen years old, I was extremely ambitious and yet unable to attain what I really wanted. So I had fallen out of love with life. Concerning God's presence, however, I never experienced the slightest doubt. In fact I was more convinced of God's reality than of life itself. He was my solace and support. However, I didn't know anything about formal sadhana at the time, so I used to worship God in the traditional way I learned from my family.

When I arrived in Bombay at the age of nineteen, my heart was filled with darkness. My family's poverty and loss coupled with my own sense of failure hounded me. Although I sought work in many places, I had difficulty getting a job and earning a living.

I felt contempt for my purposeless existence and asked myself, "What reason is there for a life without ideals?" Rather than lead such a pathetic life, I thought it was preferable to die.

Four times I tried to commit suicide without success. Although I was very determined, some event would turn up each time to change my resolution at the last minute. After I came to Bombay, however, I was more determined than ever to end my life.

As a child I found great joy in worshipping the child Krishna. Born into a Vaishnava family it was traditional to worship the various forms of Lord Krishna and recite his mantras. Also as a Brahmin, I repeated the Gayatri Mantra, which was a standard part of our religious practice. At that time the Brahmins were still considered the priestly class in India. However, an old gentleman in my Dabhoi neighborhood told me that the worship of Lord Shiva was the highest form of worship, so when I went to Bombay, I continued worshipping Shiva. Therefore I had gathered a variety of mantras to repeat—the Gayatri Mantra, the Saraswati mantra, the Sri Krishna Mantra, and other mantras which I had learned from my family.

In Bhuleshwar, the large market area in central Bombay, there's a dovecote and next to it a small Mataji Temple. I used to go there every night during the special fire ceremony called *arati*. The gentleman who had drawn me toward worship of Shiva also mentioned Shakti worship (Shiva's consort) and frequently told me that the joy in believing God to be the Mother was not to be found in any other faith. This seemed to me to be very true.

On the day that I decided I would definitely commit suicide, I went to the Bhuleshwar Mataji Temple. The arati was in progress and I joined in. Before me was the picture of the Holy Mother and behind that a vision of the Chowpathi Sandhurst Bridge. Beneath the bridge, the electric trains ran swiftly and I saw my body being crushed. This vision must have come because of my strong desire to end my life. During that service I made a firm resolution to make the vision come true.

I prayed to the Mother with tear-filled eyes: "Mother, why let me lead such a pointless life, why not swallow me into thy feet?" Those who haven't prayed in front of a statue with pure heart do not know the secret of worship. At that time while I was crying and calling out to the Divine Mother, she did not look like a statue. Her eyes were moving. There was love in her eyes and she seemed alive to me.

I had planned to leave after asking her permission. When arati was over, everyone had left but I stood there crying. The priest knew me and tried to console me but my tears would not cease. At that moment a man entered the temple wearing a towel around his waist and carrying a waterpot. He took my hand, held me close to him, and patted my head lovingly. Then he said, "My son, come with me." His kind words brought me peace. It was astonishing that although he was a total stranger, he aroused feelings of boundless confidence within me. I followed him out of the temple along the road. After we walked a little bit, he took his seat on the veranda of one of the shops. He motioned me to do the same. Then in a very serious voice he said: "My son, remove from your mind the thought of ending your life; suicide is contemptible." That an unknown person could know another person's most secret thoughts was shocking.

I hid my astonishment and looked at him. His gentle and sparkling eyes were filled with love and he was smiling. Nonetheless I dismissed what he said and replied: "This idea of yours is false; I have no thoughts of committing suicide."

His eyes filled with pity and he said very quietly: "My son, you are a devotee. It does not become you to take refuge in a lie. Tonight you were planning to commit suicide by throwing yourself under an electric train at the Sandhurst Bridge."

I was tremendously affected by his words. As a student of science I was accustomed to weighing things carefully and nothing influenced my mind suddenly. Generally I gave more importance to purity and innocence than to miracles. Yet this innocent man seemed miraculous too.

To sit at the feet of such a great man was a matter of pride and I knelt before him in complete faith. Admitting that I had lied, I repeatedly asked his forgiveness.

"You spoke an untruth against your nature. I've forgiven you," he said. Tomorrow is Thursday; meet me between three and six in the evening." I was asked not to reveal the name of the place.

After that, he left me. Looking forward to the next day's arrival, I gave up all thoughts of suicide. Although I made every attempt to be there on time, I left half an hour late. On the way, it occurred to me that this saint would be giving darshan only between three and six, and whoever arrived late would be sent away disappointed. However, when I arrived, the doors were still open.

"Swami"

It turned out that for the past four months this saint had been telling his devotees that on a certain day at a certain time a youth would arrive who would become his chief disciple. When I arrived, everyone was waiting expectantly. On the way I had purchased a beautifully scented garland, but I was not rich and paying five rupees for it was very dear. Still I could not imagine paying anything less for someone who had affected me so profoundly.

After last night's events, I felt extreme reverence for this man, but the wish to be his disciple arose only later. It is not like me to accept anyone as a guru; in fact I am rather obstinate. I have many such innocent pupils who, from the first meeting, have believed me to be their guru. However it's my nature not to believe in anything without experience.

For the most part Guruji remained seated in meditation, with fifteen or twenty pupils around him. After several days he would say one or two sentences in Hindi. Everyone waited eagerly for those words. I learned that he had been there for the past six months. On entering the room I put the garland around his neck. He signaled with his hand that I should sit down by his side. When I glanced around I realized that others were seated on the bare floor without mats. Their dress indicated that they were well off, which made me nervous.

The Invitation

With a compassionate look, Guruji said: "Swami, you have arrived. My son, that's very good." His kind words made me feel proud, the word "Swami" flattered me and my nervousness vanished.

I have a dark complexion and I thought that it was because of this that Guruji had addressed me as Swami. In order to exhibit my cleverness, I said that I was not a Madrasi, who were dark-skinned, but a Gujarati. Guruji answered with a smile,

"No son, I did not call you Swami because I thought you were a Madrasi, but because I thought you were a *sannyasi* or renunciate."

I couldn't accept that so I contradicted him, "Pardon me, but it does not seem that I shall become a sannyasi. To begin with, I have no inclination to be a sannyasi and secondly I haven't the purity. The world is dear to me. I can only live within it. If I ignored my mind and its material desires and became a sannyasi, I would be one in name only and not in spirit. The sannyasi lives a closed life. He does not toil and is dependent on others for support. Rather than live thus, I would prefer to work."

Guruji had listened with his eyes half closed, looking down at the floor. When I stopped, he said: "It's true, our sannyasis here beg and ask for alms, but, beloved son, the act of begging is not begging but the receiving of an offering, a secret gift, through which they seek to be freed from this life."

"You are going to give love to the world," he said, and "you are going to receive love from the world." On that day I could not follow the meaning of his argument, but today I can say that I understand.

All the disciples were watching me closely and everyone had joy on their faces. I had become drawn to the feet of my guru. I know it's his grace, and only due to his grace that I've been able to maintain this sadhana for so many years.

Ending the conversation, Guruji urged me: "If you wish, you may stay here with me."

I had not a moment's hesitation in accepting his offer.

Mumba Mata Temple in Bombay

CHAPTER FOUR

MY GURU

Om bhur bhuvaha swaha
tat savitur varenyam
bhargo devasya dhimahi
dhiyo yonaha prachodayat.
Oh Great Light that gives birth to all consciousness,
worthy of our worship and appearing through the orbit of the Sun,
please illumine our intellect.

(Gayatri mantra)

For some time I had been staying with a relative. I managed to eat, although it was often difficult. The idea that I could escape from this difficult life brought peace to my mind. The doors of my future flew open. In serving this unusually powerful swami, I would be able to acquire the knowledge of yoga. That thought delighted me. In response to Guruji's invitation, I arrived the next day with my trunk of clothes.

The building in which Guruji and I lived had four floors and was very solemn. However, it was surrounded by a beautiful garden and the entire place had a peaceful air. I felt like someone who had died and gone to heaven.

I have not seen such loving obedience in any other ashram. Although no one was afraid of him, no one would suddenly enter the room in which he was seated. His gentle nature had an unusual strength. Those near him were afraid to talk. Not only that, in the mansion there were about two or three hundred people wandering around doing various kinds of service, but with so much caution that not a sound reached Guruji's room.

Guruji did not ask anyone his name, what he did, where he lived, or who his family was. The astonishing thing was that when he called someone he called him by name. Also I noticed that Guruji talked to Hindi-speaking people in Hindi, Marathis in Marathi, Punjabis in Punjabi and Tamils in Tamil. No one knew how he had learned all these languages. I used to puzzle over this myself.

I could do nothing but praise my good fortune. The chance to meet a real saint and know his compassion comes only after many rebirths. One day I was without support and without hope. The next day I was full of support and hope. Who can guess God's ways?

The Golden Stool, the Pile of Dust

Generally Guruji remained in solitude. In spite of that, he asked me to visit him certain times during the day. On the first day, as the clock struck eleven, a woman entered the room saying: "Gurudev, it's mealtime; the *thalis* (plates) have been served."

Guruji arose and signaled me to follow. We crossed two rooms and entered a third one. On entering the dining room, I noticed that there were two stools made of gold and two stools made of silver. On one of the gold stools there was a gold thali, some gold bowls, a golden mug, and a golden cup. In the same way, on the silver stool, there was a silver thali, some silver bowls, a silver mug, and a silver cup. I decided that the golden stool would be for Guruji and the silver one for me, so I rather shyly stood to one side.

However, Guruji took me by the hand and seated me on the golden stool. Now my good fortune knew no bounds! Yet I held back for I was embarrassed about wanting to sit on it. Invariably proud of how strong I was, I had a rude awakening when Guruji grasped my hand. I thought to myself, "How can this sixty year old man be so strong?" I was determined not to sit on his stool. I tried very hard to resist but I was completely overpowered. Not even three days had passed since my first meeting with Guruji, but here I was being treated like a king!

Of course, it's true that sitting on a golden stool or a pile of dust makes no difference to a supreme human being. However, to a worldly man it was different. I was a worldly man and it made a difference to me. After I was seated, Guruji sat on the silver stool and explained why he had changed the order of our seating: "My son, supremacy is not dependent on a golden throne but in the feet of the person.

I could hardly understand or accept these words. But when Guruji took his first bite of food, I also began eating. I have no idea how many chapatis, rice, or vegetables I ate. Today all I can remember is the golden cup, the golden thali, the golden bowls, and the golden stool.

Although I was restless, Guruji ate peacefully. After eating I followed Guruji to his sitting room and stood in the doorway. Then I bowed to him and said, "Guruji, I'm going out." He smiled with his eyes and indicated that I could go.

As I walked I had but one thought: the glitter of the golden stools, the golden thali, the golden bowls, and the golden cup. I tried to dismiss the vision of the dining room from my mind.

For a moment my mind would clear but would then resume its restlessness. This lasted about four hours until I returned that afternoon. Wherever I turned, all I could see was the dining room.

I went to Guruji and bowed. He lovingly placed his hand on my head and said, "Swami, such a small thing made you lose your mind. Let go of these thoughts. Neither this house, nor the golden stools, the golden thalis, nor the golden mugs are yours. Those who lose their heads over such things are fools. Where can you find your good fortune in all of this?"

His words had a profound effect upon me and I immediately became calm. Just as in a clear mirror, one easily sees a reflection, so Guruji could see and clearly reflect my thoughts back to me. Although influencing my mind was extremely hard, in a short time he had subdued my thoughts.

The Temptation of Money

At least ten or twelve of Guruji's disciples were millionaires. However, his extreme compassion had fallen on a poor fellow like me. That was his greatness. He, who hardly spoke to anyone, spent hours explaining to me the meaning of the *Vedas*, the *Upanishads*, and the *Puranas*.

When I went to dine with Guruji the next day, there were four golden stools and all the vessels were gold. The change was made because Guruji had sat on a silver stool the day before, which evidently disturbed some of the devotees. However, that day I ate peacefully thanks to Guruji. Despite being surrounded by such splendor, Guruji's mind was unaffected.

Since I was his favorite, the entire assembly of disciples bowed to me in reverence. They regarded my pleasure as his pleasure. Guruji could see my attraction to wealth, so he advised me when we were alone, "Swami, if you go after wealth and the wealthy, you will have to put up with all kinds of trouble. If you want to raise yourself up, then you must be pure and innocent. The temptation of money can lead you astray."

The Silver Swing

One of the rich men decided to build a silver swing for Guruji. When it was ready, it was brought to the house and put up in the best room. Then this man talked to the other disciples requesting that Guruji sit on the swing for a few minutes. However, no one wanted to do this.

Finally, someone came to me and said, "Swami, you are Guruji's favorite; he listens to you. On our behalf please ask him to sit on the swing."

Guruji often talked about my future to his inner circle of pupils and told them I was his chief disciple. Once or twice in front of me he said the same thing. When I heard this, I was rather surprised, for I felt I did not have the purity. However his disciples believed him and respected me.

Once I contradicted Guruji and said: "Do you want to make this monkey drunk with praise? One cannot pour the ocean into a small pot."

He replied: "My son, I have planted a mango seed. In time that's what it will become." At that time I believed myself to be the seed of a fruitless tree. Since the result was in the future, disputing it was pointless. After listening to my guru brothers, I said: "All right, I'll go and ask Guruji."

The next day I went to Guruji's room where the others were also present. After greeting him, I said, "Guruji, it is every-body's wish that you sit on the silver swing for a few minutes. Even one minute will do; your touch will make it holy." I thought Guruji would do as I requested, since he had great compassion for me.

After listening to my request, Guruji asked me, "Why? Are you fond of this swing?"

Since I was his favorite, I had become rather cheeky and would say whatever came into my mind. "Yes, I like the swing very much. If you tell me to sit on it, I will." The words had barely left my lips when I regretted what I'd said, but it was too late. Immediately Guruji got up and grabbed my hand. When we came to the room with the swing, I tried to remove my hand from Guruji's grip, but it was useless. Since the day he had seated me on the golden stool, I had great reverence for his strength. I looked at him with pitiful eyes, saying, "Please don't make me sit on this swing." In spite of that, he took both my hands and seated me on it. At the same time, he was aware of my pain.

There was an ant walking on the swing and Guruji pointed to it, saying, "Look at this ant; it's also seated on the swing, but it does not take into consideration that it's a silver swing or that only a holy man has the right to sit there." Then Guruji burst out laughing.

I quickly got off the swing and, before anyone could say anything, Guruji sat down on it. Immediately everyone smiled.

"All right," he said, "what pleases the people pleases the ruler."

My Mantra

During my training Gurudev gave me the mantra *Om namah shivaya* to repeat. Once I began the repetition of that mantra, I must have repeated it approximately 1,000 times. Then it occurred to me that the meaning of this mantra was, "O Lord Shiva, I bow at your feet."

I was perplexed that despite the fact that I was saying this, I wasn't really bowing down to Shiva. Also I couldn't understand why I had to say it so often. Couldn't I just tell God once? You'd think he'd understand. Besides, if I said the same thing hundreds and thousands of times, I imagined the listener would get really bored.

With these thoughts I became disturbed. Putting my *mala* (Hindu prayer beads) down, I went and asked, "Gurudev, there's something I don't understand. I say, 'Lord Shiva, I bow at your feet.' And yet I'm not bowing at his feet when I do japa, repeating these words. Truthfully, if I were doing this properly, every time I say, Om namah shivaya, Om namah shivaya,' I would bow down on the floor."

Gurudev said, "My son, you're mistaken. Although it's appropriate to consider one meaning of Om namah shivaya to be 'Lord Shiva, I bow down to you,' the true meaning is 'Lord Shiva, I surrender myself to you.'"

Then I asked,"How often do I have to say I surrender? Won't He understand the first time?

"Here also you are mistaken," Gurudev said. "God is so merciful that if you say it just once, He will accept it, but your mind is so cunning that even saying it hundreds of times, you still don't mean it. That's why you have to repeat it over and over. When the mind truly surrenders to the Lord, you don't have to do any japa."

Our Fight

One morning I woke up early, bathed, and did some exercises. My body was alert and active and my mind was full of joy. Since I had so much energy, I felt like wrestling with someone.

When my practices were completed, I went to bow at my guru's feet. Gurudev used to sit in meditation all day. He just sat on his seat without moving. After I bowed down, I gazed up into his face. There was so much love in his eyes. Smiling and beckoning to me, he said, "Come on, let's fight." It was amazing how quickly he picked up on my thoughts.

I said to him, "You're old, and if you wrestle with me, I'll defeat you."

"Don't tell me the results; just wrestle," he responded.

It was not in any corner of my imagination that he would do this. Yet because he was happy, I became happy. I considered him like a father. When he loved me so deeply, I was half-crazed with love. As I punched my fist against my palm, I said, "Do you really want to fight?"

"Yes."

He stood up, saying, "Come forward. I'm not going to do anything. Just wrestle with me."

I quickly attacked his body. I put my hand over his neck, then around his waist, and then I tried to entangle his legs. But he just stood there. This sixty-year-old man was strong! When I tried again, he didn't even budge.

Perspiring all over, I was about to cry. How is this possible? He was standing there like a steel post. Finally I had to admit defeat. That day was the first time I heard the words *katori karana*. He described that they meant a state of extreme rigidity and firmness, and added, "This is an ordinary *kriya*, a practice. This is not a big *siddhi*, or miraculous power."

At Gurudev's Side

I was fortunate to take my meals right by Gurudev's side. Since he ate only one meal, we sat together for that one meal while he attempted to train me in moderation. He told whoever was serving us, "That's enough. Don't give him anymore."

Seeing my condition, the serving lady would look at Gurudev and cry. "Please let me give him a little more."

But Gurudev would simply say, "Time to go." So I had to wash my hands, and she had to wipe away her tears and leave us. Meanwhile, my tummy felt empty.

In the evening Gurudev did not take meals. For my evening meal, he instructed the servers, "When you serve him, I'll be there."

Believe me—that was true. I had no control. As soon as a signal came from him to stop, I had to wash my hands and leave the table. Some might consider that fanaticism, but to me it was a great training in moderation. He took such good care of me in every aspect of my life! When I remember that love, I am so in awe that I almost lose consciousness.

Every day I was accustomed to having two meals and two or three snacks. First Guruji stopped the snacks, and then he reduced the meals to one a day.

Now consider if a boy of ten could not tolerate hunger, how much less would he be able to tolerate hunger at the age of nineteen? However, by his grace, I was able to adapt myself to one meal a day.

After that he said, "For three months you'll take only cow's milk."

And I responded, "That will happen by your grace alone."

It is true that a little baby can live on milk, but a nineteen-year-old-boy? However, by the grace of Gurudev, I completed that as well.

My Discipleship

In my spiritual preparation, I regarded Guruji as my spiritual father. Later I regarded him as a guru, and now as God.

After eight months he said to me: "I'm going to give you training for sannyas."

"Training for sannyas?" I asked in astonishment.

"Yes, training for sannyas. Is that worse than suicide?" In this way he reminded me of the past; and of course I was embarrassed.

I said "Guruji, I have tremendous desire for women, wealth, and fame. How can I become a sannyasi? Although I have complete faith in your word, still it's discouraging when I consider my mental state."

I continued: "The fact that you have made me your chief disciple has been my great good fortune. Training for sannyas is an added boon and an extraordinary one. But answer me one question. How can a crow become a swan?"

He replied, "My son, whether you are a crow or a swan, you'll know the answer when the spirit of sannyas and the delight of yoga are born in your soul." This answer brought peace to my mind.

The day of my training for sannyas was fixed. Guruji had told me that before the training I would have to go on a strict fast for forty-one days, taking nothing but water. Gurudev knew me inside out and I had unflinching faith in his wisdom. When I approached him, I bowed at his feet and said, "Gurudev, fasting for such a long time seems impossible to me, but with your grace, I'll give it a try. Then he gave me my training for sannyas. Explaining the purpose of the fast, he said: "In your mind are the impurities of many births and in your body are the impurities of one mind. The fasting and repetition of mantras purifies your soul and subdues your body and mind," he said. He placed his hand on my head and said, "Son, I bless you." Immediately I felt energy transmitted through my whole body.

Then he gave me comforting guidance, "My son, the first three days will be difficult for you, but this discomfort will diminish by the fifth day. By the seventh day you'll have no difficulty at all."

And that's exactly what happened. On the fortieth day of the fast, I was still able to walk although I felt very weak. Nevertheless, my mind was alert and strong. Gurudev had given me japa to do during this fasting time, so I acquired a deep love for it. I was very much engrossed. Even today, when I think of my guru's love I lose consciousness. I know for sure that whatever I have received in this world is because of him. To me Gurudev is life itself; he means everything to me. By his grace I was able to finish the fast with no difficulty.

A small room in the house had been chosen for me to spend forty-one days repeating mantra. I used to come out of the room only twice a day, to kneel before Guruji. Solitude, strict fasting, silence, repetition of mantras and concentration were the chief features of this path. Although he gave me the mantra *krishna govind gopijana valabha namah*, Guruji did not give me saffron robes. Instead he instructed me, "In the future, when your mind has risen above worldly thoughts, you will receive the saffron robes from a great learned man."

With the training for sannyas, he also gave me training in yoga. He said, "Today I shall teach you something about the ancient practice of yoga and make you a yogacharya, or spiritual master. I give you the choicest blessings. You will be one of the incomparable yogacharyas of the world."

Bapuji as a young bearded pilgrim

Krishna statue at the Taj, Baroda

CHAPTER FIVE

OUR PILGRIMAGE

Asatoma sada gamaya

tamasoma jyotir gamaya

mrityorma amritam gamaya

Lead us from the unreal to the real.

Lead us from darkness to light.

Lead us from death to immortality.

(Ancient Sanskrit prayer)

After staying in Bombay for a year and three-quarters, Guruji took leave of his pupils. The whole assembly of disciples wept. That day the millionaires, who could acquire anything with their wealth, could not acquire the opportunity of serving Guruji. It was then they understood the futility of their wealth.

Guruji instructed us, "Tomorrow night I shall leave Bombay, only the Swami will accompany me, and no one else. There is no need for anyone to come to the station." On hearing this, the entire assembly was upset, but since they were used to obeying his wishes, they remained silent. They neither debated nor expressed disappointment.

Guruji had requested two third-class tickets. Convinced of his lack of interest in worldly things, no one debated this either. When he arrived in Bombay, Guruji had brought with him two towels, one pair of pants, and a waterpot. When he was ready to leave a year and a half later, he had the same two towels, the same old pants, and the same pot. Although Guruji had innumerable millionaire disciples, he had never asked for anything, nor had he accepted anything that was given to him that was unasked for.

To be totally detached from wealth was his nature. And I'm the disciple of that great man.

Our pilgrimage began at the Bombay train station. Guruji and I had been taken by car, and we boarded the train and sat together in a very dark coach. We had two tickets to Mathura in central India. Guruji had asked me not to carry any money in my pocket. He alone was my source of wealth, so I was not worried.

The train started and we were on our way. Seated near the window, I was trying to take in the scenery in the darkness.

Guruji sat in concentration. For him any place in the world was suitable for meditation. Like a succession of births and deaths the stations came and went until finally we arrived at Mathura. There we got out, drank and bathed in the waters of the Jamuna River. A kind gentleman invited us for a meal and we ate together.

During the next three days we completed our pilgrimage to the birth and early childhood places where Shri Krishna lived. We visited Mathura, Gokul, and Vrindavan. On the fifth day we set out for Delhi on foot. The distance from Mathura to Delhi is ninety miles. Resting for an hour at midday, we continued our journey on an empty stomach. In this way we reached Nizamuddin in three days. During that time we received one meal without asking.

I was young and energetic, but I had never walked thirty miles at a stretch. Since I didn't understand the purpose of this journey, I didn't have much enthusiasm. At one point I tripped, and the strap on one of my sandals broke. Since I had no money, I couldn't get it fixed. So I placed my sandals in my bag, and I continued walking barefoot.

My Storehouse of Conceit

At the beginning of our journey I thought this old man wouldn't be able to walk very far. However, when he walked without stopping for thirty miles on the first day, I regarded old age as praiseworthy and my youth as contemptible.

I did not imagine that Guruji would walk thirty miles the second day. However, when once again he proceeded walking rapidly, I imagined his feet were made of iron, not flesh and blood. My vanity stopped me from saying "I'm tired," for the strength of my youth hoped to vanquish the strength of his old age.

So I ground my teeth and continued walking. On the third day we started out again. Utterly exhausted, however, I sat down under a tree and cried loudly. I said to Guruji, "I can't walk anymore." Thus on the third day, my pride collapsed. Was Guruji unaware of my difficulties? Oh, he knew them only too well, but he wanted to bring down my pride, for he said to me, "If you had told me from the beginning, I would not have walked more than ten miles a day. But you're extremely conceited, which is not a good trait; you must be more humble."

Even in that state my temperament asserted itself as I blurted out, "Tell that to God, not to me. He alone made my mind a storehouse of conceit."

Smiling and pinching my cheek, Guruji sat down and began massaging my feet. His gentle touch made me feel like a child. I would have liked to tell him to stop, but I couldn't. Seeing his greatness and extreme kindness, once again I cried like a baby.

I don't remember how long he massaged my feet, but in a short while, the aching ceased. In this world no one has loved me the way he did.

Following Disappointment

After massaging my feet, Guruji massaged my body. When he thought I was recovered, he said, "My son, do you want to eat?"

I laughed and said: "I certainly want to eat. However, without your assistance, what good is this desire? In forty-eight hours, not a grain has entered my stomach." He patted me lovingly and with a laugh we started out for the closest village.

Guruji's heart was a combination of mother and father. From ancient times it's accepted practice that the disciple goes to a town or village and begs on behalf of his guru. Though I had no desire for him to beg for me, I was in no condition to beg myself. Here the order was reversed. The guru begged from house to house for his disciple.

I had never begged and did not know how. Nonetheless, had Guruji wanted to eat, I would gladly have found a way to beg on his behalf. After an hour, he came back from the village bringing twenty-five thalis made from leaves. There must have been a group eating dinner but much of the food remained uneaten.

As he sat beside me, he started to arrange the food onto separate thalis. This same man who had golden vessels and a golden throne at his disposal was now eating food he had begged from others.

Truly that was supreme nonattachment. In his noble vision the idea of clean and unclean did not exist as it did for us Brahmins. Although I felt Guruji could eat leftovers, because he was unattached, I couldn't because of my tradition. He was an unshaken, equanimous saint as related in the sacred scripture, the *Bhagavad Gita*.

After arranging the food onto thalis, Guruji said, "Look, son, eat your food."

On hearing such kind words, I thought, "Guruji is a great man, a solitary man. I am his chief disciple and I should follow in his footsteps, for he has enriched my soul. There's no sense in making a fuss for I'm extremely hungry."

Then my feeble mind gave me further advice, "No one's going to see you here, so be quiet and eat your food." I sat down and found the food very tasty. Guruji and I ate from the same thali.

That night I ate and slept soundly. However, when I awakened the next morning, I found myself alone under a tree. Guruji had left and gone away. For two days I stayed under the same tree and waited for him, but in the end I was disappointed. This story is more than forty years old today. Guruji never contacted me. He never wrote to anyone and, in spite of my being his favorite, he never wrote a letter to me. For this reason, no one knows where he is or whether he's alive.

Yet today I have been in continuous yogic practice for over thirty years. I do not believe it is courage that has propelled me, but the supreme compassion of God and guru. In truth, Guruji fed me with a mother's love.

The newly initiated swami

CHAPTER SIX

A SWAMI'S LIFE

Om namah shivaya
I surrender to Lord Shiva.

(*Shiva Mantra*)

Many things at first regarded as coincidences often turn out to be the fruits of a celestial design. After I completed my training with Guruji, I lived in society for more than eight years. Suddenly one day my illusions about the world ended, and I went to seek sannyas. I received initiation from Swami Shantanandji Maharaj, a solitary learned man, and then donned the saffron robes of a swami. Thus Gurudev's predictions came true.

Swami Shantanandji Maharaj was unattached and gentle. He worshipped cows, and he used to tell everyone that the cow alone is the Holy Spirit. He left Uttar Pradesh and came to the banks of the Narmada, in Gujarat, for the purpose of yogic observances.

From childhood I had been brought up to believe in one God. In the tradition of my first guru, all the mantras held the same intrinsic power. However, each one is used during a different stage of life or different occasion. To the married, we give the Gayatri Mantra, single people are initiated on the path of yoga with the Vishnu Mantra (*Om Namo Bhagavate Vasudevaya*), and the sannyasis receive the renunciate's mantra or the Shiva Mantra (*Om namah Shivaya*).

Without performing a mantra, it cannot be understood, yet its power to purify is overwhelming. So when I was given the Shiva mantra to repeat, I could immediately sense its power. Even by relating these incidents about Guruji's life, I've purified my speech.

Now I'll relate something about my silence. In 1958 there was a big celebration for my birthday. After that I took up vows of silence so that I could make sadhana the sole focus of my attention. By the time my birthday rolled around in 1970 that silence was twelve years old.

It has protected me well, but I've only been able to observe silence through the grace of God and guru. Since I'm a seeker of salvation, solitude and meditation alone are dear to me. Truly there is only one thing I want to do in life, and that is to do sadhana as far as sadhana will take me. Silence has been the means to devote myself wholeheartedly to yoga sadhana, so that now there's no more attraction for money, fame, or fortune.

In spite of my love for solitude and silence, God pushed me into a stream of activity. When I went to Kayavarohan for the first time, I realized it was an ancient place of worship. I read its history, and went and visited each temple on the site. Then I got the inspiration for the rebirth of this holy place. It may have seemed courageous to take on such a monumental task, but I don't believe in courage. However I am a great believer in God and I believe that God willed me to take up that mission.

After ten years I founded the Society for the Preservation of Kayavarohan and announced before everyone: "For the rebirth of this holy place a total of fifty million rupees will be required." When the people heard such a large sum announced, they felt faint. However, I have an abiding faith in God, so if he asked me to do this, then in some inexplicable way it will get done. This work isn't mine. It's God's. I'm merely performing His service.

A holy man once said: "I've never known anyone shamed through worshipping God. He whose mind is with Krishna speaks the language of the Vedas." Saints' words are never false. If I'm not a saint and if God has not willed me to begin the rebirth of this holy place, then I've just been suffering from illusions and the consequences will be disappointing. Without any hope for self-gratification and only believing it to be God's will, I carried out the work of rebuilding this temple. When I had no more pride, I truly became a sadhu. Today there is nothing on my books to my credit and the debit side is also blank. One could say in the land of the unclothed, what need is there for a dhoti?

After taking my sannyas training, for the purification of my soul I performed many small constructive deeds in the villages I was visiting. This went on for about eight years. Cities no longer held an attraction for me and I was neither drawn toward their rich dwellers nor toward the successful life. Good behavior, restraint, praying to God, service, dedication, repeating mantra, studying, and teaching from the scriptures—these are what I enjoyed the most.

Guruji taught me that these acts could banish sorrow. He also put extreme importance on celibacy. He used to say that celibacy alone increased the value of worship and that through the combination of physical and spiritual virtues one became holy. Celibacy alone brought out the highest in a person. I later became convinced that this premise was even scientifically true.

Earlier, when I saw rich men traveling around in their cars, I considered that there must be other ways of reaching the highest apart from celibacy. When I put this to Guruji, he said: "My son, you only know the superficiality of this premise, and not its root. Any form of spiritual practice must be firm at its base. It's this firmness which gives rise to all results." Only after many years did I understand the importance of his statement.

By the time I was thirty-two, I had left worldly attachments behind and moved about freely as a swami. After receiving *swami diksha* or initiation, I traveled along the shores of the Narmada River in the state of Gujarat. I would spend no more than a day or two in each village and then move on. I was detached from everything that had been part of my life prior to this time— my relatives, my home, my town, everything.

The purpose of being initiated, dressing in swami clothes, and carrying a begging bowl, is to learn to trust in God. Although a swami begs for food to sustain himself, he must go not to one but to seven homes, in order that families not be depleted by what they give. A swami also has to be prepared to sleep under a tree. He depends upon God for all necessities of life. At the same time as part of his practice, he may not place any wants or conditions on God.

Since I had never asked for alms, I was a little bit hesitant as to how to go about begging for food. After leaving the ashram I walked about three or four miles. I came to a small town with a temple. I went in, bowed down, and took my seat in the corner in order to pray. It was exactly twelve noon— time for a meal. Although I didn't desire food just yet, I was beginning to be preoccupied with the way it would work.

"If I do not ask for food for two or three days, it will be all right," I thought to myself. "But I will definitely have to go for alms on the fourth or fifth day."

In the temple compound there was another temple next to the one I was in. A mother and her son lived there and performed puja for both temples. All of a sudden I heard the son tell his mother, "Yesterday auntie told me that she would come for a meal today. Yet today when I went to call for her, she said she'd been joking. In fact, she had already finished her meal."

"What will I do with all this food that I prepared?" his mother wondered aloud. "Never mind, son; finish your puja."

So he came into the temple and began worshipping God. Seeing me, he finished his puja in a hurry and returned to his mother.

"Mother, there's a swami sitting in the temple," he told her.

"Ah, my son, then this meal has been prepared for him. Go and tell him not to seek alms anywhere else, because his food is already here."

Her son quickly came to me, bowed down, and asked me to go to his home for a meal, so of course I accompanied him. His mother was standing on the steps with a bucketful of water, and, as was the custom, she washed my feet. Then her son took a towel and wiped them off. Once inside they seated me on a wooden platform. Incense was lit and a beautiful meal laid out. As soon as I began eating, both mother and son started fanning me. Tears rolled down my eyes for my first meal as a wandering swami. I offered thanks to God and prayed that I would never, every worry about myself again. The Lord is truly the well-wisher of us all; it's His goal to bring happiness to everyone.

In the early days I bathed in lakes and rivers and washed my clothes by pounding them on nearby rocks. Shantanandji had given me my swami provisions: two dhotis, several loincloths, a towel, a sheet, a blanket, and a mat. Since I didn't accept money, I couldn't afford to buy soap. Often when I was resting, however, one of the local sisters would take the clothes I'd just washed and wash them again in the river with soap.

Once I'd begun my yoga sadhana, however, I was fortunate to stay in the homes of my disciples. Each day they'd take my clothes and carefully wash and press them. Feeling embarrassed, I'd ask them not to do that, but they replied, "Bapuji, our children are fighting among themselves to press your clothes and will not listen to us."

Motioning them to sit down, I said, "My children, we sannyasis are required to observe certain restrictions. What you consider service is a luxury for someone else."

They swiftly replied, "Whoever visits is coming only for your darshan. No one cares whether you wear pressed or unpressed clothes. Let us serve you in this way and don't worry about what others think."

In time I learned to be tolerant even in such matters as how to dress. When the ashrams of Malav and Kayavarohan were established, however, nonattachment became displeased and left me altogether. Heaps of dhotis, kurtas, sweaters, shawls, towels, napkins, handkerchiefs, sandals, and shoes piled up. Whenever a brother or sister disciple brought newly made clothes, I would lovingly scold them. "Why have you gone to such trouble without consulting me?"

They replied, "We don't need your instruction in such mundane matters."

"But I have many clothes."

"That's okay. We'll simply give the old ones to a needy person. You don't need to worry about it."

I never had time to consider my worthiness or unworthiness in these matters. Yet it was my strong desire to remain steadfast on the path of love. Reflecting upon the feelings of my disciples, however, I absorbed the love from their pure hearts. For in truth, love is the most pious pilgrimage, and purity can be acquired only by bathing in it.

Before my first year of official yoga sadhana, I was totally satisfied studying and chanting the *Gita* daily and reciting various hymns in praise of God. By then I was practicing yoga in the town of Rajpipla; later I went to Halol. I had established an organization called Shri Krishna Gomandir and remained there approximately eight years after my sannyas initiation. I was thirty-eight years old.

When Gurudev had initiated me at the age of nineteen, he taught me only one yoga posture: the lotus position. He said to me, "This posture is the seed of all postures; you will accomplish countless postures through it." And the only pranayama he taught me was alternate nostril breathing. He said, "This is the key to yoga; by practicing it properly, eventually you'll learn all yogas and tantras."

Although I did not grasp what he meant, I listened very carefully and had unflinching faith in his teachings. When I moved to Halol, I began practicing pranayama according to Gurudev's guidance. At first I practiced in three one-hour sittings in the morning, afternoon, and in the evening. By the second or third month I began practicing for one and a half-hours at each sitting.

Since there were many mosquitoes, I sat on a bed covered with mosquito netting. However, one day I slid into psychic sleep unexpectedly and could not remember anything when I awoke an hour later. Strangely enough, my body was in the lotus posture with my chin touching the floor. This was a new posture to me, and since I knew nothing of *yoga nidra* (a yogic or psychic sleep), I imagined that I had either been sleeping or unconscious.

I began to explore what was happening. The next day I decided to let the mosquitoes bite; I would not do pranayama under the mosquito net anymore. I placed a mat on the floor, and I began my breathing exercises that continued for an indeterminate period of time.

All of a sudden I found myself standing up and performing various postures, *mudras* (spontaneous movements) and dances. Overjoyed at these experiences, I was amazed at their spontaneous quality. Later on I learned their connection to *shaktipat*, the awakening of divine energy.

I had only heard the expression "shaktipat" when someone visiting Gurudev requested shaktipat initiation. Although he turned him down, I asked later, "Guruji, what does shaktipat initiation mean?"

Briefly he replied, "It's the final initiation given to a seeker of liberation. After receiving this initiation, various yogic actions manifest spontaneously in the *sadhak* (spiritual seeker), and from then on, he need not learn any of these actions from anyone."

Earlier a fellow disciple had presented me a large book on raja yoga written by Swami Vivekananda. I read everything carefully. Before this I had never read a single yogic scripture. In fact I didn't even know their names. After that incident, however, I became very interested in yoga sadhana as new experiences manifested each day of my practice.

Reading scriptures like the *Upanishads* and the *Darshanas* has brought about an amazing change in my temperament. They have converted me from an ordinary reader into a contemplative thinker. I can no longer read much. The moment I read one verse, I fall into deep contemplation. Yet if my study were without books, I'd feel like a bird without wings.

The varieties of yoga experience continued to amaze me and new postures and movements surfaced each day. One day I experienced severe itching under my tongue during yoga practice. It became so severe that I rubbed my fingernail on it. Since my fingernail had grown quite long, it cut right through the tendon and blood began flowing. After meditation I examined my tongue in the mirror and was amazed to see that the tendon had been cut. I had not heard of khechari mudra, an advanced yoga technique in which the tongue ascends through the soft palate. Gurudev had never given me instruction about it, but that's what was happening to me. Later I learned of its extraordinary significance through yoga books and scriptures. As I read descriptions of various asanas, mudras, and pranayams and saw how my own experience precisely matched those described in yogic scriptures, my joy was boundless.

On Sanatana Dharma (Eternal Truth)

The scriptures explain all the stages of life from birth to death. What are the duties of a student and a householder? And what are the duties of one who reenters spiritual life or who enters the final stage of life, called sannyas? Described in great detail, these stages are designed in such a way that no matter what nation you belong to, nothing poses as a barrier because you're following the path of truth. From childhood my thoughts about religion have been unique. I believe in one God, and I believe in the unity of all beings. If we're worshippers of truth, then all gates of religion should be open.

The spiritual path that I teach is called *sanatana dharma*, which means "the way of eternal truth." First practiced by the *rishis* of ancient India, sanatana dharma is not a sectarian creed or point of view. It is the performance of skillful actions that lead one to the direct realization of truth. Truth cannot belong to any one race, sect, or nation. It does not recognize such narrow distinctions; it makes itself available to the whole world. Once a seeker has experienced and realized the truth, his whole life is guided by that truth. Truth becomes his only guide, his only guru, his only God.

Religion is like a needle that sews two things together. On the other hand, irreligious behavior is like a scissors, cutting everything in two. To determine whether a religion is true, all you need to know is whether it teaches love and creates unity among all beings. For religion has one identifying characteristic — it can be eternally relied on to evoke the true experience of oneness. You can only consider a religion immortal if its truth cannot be destroyed. Everything else is destructible.

So the old rishis or visionaries gave sanatana dharma its name by studying its character. Sanatana dharma was born in sacred places in the woods, and it has been sustained in every sacred place on earth. You won't find missionaries of sanatana dharma. It's not a religious sect; it's the supreme human experience. For that reason it's never been necessary to propagate it. Even the great masters, who wrote scriptures once they perceived the truth, remain unknown. When I practice the sadhana of truth, I never take into account my nationality or religion. I never think of myself as a Brahmin or a swami—a follower of truth has no such ties. Conveying the beauty and magnitude of sanatana dharma is not only beyond my capacity but also beyond that of any great master. You cannot understand it without direct experience.

The expression *vasudhaiva kutumbakam* means, "the whole world is one family." Sanatana dharma prescribes that we continually develop this familial feeling. Thus the renunciate cultivates a more expansive feeling of love for his world-family, to which he subordinates his feelings of love for his original family.

Not long after I'd become a swami, the people of Halol extended a special invitation to my mother, who visited us for several days. Before returning home, she expressed a strong desire to me, "Swamiji, now I'm old and cannot follow you wherever you go. If you come to Dabhoi just once a year, I'll be happy."

Affectionately I gave my consent. Then a year later when I was on my way to Rajpipla, I suddenly remembered that promise to my mother. Since Dabhoi was in the same direction, I stopped in to visit my mother. It was noon and she was performing her daily ceremonial worship. Overjoyed to see me, she completed her worship and ten minutes later carried a ceremonial tray to the chair where I was seated. When she sat down in front of me and asked me to extend my feet, I was shocked. I asked her what she was doing.

"Today I would like to wash your feet, Swamiji, and I want to receive mantra initiation as well. I have great faith in you, for you have never deceived me. My husband was a devotee of the

Lord and both his sons are now renunciates. Now like a solitary tree in the desert, I am alone in this world. I want to pass the rest of my life in devotion to God. Please give me guidance so I may die in peace. I have spent all these years without a guru just to meet you, the *sadguru* (the highest master). Please be my guru. I am illiterate and foolish, but I have faith that you will take me to the opposite shore."

Her throat was so choked with emotion that she could no longer speak. Although mother had always tolerated pain well and rarely cried, now she was crying profusely. Each word pierced my heart. During my youth she spoke very little for the most part and would mostly listen to family members, since her husband and sons (myself included) tended to dominate the conversation. In fact I had never heard her speak so soulfully. My eyes overflowed with tears, and I got up from my chair and embraced her.

In that moment I instinctively realized that the mothers of the saints in ancient India must have been this simple, affectionate, and devoted.

Immediately I bowed at her feet and said, "Mother how beautifully you've spoken; it has touched my heart. Yet you should not speak this way, because you are *my* guru. You have inspired me, and you are the boat that takes us to the opposite shore. A boat does not require another boat."

Nevertheless, my words did not change her mind. "Even after being initiated as a sannyasi, do you still consider me your mother?"

"Of course. How could I forget to honor you as my mother? You are an extraordinary being. Not only have you fed me milk; you have fed me liberation itself."

As she usually did, mother remained firm, "Give me mantra initiation just as you've initiated others."

To satisfy her pure feelings, I seated myself on the chair and allowed her to wash my feet. After puja, I gave her mantra initiation and the appropriate guidance. Finally she bowed down reverently and made the traditional offering of rupees to the guru and then cooked the foods that I liked the most. Whenever I remember that special event, I drown in the depths of my mother's greatness.

If you want to worship truth at all, then begin with the sacred commandment: "Know your parents as gods." The first truth is that your mother is divine, and your father is divine. If you can follow that much, you will bring sanatana dharma into your life.

A Swami's Needs

Since my nature is to submit to the wishes of loved ones, I imagine this has also made me prone to surrendering to the Lord. I have another unique personality trait—I will never compromise my deepest-held values, nor do I consider anyone my friend who attacks these same beliefs.

On the other hand, to be utterly supported in carrying out my work is a great gift. Therefore I wanted to praise the village of Malav in Gujarat, which looked after me with love during my twelve-year stay many years ago. In my experience, the people of Malav are simple, generous, loving, and always ready to satisfy one's wishes.

In 1958 I came to Malav for my birthday festival and thought how good it would be to live in a hut and carry out my yoga observance. I told the elders I wished to stay and asked if I could have a hut built in a quiet place at the edge of the village. I asked that it should have cane walls and a palm-leafed roof, but made so that mice, ants, cockroaches, mosquitoes, and other insects could not get into it.

I suggested a hut for the reason that if I left, no one would be disappointed. Leaving a solid house behind would be more difficult. On hearing my concern about insects, the elders put up solid walls and a roof of tiles. When the monsoons came, however, torrential rain fell and water seeped through the tiles. Thus, while I was seated in meditation, the room gradually filled with water. When two of the elders came to see the hut, I opened the door and immediately began crying, for not only had my meditation been interrupted, but also there was no place to sit now that the rain was falling.

The elders consoled me immediately and took me to the village to find me a quiet, dry place. Within several days, they had patched the roof. After that, alterations were made, and the ugly hut turned into a beautiful home. Truly, I cannot paint a picture of the kind of service offered me by the town of Malav. The day before the festival, I told the workers that when I gave my speech, I would relate some of the events of my guru Pranavanandji's life and of my silence, and also the service done by the village.

Immediately they said, "There's no need to speak of our service. Please do not waste time talking about it." These were the sentiments of pure souls, hard for me to put into words.

In the village, everyone remarked, "Bapuji's footsteps have made our village a happy one. A canal was constructed, a new school for boys was built; and rooms were added to the girls' school. The Town Hall and clinic were built, the water tank added, and many other things took place."

The people of the village gave me credit for these good works. However, what happened was the result of their efforts and the grace of God. My feet have trodden through many villages. If there had been some kind of magic in my feet, then everywhere I've gone, you'd see the same results. But it didn't turn out that way. What happened, instead, came as a response to their beliefs, their love, and their kind feelings toward me.

My training for sannyas took place more than thirty years ago. Since then I've never had a coin in my pocket, and society has taken care to see that I've never needed one. I've regularly received one hot meal and one hot drink a day. Thus I'm fortunate that society has provided for my needs without my having to ask.

In fact I have more than I need. Although I had no need for a hot drink, my closest female disciples insisted that I have one and brought it each day so there was no choice but to drink it. At first the milk contained a lot of water mixed with it, as I requested. But little by little, my beloved daughters decreased the proportions of water and increased the milk. Since I didn't want to hurt their feelings, I kept quiet about it.

It's hard to convey the simplicity of a swami's needs. When I eat, for example, I always close the door of my dining room. If too many dishes have been prepared, I'm careful not to overdo it, since I eat a very moderate amount. Usually I put the food I need on one thali and the extra food on another.

When the disciple who prepared my meal came to pay her respects and saw the food left over, she thought I didn't enjoy the meal. Seeing her so dejected, I asked, "Why is your face so sad today?"

She blurted out, "Because of how little you ate. Didn't you like the food? I can always prepare something else." I explained about my diet and yoga practice and assured her that the little I'd eaten did not reflect upon her good cooking. Immediately she became calm. It's truly the grace of God that my disciples take care of me in situations like this, especially when they're innocent as to the nature of my practice.

Moderation in Diet

Looking back on those days, I realize how hard it was to set good habits in motion, especially around food. Moderation in diet must be practiced until you attain complete liberation. However, it's difficult to fast if you're in the stage of sadhana that I'm in. In fact, it's difficult even to eat moderately, because my disciples bring me fruits, nuts, sweets, and a whole variety of foods as an expression of their love.

Although I eat a little bit of everything, still it gets to be too much. When I came to America, Urmila Desai, my disciple, had placed different jars of almonds, cashews, and figs in the house, saying, "In the evening, you can take a little bit," but I told her to please take it all away. Wisdom stays alive when excess food is absent.

Now I take only one meal a day, and I've made arrangements that no food is kept in my room. I'm old. God has given me some wisdom, so my mind is not as mischievous as before, but if it acts up, I avoid what it likes the most. Without such wisdom, how can we grow? I've given you this background so you can understand the conditions of my sadhana and what brought me to this stage of my life.

In the yoga tradition there are certain guidelines to help you. If you want to keep up your health, fast on water at least one day a week. If you can't do that, then take only juice. If that's not possible, then drink milk. And if that's difficult, take one fruit with the milk. If you can't do that, then eat one moderate meal during the day. And if you can't do that, then just sit in the kitchen and eat whatever you want all day long.

In the beginning of my life as a swami, I only drank milk when I delivered discourses in the small villages, even if I remained there for a month. That made it easy for me to lecture, since my body was alert and my mind one-pointed. Invariably the townspeople gave me so much love I forgot I'd been fasting.

In order to support my yoga sadhana, I've made innumerable experiments with diet through the years. For instance, for six months I ate only two small bowls of mung bean soup daily. For three years I fasted on milk alone. I also lived on a small amount of popcorn for six months.

I liked that spiced popcorn very much. Always coming out of meditation at ten o'clock in the morning, I would eat as much popcorn as I could, chewing thoroughly, till 10:30. Then I washed my hands and mealtime was over. Although I've conducted many experiments on diet, I've come to the conclusion that the best thing to do is to eat only one meal a day.

The Buddha also experimented with diet. He began by taking a handful of rice and counting the grains, each day subtracting one grain from what he ate until only one remained. However, on the very last day of his fast he fainted from weakness. What saved him was some rice pudding graciously offered by a peasant woman. After that, he said, "One should follow the path of moderation. If the strings of an instrument are kept too loose, they cannot produce music, and if stretched too tightly, they will break. An instrument can only give music when tuned moderately. Similarly, the amount of food one eats should be moderate — neither too much nor too little."

Living Religion

Never forget that an unshakable and virtuous way of life is the essence of living religion. No matter whether you believe in Krishna, Rama, Shiva, Christ, Moses, Buddha, Allah, or God — you may believe in anything — if this worship does not produce an unshakably virtuous way of life, then your belief is useless. Unshakable virtue is the foundation of religion; seeking it alone constitutes the true search.

The deep meaning of yoga cannot be understood by reading volumes or listening to tales. For such understanding, one must have endless concentration. I'll give you an example: Mr. Mashak from France was twenty years old when he came to India to study yoga. He used to meditate in Rishikesh. There he met my disciple, Amrit Desai, who was on a pilgrimage with some of his American students. Mr. Mashak had made a list of all the yogis to visit in India and Amrit added my name to his list and begged him to come see me. After talking to me, Mashak humbly asked: "Guruji, please accept me as your disciple."

I answered him saying: "My son, first go and meet the yogis on your list. If after that, you feel inspired to come to me, then do so."

A few days later he went on his journey and, after meeting all the yogis, he returned and offered himself to me saying: "Guruji, I accept you alone as my guru. I left my country, my relatives, and all worldly things to come to India. Please give me training in yoga." He continued, "I've made a firm resolution. Only when I become a yogi will I return to my native land. If not, I'll die here in India. I've heard that great yogis give instruction in shaktipat, which quickly puts the disciple on the road to yoga. Guruji, please give this child instruction in shaktipat and do not scorn him as foreign and unholy."

Seeing his love of yoga, I felt great love for him and gave him shaktipat training. I had known about shaktipat for the last twenty years but had never given it to anyone. Since the yogic scriptures say that this training should be given only to the highest seeker of salvation, I thought I would reserve it for a true and honest disciple. However, it seemed that his being there must be God's will, and I did not question it anymore. In giving shaktipat, the meditator is seated in concentration and sent off on the path of yoga. This meditation is very enlightening and it does not take one long to be completely absorbed in it.

First, I taught Mashak asanas, pranayama, pratyahar, dharana, dhyana, and elements of the eight-limbed path of yoga. Finally, I told him to chant the Ram mantra constantly. After learning how to repeat it, he said to me: "Who is Ram and why should I repeat his name? I have no faith in it."

He was a foreigner and, for him, the Ram mantra was new and strange. I made an effort to explain to him that Rama is the name of God that one repeats in order to purify one's mind. I instructed him that this sound originates in yoga and comes from the sound of the infinite. Only when one hears this sound through the study of yoga can its essence be conveyed.

At that time I also gave him the name Shubhadarshan. Beginning his practice of yoga, on the third day, he started chanting *"rama, rama, rama,"* loudly. When he came to pay his respects to me, Shubhadarshan said: "Guruji, I want to ask your forgiveness for my stupidity in not wanting to repeat the Ram mantra. Truly this Ram mantra amazes me. Now I clearly understand that the essence of yoga is not revealed through the strength of imagination, but through the strength of study."

A year later I asked him: "Well, my son, are you still repeating the Ram mantra?'

Laughing, Shubhadarshan replied in Hindi: "Gurudev, each hair of this body is filled with Ram mantra. From the moment I get up till the moment I go to bed, the mantra repeats itself continuously."

The Victory of Ideas

Our ideas are colored by our previous way of life. But we can choose a desirable idea in order to cancel the effects of an undesirable one. This reminds me of an event that took place some thirty years ago.

I lived in the village of Avidha near Rajpipla in the state of Gujarat. In the morning I conducted *Bhagavad Gita* class and in the evening I gave lectures on the *Gita*. Since members of the village were well educated, the hall was always filled to capacity.

At that time I was newly a sannyasi, and so a bit more proud of my renunciation. Moreover, I was an intellectual who often enjoyed displaying my learning. After one month, the village people took me to their hearts, so that any time of day a group of twenty-five to fifty men and women were sitting at my residential place. I was staying on the upper floor of a villager's home. The whole family served me heartily.

One day I was sitting on a swing lecturing to ten or twelve men and women. I was used to speaking in a light vein and everyone was pleased with the talk. In the midst of our conversation, however, the wife of the household suddenly entered, carrying bowls, plates, and other material with her.

I asked her, "What's all this?"

"It's material for remedying the evil eye," she replied.

"The evil eye?"

"Yes."

"For whom is this remedy intended?"

"For you."

I laughed and said, "For me?"

"Yes."

The woman was a very good and pious lady. She loved me very much, and I also loved her. Although she was older, she behaved like a young daughter.

"What did I do to catch the evil eye?" I asked.

"Narayan! Your speech is very sweet. That is not just my experience but that of the whole village." Then I became serious, considering that too much talkativeness or display of enthusiasm may not have been good. I asked her, "What has my speech got to do with the evil eye?"

"Narayan! You've been suffering from fever for the last two days. I think your speech attracted someone's evil eye."

Although I wanted to laugh, I suppressed it, and instead kept mum as she prepared to remedy the evil eye. When the inverted bowl stuck firmly to the plate, she smiled and said, "Narayan! See how the bowl stuck to the plate! Didn't I say it was the evil eye? I was afraid you wouldn't allow me to treat you, but I was determined to remedy this."

While it was often my habit to joke and make fun of things, I restrained myself and said, "Now the fever must surely disappear." My reply satisfied her and in a short time she took everything with her and returned downstairs.

An elderly gentleman among the graduates sitting before me spoke out, "Swamiji! You belong to the new age and your views are liberal. I'm shocked to see you falling for this superstition."

I argued, "I'm a scientist. I don't believe in superstition."

"Was there any science in remedying the evil eye?" he asked.

"Yes."

"Please explain it clearly."

I replied, "I've been suffering from a little fever the last two days, and this woman thought I'd fallen prey to someone's evil eye. If I'd entered into a discussion with her to try to remove the notion, we would have wasted a lot of time, and she would have been offended. Even then her idea would have remained intact."

"However, when I saw that she'd brought up the remedy, I remained silent. She believed I was suffering from the evil eye, but she also believed that treatment would help. One thorn removed another. If the presumption of the evil eye was a superstition, the presumption that a cure was possible was yet another superstition, canceling the first. I loved the good result more than the victory of my own ideas."

Seated in meditation

Statue of Lord Brahmeshvar (Dadaji)
in Kayavarohan Temple

CHAPTER SEVEN

A MONUMENTAL RESOLVE

Om namah shivaya gurave

sacchidananda murtaye

namastasmai, namastasmai,

namastasmai, namo namaha.

O Lord Shiva, I bow to you

in the form of the Guru,

and surrender to your bliss, consciousness, and truth.

To you I bow, to you I bow, to you I bow with great respect.

(Bapuji's Mantra of Surrender)

In the process of purifying the mind, a resolute will is of prime importance, for the power of will is synonymous with the power of the self. A will that is self-possessed has a rock-like sustaining power that fends off any disturbance. By developing willpower, one acquires a strong mind and point of focus.

A person with a strong mind does not harbor many little resolutions. Rather a single, monumental resolve inspires and drives his actions. An all-encompassing resolve defines his life's vision, and every aspect of his life unfolds that resolve. As a result, his life exemplifies his vision as much as his vision shapes and defines his life.

That describes a Shiv-resolve. Dedicated in name to the most resolute yogi of all, Lord Shiva, a Shiv-resolve is equivalent to a solemn vow or oath. Unexpectedly I came to know the power and magic of a Shiv-resolve. It was over twenty years ago that a friend invited me to Kayavarohan for two days during their devotional song festival or bhajan week. Although by that time I'd stopped traveling and had lost interest in delivering lectures, I said yes. Looking back, I deem it a gift of Lord Shiva.

On the appointed day, I arrived. Although my hometown Dabhoi is quite close to Kayavarohan, I had never seen the village, so I visited for the first time on a lecture invitation.

The next day some residents called on me to invite me on a tour of the holy and ancient temples of Kayavarohan. While someone narrated the history of each temple and residing deity, we walked from one structure to the next. If any facts were missing, another person spoke up and provided key information. This warm and sincere invitation touched my heart.

When they excitedly told me that Kayavarohan was considered a second Kashi or home of salvation, I became intrigued. In present day India, Kashi, now known as Benares, is considered the highest place of pilgrimage. Now these townspeople were telling me that this was in fact *another* Kashi. The amazing thing was that this *Mahatirtha* or great pilgrimage place was only ten miles from my birthplace and I didn't know anything about it.

All this time I had been intensely concentrating on the subtle physical forms at this site. My ears were focused on the narration, my eyes were focused on the beauty of the place, and I had no idea that three hours had elapsed. It was sunset and in a very short time, darkness would envelop the earth.

As we entered a temple, one of the guides said, "Our tour comes to an end with this last temple which is the abode of Lord Brahmeshvar. Your lodging place is some five hundred steps from here." As soon as I entered the temple, my eyes fell on the black linga with the beautiful statue of Lord Brahmeshvar embedded on the front of it. Immediately my heart sped up. Copious tears filled my eyes and I felt like I was going to faint, so I leaned against the wall. Taking hold of myself, I then lay prostrate at the feet of the statue, completely surrendered to the Lord. Absolute peace descended on me.

After a few moments I stood up. It had taken me about four hours to visit the different temples, and I was exhausted. But there was no doubt that the form on the front of this linga was the same as my beloved Guru Pranavanandji. I related this to the guides who were with me. Then I told them about my guru. I explained that as a swami I had traveled to the Himalayas many years ago and spent the winters there. There's one pilgrimage place I frequented called Rishikesh. It's a place where many yogis lived, and I studied Sanskrit and practiced my sadhana there. At the time I must have been thirty-five or thirty-six. One day while cutting a small branch off a tree to clean my teeth, I saw an individual with a cloth wrapped around his waist coming down the hill. Because there were so many wandering monks and swamis, I paid no attention to him.

Suddenly hearing the sound, "Swami," I turned around. That voice was identical to my Guru Pranavanandji's. Yet his body was different. The 18-year-old body of his was identical with the one I saw before me on that statue. When I looked at him, he smiled and his eyes twinkled. Despite being disoriented by his form, I realized he was in fact my Gurudev. His voice was exactly the same. I knew he was the only one who could address me in that way. Immediately I hugged him. He stroked my head as I bawled. Then I remembered that I had not bowed down at his feet. "Gurudev, please excuse me," I said as I bowed down.

Although it was winter, he was wearing only a cloth around his waist and the rest of his body was bare. I on the other hand had lots of woolen clothes on. I wanted to give him something warm, but he sat comfortably on a stone and began talking to me. Since I had asked him long ago what the divine body looked like, he had told me that some day I would be able to see it. Now I asked him, "Gurudev, is this the divine body you mentioned long ago?"

"Yes, this is the divine body," he said. I asked him how many years old it was," and he replied, "My son, you'll have to find that out for yourself."

"Gurudev, how in the world can I find out such a thing?"

Again he looked at me with those sparkling eyes but said nothing.

From the brief history I received from the residents of Kayavarohan, I now knew that the form of Lord Brahmeshvar was ancient. On the other hand, my Gurudev lived in recent times. How could I reconcile these contradictions? As we made our way to our lodging place, no one uttered a single word. I arrived at my residence, took a bath, and entered my meditation room. Sitting on my meditation cushion, I prayed to the Lord, as was the customary opening to my practice.

For a long time I had been endeavoring to master one specific stage of yoga, but I was unable to succeed. That day I mastered it effortlessly. Every cell of my body felt the impact of attaining it, and my mind danced with joy. When my normal period of meditation was over, I didn't feel like getting up. Yet I knew it was important to abide by the rules of sadhana. There's a yogic discipline that after a fixed period, you must stop because the nerves undergo extreme purification while you're meditating. If you tire them too much, you'll go crazy. So with great difficulty I got up and went to bed.

However, the meditative state continued. All of a sudden, I saw the morning sun rising over the horizon. In its light I could clearly see a big and beautiful city of innumerable *shivalayas*, places for worship of Lord Shiva. The darkness spread out and that vision gradually faded. Yet the darkness did not completely vanish. It lasted quite some time. Then I saw the sun rise again, and that same city appeared for the second time. However it appeared to be different from the first, though there was a resemblance between the two.

Some invisible divine power was inspiring me through these visions: *Son, the first city you saw was Meghavati and the second was Kayavarohan. Both were located at the same place, yet they appear somewhat different because of a long passage of time. You are our choice to revive Kayavarohan.*

Following these words, I immediately received the darshan of two great sages—Maharishi Vishvamitra and Lord Lakulish. I bowed to them with immense faith and devotion. Tears of joy filled my eyes. In utter humility, I said, "My Lords, your darshan has made my life sublime. I am poor and without resources. How shall I ever be able to carry out the revival of this Mahatirtha?" Back came the divine reply, *Our chosen son, you have only to act as an instrument of divine will. The task will take care of itself.*

The next morning at 7:00 AM, I left my meditation room and sat in the living room. At that time a firm resolve took root in my mind to build an imposing temple and set up a Sanskrit university. When local friends called on me. I asked them, "Who's the most respected person in this area?"

"Sri Hirabhai Patel, who owns the cotton gin," was the reply.

"Please send for him. I want to talk to him," I told them.

Fifteen minutes later they returned with Sri Hirabhai. As he took his seat, I gave voice to my inner thoughts, "Dear friend, I have visited this place for the first time in my life. Yesterday these kind people took me on a tour of the local temples and helped me to have darshan with the deities. They narrated a brief history of this tirtha. Yesterday I found out that the residents of this town refused to depart with the Shiva Linga when someone made a proposal to install it in his new temple. With that in mind, I'd like to suggest that if the residents agree to place this statue of the Lord at my disposal, I will build a grand temple on the outskirts of this town."

Sri Hirabhai had never met me before. I was a complete unknown to him. Yet, with a voice choked with emotion, he replied, "Swamiji Maharaj, you have given expression to my heart's desire. To build a grand temple for Lord Brahmeshvarji and revive this town as a pilgrimage place is my life-long ambition. I thank the all-merciful Lord who's sent you for the fulfillment of this Shiv-resolve of mine. From the cotton gin earnings, I can afford to build a simple temple for about 50,000 rupees, but that's not my preference. My inner resolve is to construct a grand temple of stone in honor of Lord Brahmeshvar.

Sheer insanity marked these thoughts, which then became rooted in both our Shiv-resolves. It appears that two crazy men met and merged into one another like salt in water. Although my insanity was newly born, Hirabhai's was long standing. Our mutual passion made us all the more emotional and bound us together in love and mutual regard.

Clarifying my position, I said, "Hirabhai, at present I'm practicing yoga and will not be able to act on this project immediately. I'll begin work immediately after attaining a certain stage of yoga."

Hirabhai paled and then asked, "Could you give me an idea how many years that will take?"

I replied: "It all depends on God's will. It's difficult to fix an approximate time limit."

Crestfallen and dejected, he asked, "Will I live until then?"

This question made me pause and think. After a few minutes, I said, "Perhaps neither of us will live long enough, but if it's a Shiv-resolve, it's bound to triumph."

Ten years later I founded a committee to develop the project and drew up a brief outline. The total estimated expenses for this project were around fifty million rupees. It was a highly ambitious plan.

One day Hirabhai confided, "Swamiji, people do not believe this can happen. They believe in miracles. But you're a yogi. Even a single miracle will attract innumerable people and generate faith in them."

I laughed aloud." I would not have set up this committee if I thought I could carry this out by performing miracles." Then I added, "Let's both take a vow today to share the burden of building an imposing temple for Lord Brahmeshvar. We will suffer jointly and equally in this religious venture. In the matter of setting up the university, I will bear the lion's share of hardships, and you'll be spared."

He listened very respectfully. At last in a choked voice he said, "Narayan! I deem you as my Guru. I have full faith in every word of yours. Right now I take a solemn vow not to part company with you until I die. What's more, I will cooperate with this mission in every way possible."

For these words of a faithful devotee, I thanked the All-Merciful God, saying, "Lord, you have given me a high-spirited companion." And indeed, Sri Hirabhai was a religious minded, pure, and devoted person. He observed his vow till the last.

When disease overwhelmed him, he became somewhat dispirited and upset. He said to me, "Whoever is born has to die. I'm not afraid of death. I'm ready for it. But my only wish is to see with my own eyes the sacred temple of Lord Brahmeshvar completed and the idol of Lakulish installed there." He passed his last years with this burning passion.

As his time approached, his relatives and well-wishers gathered around and prayed, waiting for him to utter his last wishes. With half closed eyes, he understood the situation. "Why have you come here altogether?" he asked.

All averted their eyes. A few moments passed without words. At last his brother-in-law took courage and in a soft voice requested, "Please tell us what your last wish is."

Hirabhai closed his eyes in introspection. After a while, he opened his eyes and instead of replying, asked them, "Do you promise you'll fulfill my last wish?"

All four of his sons spoke up simultaneously, "Indeed we will!"

"Then listen. The installation of Lord Lakulish's idol must be done in the new temple. This work must never stop."

The sons replied in a firm tone, "This is our vow. The temple construction will be completed. We will see to it that your wish is fulfilled."

Instantly a glow of satisfaction came over his face. "Please send for the leading persons of the tirtha."

In a few moments, the entire room was packed with people. Someone whispered in Hirabhai's ears, "The village leaders have arrived."

He opened his eyes and surveyed the scene. Then he spoke in a feeble voice, "Do you know why you've been called?"

"Yes."

"Have you thought about it in all seriousness and have you arrived at a decision?"

"Yes."

"What is your decision?"

"We will not allow the temple construction work to stop. It shall be completed."

Despite this assurance, he asked again, "Have you made this decision of your own free will?"

"Yes." When he received this final assent from the village aldermen, he folded his hands in gratitude and commenced his last journey.

The whole village was in tears and grief-stricken. When I received the news, I mourned his parting. Whenever I think of him, my heart goes out to him again. I feel his absence with agonizing pain.

I want to convey this holy message to the soul of the late Sri Hirabhai, wherever he might be: "Dear brother, the temple of Lord Brahmeshvar has been built. The idol of Lord Lakulish has been installed. Your Shiv-resolve has been realized. Your sons and friends of the tirtha have fully cooperated in the fulfillment of your last wish.

The Foundation is Laid

After the death of Sri Hirabhai, I visited Kayavarohan. His son Sri Dayabhai presented himself at my service and looked after me very conscientiously. In the course of only four or five days, he won my affection. I started calling him my son. Dayabhai had been appointed head of the board of trustees. Despite the weak financial position of the institution he wasn't negative. On the contrary, he was full of optimism, enthusiasm, and confidence. He was always ready for service. Seeing this, I thought, "Sri Dayabhai has been seized with the Shiv-resolve as well."

I felt that God had given me new strength. The activity of any person possessed with a Shiv-resolve constitutes an open book. Service becomes his prime objective in life. Day and night have meaning to him only insofar as they assist in helping him reach his goal.

Some capable persons pass themselves off as social servants. In fact, they are like greedy traders, who do not relish giving any service unless it brings them renown or other worldly gains. There is a vast difference between an ordinary resolve and a Shiv-resolve. An ordinary resolve cracks under the stress of a single adverse event. On the other hand, the Shiv-resolve assumes more and more firmness as it encounters difficulties. Sri Dayabhai was called to do many different types of service. Indeed, on the altar of this resolve he sacrificed all his resources—body, mind, and wealth—in about equal measure. Not only that, he assigned the utmost importance to this vow, casting aside all personal considerations.

After my birthday festival, I told the villagers of Malav, "I'm moving to Kayavarohan," and they became very sad. I, too, felt sad at the thought of leaving.

Many said, "Bapuji, it will not suit you there." I assured them I had no wish to go anywhere, but that God had willed me to tend the shrine and so I had to go. They became silent. To console them, I explained that Kayavarohan was the seat of the most ancient shrine. Not only that, it was one of the most important places in Aryan culture. Its glory cannot be described in words. According to my understanding, the number of such shrines remaining in

India today can be counted on the fingers of one hand. During the Aryan civilization, however, these great shrines developed and maintained a very sacred religion and pure culture throughout the country.

In the surroundings of these great shrines the holy essence of that age remains intact. It is the holy essence that has inspired me to carry out service. In India, in ancient times, there were said to be only twelve *jyotirlingas*, or light-filled lingas. To find an explanation for the thirteenth, I investigated history books and, thanks to God, solved the problem. Eons ago the great sage Vishvamitra had established this town as Kashi. For this reason, the linga made famous at this shrine had to be a jyotirlinga. It was into this linga that Lord Lakulish was merged, after finishing the work of his avatarship. That is why one sees his outline on the front of the statue.

For fifteen hundred years, disciples of Lord Lakulish managed the shrines of all twelve jyotirlingas throughout India. These sadhaks used to live at Kayavarohan, teaching about scriptures and rituals. It was inconceivable that that shrine, which managed all the shrines of the twelve jyotirlingas, should not itself have a jyotirlinga. One had to assume, therefore, that, the jyotirlinga was hidden somewhere in Kayavarohan. In fact it is this very same jyotirlinga which had been found 100 years ago, buried in a field.

When the head of the Dvarka Temple came to Kayavarohan to lay the foundation stone of the Temple of Lord Brahmeshvar, he said: "Once I wondered why the twelve shrines were called jyotirlingas and what was so unusual about them. On investigating, I found that only those lingas made from meteors are called jyotirlingas." On hearing this, I was filled with joy, for the Brahmeshvar jyotirlinga is made from the substance of a fallen star.

Those who heard me speak with such deep feelings, said, "Bapuji, we have confidence that God will fulfill this work of yours."

A Mighty Force

There were many conflicts with this project. Some residents of the town did not see eye to eye. Labor was scarce. People with only limited capabilities and resources came forward to volunteer their services. On one hand, they had to work hard for their livelihood and on the other hand, they had to find time to assist a spiritual cause. By the grace of God, however, feuding came to an end and local residents gifted land to the institution and cooperated wholeheartedly in developing the project further. Plans for the institution included a temple complex, a library, a university and ashram facilities for study of yoga.

Finally we began making progress. But then we were confronted with elections, famine, drought, heavy rains, and floods — each one slowing us down. I had no idea how we'd ever complete the project. However, with the appointment of new members to the executive committee, the Shiv-resolve gained added momentum. In a short time, it paid off Hirabhai's debt and increased overall donations. This brought new vigor to the members and the project.

When the Shiv-resolve had sprouted in these humble people, it provided them with new impetus. Disciples, friends, and well-wishers made sacrifices for the development of this institution and the attainment of its goals. Strong and beautiful as our edifice is, it has been built on an even stronger foundation.

After a good bit of discussion, the executive committee made a vital decision to install the idol of Lord Lakulishji in the temple. The choice fell on Baroda's noted industrialist, Sri Nanubhai

Amin. My disciple, Sant Muni Rajarshri agreed to assist with this phase of the work. When they started working enthusiastically, it made me feel that both had been possessed with the Shiv-resolve and I was extremely pleased with their service.

By the grace of God, this temple was finally inaugurated in 1974. The auspicious occasion of the *Pranpratishtha* of Lord Brahmeshvar was a day of grand festival. *Pranpratishtha* means "putting life" into the statue. This ceremony went on for four days with about 25,000 people participating.

I was absorbed in this service, without any wish for the fruits. Then after nineteen years, my divine dream — once considered difficult to attain — came true before my eyes. I no longer think of it as a dream, however. I deem it to be a great favor of Lord Shiva. When this Shiv-resolve first germinated in my mind, I didn't have a cent. Nor did I have well-to-do disciples or well-wishers or the necessary strength in body, mind or intellect. I had only one thing — unshakable faith in the Lord. Truly, the Shiv-resolve is a mighty force.

Bapuji with disciples in America

CHAPTER EIGHT

IN AMERICA

Sarvetra sukinah santu
sarve santu niramayha
sarve bhadrani pashyantu
mah kaschid dukkha mapnuyat

May everyone here be happy.
May everyone here be healthy.
May everyone here be prosperous.
May no one experience unhappiness.

(Ancient Sanskrit prayer)

In May of 1977 I arrived in America. I did not come to preach religion or yoga — or any path, for that matter. I came here only to meet my disciples' students. That also happened by chance. For years, Amrit Desai, Yogeshwar Muni, and other disciples kept inviting me here. In India all I did was travel from one room to the next, from the hallway to my sadhana room, not even an eighth of a mile. Under such circumstances it was impossible to imagine coming to America. But, as distractions arose in my practice, I felt it would help to go somewhere far away.

Now that I'm here I wish to address the disciples directly. Owing to the unusual occasion of my travel and because I've broken my customary silence, I will now speak directly to your questions and concerns. After all, I came to America drawn by your love, like iron filings to the magnet. It can be said that what was impossible then became possible. As soon as I arrived and took in the natural beauty of this country, I was extremely pleased. It seems if one meditated under any tree in America, one would immediately sink into a deep state of peace. This is a beautiful country. I am happy to have met you, and I see that you have tremendous love for spiritual growth. A new India is being born here in America, and I hope that it grows and fulfills your needs.

When I started on the path of yoga, I believed I would reach the highest samadhi in six months. As I penetrated deeper into practice, one year passed, then two years, then ten years, and finally twenty-seven years, in which I practiced more than ten hours a day. I made only one decision and that was to travel this path. Anyone who chooses a spiritual path has to give up distractions from the outside world, for as long as one's mind is attracted toward worldly pleasures, it won't be inclined toward God.

Indeed, maya, the Lord's play, is totally beyond our grasp. I'm surprised that I who am accustomed to being confined within the four walls of my residence have managed to travel such a long distance. It must be the strong force of your love; otherwise, what else would drag me thousands of miles from India to America?

This Life of Maya

You've been very kind to me and have given me comfort and happiness. I am pleased with your loving service. In many ways it seems like a dream, which brings to mind the story of Lord Krishna and Sudama. One day Lord Krishna visited

Sudama, his friend and devotee. As soon as Krishna entered his hut he told Sudama's wife that he hoped to stay for a while. She was greatly pleased. Both Sudama and Krishna got together in a small room and began a lively conversation. They kept on talking, oblivious to their surroundings and forgot to bathe or even to eat. Accustomed to their lengthy conversations, Sudama's wife went about her affairs.

After several days, the two friends went to bathe in a nearby river. When they arrived at the riverbank, Sudama remembered his deep longing: "Oh Krishna, I have heard that experiencing your maya is miraculous. Show me that maya."

"It's not worth seeing," said Lord Krishna.

"But everyone says that your maya is unique," Sudama continued, "and you're my friend, so you must show it to me."

"I told you it's not worth seeing. It's just an illusion."

But Sudama insisted, so Krishna said, "Okay, let's bathe first." After diving in, they had a competition as to who could stay under water the longest. After a short period, Sudama crossed the river to the opposite bank. He found that he had come to a different city. Entering the city, he traveled around making inquiries to see whom he might know. Shortly after arriving, he got connected with a certain family and was able to live with them as he studied various subjects. Then he began earning money, engaged in a new business. Years passed. As he was very successful, Sudama built a big palatial building, got married and started a family. He and his wife happily raised their children and the family prospered.

However, there was a special custom in that city. If the wife died, the husband would be cremated along with her. So on the day that his wife died, he was seized and taken to the crematory. They arranged for him to lie beside his wife on a pile of dry wood and a fire was lit around him. Shaking with fear, he called out the name, "Shri Krishna, shri Krishna, shri Krishna."

All of a sudden Sudama came out from his dive under the water and stuck his head above the surface.

"Did you see it?" Lord Krishna asked.

Sudama replied, "Yes, my lord; don't show it to me again." Such was the power of Krishna's maya.

The same thing has happened in my life. Almost like a dream, God has brought me here, and I never believed I'd surface on these shores. But this version of maya is more beautiful than I could ever have imagined, and I'm grateful to be here with you.

Needless to say, this world is an ocean of pain; the Lord alone is the source of bliss. Since everything we perceive is the Lord's maya, under these circumstances it's good just to be able to say a few prayers.

The Fearless Stage

While I'm here visiting the Pennsylvania ashrams, I'll also go to Toronto and California. As I told you before, the purpose of my travel is to meet devotees. I haven't come with a mission of spreading knowledge, religion, or yoga. Originally I came for only three months. After arriving, however, I felt I should stay longer and do more sadhana. So that's what I'm doing. Returning to India after completing this journey, I'll simply enter my sadhana and not come out. With the grace of God my sadhana is progressing well. In fact I may soon achieve the highest stage that I've been hoping to attain for many years.

This stage that I am talking about is called the stage of complete fearlessness. Once you achieve it, you are firmly there and nothing can dislodge you. What I understand about the fearless stage is that the Lord himself takes hold of the devotee's hand and from there on takes care of him completely. After my supreme Samadhi is completed, the remainder of my life will be spent in service to the universe. Even after that stage and regardless of what happens, I will continue my sadhana for a very long time.

The Sadhana of Love

Today I accept your *pranams*, signs of respect, with great love. That is not just the offering of your pranams, but the love of your heart. Utilizing the yogic *kriyas* (actions), *prana* can go wherever you want guide it. Prana is the life force. However, there is another kriya very similar to it that is called love. Once we have love in our hearts, we can direct it wherever we desire. If there is any power considered the highest, it is love. We can get rid of most of our possessions and still survive. However, take away the experience of love and we're dead.

Prana is the animating force behind all thought. Today's science says that whatever we think, we'll attract the same kind of thought from different directions. If we're thinking of the Lord or of saints, engaging in pure thoughts as much as possible, then those same qualities are pouring into us from the universe. One who loves God is imbued with love. Everything he does and everything he is—his movements, his speech—every cell of his body emanates love.

Thoughts and actions filled with love create love in others. When you look at me with love in your eyes, you create balance. Understand the power of your love. Wherever you direct your loving glance, it brings someone into balance and peace. And the first place to conduct that experiment is within your family. This is not meant as a drama or a charade, but as a real undertaking—you love one another consciously by giving up violence and directing words of kindness to each other. If we cannot innocently love those we're close to, then there's no way we can love anyone in this world. If someone doesn't love you the way you'd like, then the real cause is that you do not love him with pure love. If you understand these principles, pain and suffering can be transformed into joy and happiness.

I enjoyed the experience of having an American Father's Day celebration with you. It was perhaps the most memorable day of my life. Better yet—call it "Grandfather's Day!" I was moved by the way you came to me and offered your pranams full of love and humility. It was as if you were children of five or six years old and I had the urge to pick up each one of you and hold you.

When you approached me walking on your knees during the processional, you went to such levels that your love arose from the depths of your being, I felt it clearly. You must learn to keep that feeling steady in your heart. Imagine approaching each person in your life with that same humility and loving-kindness.

No sadhana in this world compares to the sadhana of love. When that love is showered upon the Lord, it becomes devotion or bhakti. When it's showered upon the guru, it becomes guru bhakti. It's written in the scriptures of India that one's father is to be considered a divine being, one's mother is also a divine being, and the guru is a divine being.

In much the same way, that's how you've received me. Early in life I received the mantra of love, which is the highest mantra. Truly that spoiled me. Today I'm the father of innumerable children who love me very much. If you learn to love others the way you love me then it will not only help you, it will help the entire world. For then you will realize that the only source of true happiness in this world comes through love.

Full Attention

In truth, the greatest asset for a student or disciple is a deep desire to acquire knowledge. This goes beyond mere interest. Once, Ramakrishna Paramahansa, Swami Vivekananda's guru, was asked, "How can I create a burning desire that will bring me immediate results in my sadhana?" This discussion was carried out on the banks of a river. Ramakrishna replied, "My son, I cannot give you that answer here on the riverbank. I can only respond in the river." As soon as they entered the river, Ramakrishna held his student's head under water. He started struggling and couldn't speak. Clearly his eyes were saying, "Save me." Then Ramakrishna brought him up again. "So long as we're not drowning, we don't have a desire to be saved," he told him. Truthfully, when we are in great difficulties or profound pain, our heart cries out and God's help comes immediately.

In order to receive knowledge, every part of your attention must be absorbed in the learning process. Once a student reported to his guru, "I passed my test with thirty three and a third percent," evidently pleased with the results. However, the guru responded, "Well, consider this. If you were a businessman, interviewing cooks for your new restaurant and someone said, 'Sir. I cook 33 out of a 100 chappatis perfectly; the other 67 get burned.' Would you hire him?"

Thirty-three and a third percent equals small progress. You must apply yourself one hundred percent to the task at hand. That's true in yoga as well as in other endeavors. In the *Bhagavad Gita*, Shri Krishna says, "Yoga means perfection in action." In order to achieve mastery then, one must fully concentrate and be fully present. The greatest spiritual teacher remains, above all, the student.

In all these years I have taught only three or four students, but they have taught thousands of people. In essence I've prepared the captains. It's their job to train the armies.

The Spiritual Teacher

From my perspective, if there is any work in this world of supreme value, it is the work of the teacher. Only one who has great love can become a true teacher — love for the student and the subject.

In India those who teach kindergarten through college are called teachers. But one who has attained a higher level through practice and who teaches others through his own life is called an *acharya* or spiritual teacher. The character of a spiritual teacher must be very pure.

If a symbol is woven into the flag, it has great value; but on a piece of paper it's ordinary. In other words, you must be what you are teaching. For many years I have been an acharya. I feel that my life has greatly progressed because of it. Before I became a swami, whenever my mind was disturbed, I used to go and play with small children. Then I would become silly and make them laugh. As a result I myself became very happy. That's how I feel about teaching. I love this work very much. In fact it's hard to imagine doing anything else.

Once when I was about to give a lecture in a small town, a doctor came to accompany me, and his hand touched mine as we were walking. All of a sudden he got concerned and said,

"Guruji, you are hot. You must have a fever!" Immediately taking out his thermometer, he took my temperature and said, "No, you can't go, you must lie down because your fever is very high."

"My brother," I replied. "I'm going anyway, for it's good medicine. When I teach I forget my fever. That's as good as lying in bed."

The lecture started out beautifully. Ordinarily I would speak for an hour and a half. That day I talked for two and a half hours. I must have gotten a fever of the tongue. At any rate, when the lecture was over, the doctor was again worried that I was suffering and took my temperature. This time it was normal.

Because I love teaching so much, whatever troubles come my way I accept as friends. That's an important part of spiritual development. Whenever you're completely engrossed in something, no disturbance troubles you.

Teaching is a spiritual practice. Whenever someone is teaching, he is truly carrying out a deep study within himself. So the work of a teacher is of the highest nature—like a farmer sowing seeds in the field. Each moment he must be aware of his students' state of mind to see whether they have received what has been sown. As he continues planting seeds, they sprout and open, eventually bearing fruit in the student's lives.

The Music and Dance of Sadhana

When I left my residence to join you here in the meditation room, I had no idea that you were going to perform the play of my life before my eyes. I was very moved as I recognized many incidents from the past. Immediately my thoughts turned to earlier years and the pleasant memories of my guru. I found myself thinking about him and then about the purpose of plays in general.

The play was born in ancient times. Although plays were centered on some type of external conflict, they were meant to represent the internal conflict taking place within each person. For example, the battle between angels and demons really depicts the battle between our lower impulses and our divine nature.

I played out that same drama behind my house in Summit Station. I did some brief movements and then some mudras or different positions of the hands. Years ago I had done spontaneous mudras and all sorts of meditative dances, but these disappeared after a long while, evidently no longer a necessary part of my sadhana. However, as I experimented with the mudras on a recent afternoon, all of a sudden a dance began to flow spontaneously and I allowed myself to be carried along by its movements. There was a strong difference between the dance movements I had done before which were quick and speedy while this time the dance was slow and rhythmic.

When such a dance emerges from your sadhana, many changes occur in the nervous system and in the body as a whole. Nerves are strained and stretched to such an extent that most people would collapse after five minutes of such intensity. However, at the age of 65 I danced continuously for one and a half hours. After a period of time it felt like the earth was moving under me and I was just sliding along, effortlessly carried by its movement.

The supreme yogis of all time, Lord Shiva and Lord Krishna were both the best of dancers. Both of them taught me how to dance. Understand music and dance as the very highest sadhana. Applied with deep reverence, both music and dance are methods through which true purification of the body can be attained.

Nonattachment

A principle that's very important for purification and for the practice of sadhana is to gradually let go of those things you crave and to develop a solid foundation in nonattachment. Freedom from material things is only the beginning, however it's an important first step to take in becoming free in other realms.

For years my pupils clothed me in silk. However, at one point when a disciple brought me an expensive garment, my eyes were opened. I said to myself, "You are a sannyasi, and in a year you'll be sixty. This does not become you. Today India is poor and sad. It's not appropriate to have expensive clothes or expensive things."

I built an ashram because the practice of sahaj yoga didn't conform to people's beliefs. Even there I had to let go of pleasing people, so nonattachment became essential. The observances I did were so unusual, they could not be done in any old place. For years I used to roar like a lion, cry loudly, laugh heartily, sing Ram dhuns, dance, clap, or bang my hands and feet hard on the ground. This spontaneous routine would start around three in the morning and continue until ten the following night.

The neighbors were tormented and the uninitiated thought it was madness. It was madness, the madness of the love of God. During that time, I would frequently jump into the waters of the Narmada, swollen by monsoon rains, and plaster my body with mud. For a time, I even wandered naked through some villages because I didn't feel that I had a body.

When I finally decided to build an ashram near Odi on the banks of the Narmada, it started off well, but I did not remain there because the work started in Malav, where my only intention was to perform religious observances. Out of practical necessity, I kept contact with wealth — whether I'm attached or unattached is known by my close disciples who serve me. For the sake of my own salvation, however, I'm determined to remain unattached.

Those who don't know me think the company of rich men altered me in some way, but in truth only religious observance changed my life. Because of my rigorous sadhana schedule, I kept track of every minute. Therefore I couldn't give a lot of time to anyone wishing to speak. Furthermore I didn't correspond with my disciples very much, nor did I spend much time clearing up their troubles or confusion when they came to visit. For this reason many of my disciples were fed up. At such times I put a loving hand on their head and gently explained my state to them, and that gave them some consolation.

In practicing sadhana, all sorts of attachments crop up, and sooner or later they all must go. At last I've come to realize that if we must harbor some attachment in life, it's helpful to place it in those things that will ultimately lead us to freedom.

Miracles

Now that summer has arrived, and we're celebrating Guru Purnima at this Pennsylvania ashram, I think it's a good time to show you a miracle. Don't you agree?

Even though you don't have the kind of fans that we have in India, still you'll sense my mysterious powers as a result of this experiment. If we turn on an electric fan, immediately it blows cool air into the room and everyone's hair starts flying around. However, mine does not. Isn't that a miracle?

Of course I'm bald. But honestly, I don't understand why you love miracles so much, because there's no miracle on earth that compares with chanting the name of the Lord. Thinking about God or chanting mantra provides miraculous effects. In fact, no other technique produces as many miracles as mantra does.

In Malav there was a sister who used to serve me faithfully. One day she came in, bowed down, and then immediately burst into tears. I said to her, "Why are you crying, my daughter?"

With great pain, she said, "Oh Bapuji, I've lost my buffalo."

Now in India that is no small thing. A buffalo easily costs six or seven hundred rupees, which was a huge amount in those days. In order to ease her pain and help her laugh, I told her I'd go into samadhi and try to find where her buffalo was. Can anyone really go into samadhi to find a buffalo? If you could find buffaloes in samadhi, where would you search for God? But I told her this to ease her mind and we all began laughing.

The sister sitting beside her replied, "You'll definitely find your buffalo now that Bapuji is laughing." The next day she found her buffalo. Well, God is the real comedian here because He gave me credit when the real credit was His. A true saint does not lay claim to magic or miracles, so you must be careful about such things

In my childhood I used to read about magic and came in contact with people who knew some tricks, but I never had the slightest belief in it. Nothing happened without some material basis—that was my firm belief. Nonetheless I continued to watch magic tricks and read about miracles. When I sat at the feet of Sri Gurudev for more than a year and a quarter, however, I became acquainted with the innumerable unusual powers within him.

Before parting from me, he said on many occasions: "My son, until you complete the yoga cycle, don't write my biography." This wish of his has been granted. Had I not done so, the reader would believe the stories about him and his strange appearance in my life to be a figment of my imagination. When the cycle was completed, however, I told his story. Today I delight in revealing the greatness of Shri Pranavanandji Maharaj and can say that if any yogi in the world performs a miracle, I shall not bat an eyelid, for I have seen far greater powers demonstrated by my Guru, who shone like the sun. I believe him to be an avatar of Lord Shiva.

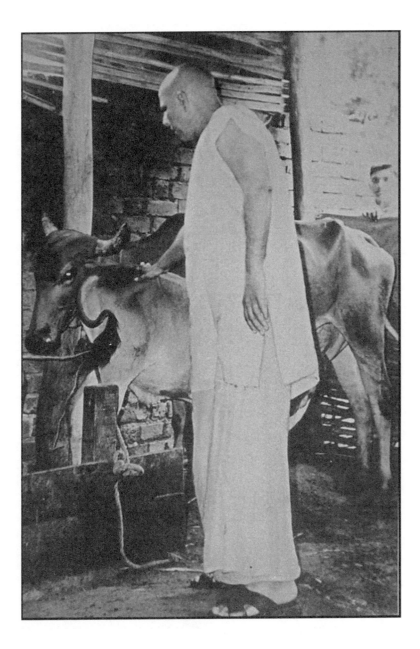

Bapuji with cows in cowshed

Chalkboard writings

PART TWO

BAPUJI'S GUIDANCE FOR
A LIFETIME OF SADHANA

In traditional yogic teachings there are four aims in life: the pursuit of kama, *or pleasure,* artha, *or wealth,* dharma, *living a righteous life, and finally* moksha, *or liberation. In this section Bapuji walks us through all these stages in no particular order. He gives instructions so that householders can live a life of greater love, joy, and receptivity, and so that yoga adepts can progress through the initial stages of sadhana and discipleship to the path of enlightenment.*

In fact, any move toward purification, spiritual practice or the pursuit of right living charts a course toward liberation. Although Bapuji distinguishes among purna yogis, those who've perfected their practice and come all the way through to completion, he also designates the pathway for the perfect follower — one who may not necessarily reach liberation, but has set the wheels in motion. Herein lies the guidebook for a practice, no matter what the path.

These teachings can be considered as scripture and are meant to be read not once, but many times, so that we may extract the subtleties of these passages and their relevance to our practice. Revisiting these readings will hopefully give us inspiration to dive more deeply into our chosen sadhana, and upon surfacing, to find our reflection in the mirror of Bapuji's words.

Bapuji with cap

CHAPTER NINE

A FOOL FOR LOVE

Although we're all acquainted with the word "love," the strange thing is that no one really knows what it's about. However, love has one defining characteristic—once you've kindled its flame, it can never be put out.

When you meditate, close your eyes and draw your senses inward. Then imagine you can enter the chambers of your heart. Resting there for a moment, sense the presence of an all-abiding love. Allow the breath to quiet your awareness. You'll find love eternally present in the human heart.

But when you consider it, who has ever loved you with the depth and strength of that all-abiding love? Of course the answer is God alone. The strangest thing is that the very incarnation of love—the Lord himself—is hungry for it. Everywhere He goes He begs for love, but his bowl keeps coming up empty. At the same time people constantly talk about love and fall over one another searching for it.

Though the path of love is available to us all, smart people avoid it. Even if they were to stumble upon it by mistake, they would immediately run away. That's because they think it's for fools. To be a traveler on this path, you must be a fool when confronted with worldly desires. That means being ignorant of their charms. Devote yourself to God and take on the challenges of this path, and people think you're crazy.

In truth this path isn't a path; it's divine fire. Also understand that a fool on this path doesn't walk but runs like crazy. There's no end to the disturbances he faces. Whether dancing on the razor's edge or balancing on the edge of a sword, it takes a fool to choose such a posture. No intelligent person would do that. In addition, although most people fear death, the fool on this path is so courageous that if death were to show up, he'd eagerly put his head into its mouth.

Even if offering love confers only a small bit of happiness to his beloved, the fool is ready to take on mountains of trouble. Constantly bent on serving, this fool has no idea whether it's day or night, afternoon or evening; he doesn't notice the season of summer, winter, or monsoon. Continual service is the constant for him and the only means to give true expression to his love.

I too am included among such fools. Although I don't know which number fool I am after all these years of sadhana, I'm certain God knows that.

Love and Nonviolence

As you may gather, love is my most favorite principle, and dedication is the core of love. Whoever commits himself to developing just one genuine life-building principle receives the benefit of the rest.

Love is the foremost principle; sadhana is second. Knowledge, perseverance, punctuality, patience, and conservation of energy combine to form the third set of principles for life development.

The highest form of non-violence is love. Whenever we speak sweetly and without selfishness, we're practicing non-violence. The lowest form of violence is jealousy or hatred. Violence is rooted in what we don't like or wish were different. When that experience of not liking expands, it becomes jealousy or hatred. Then fighting and conflict arise in our lives.

Find out what it is you don't like and make sure it doesn't grow stronger. For as your dislike increases, your mind becomes more and more restless. Instead, determine that your life will be heavenly as you increase the presence of love. Say to yourself, "I want to be happy and I want others to live happily."

One Family

You've seen how lovely flowerpots are. Don't you wish to plant and nurture seeds of love in the flowerpots of your heart? While a flower's fragrance merely perfumes the home, love's fragrance perfumes the whole world.

The highest principle of sanatana dharma is that the whole world is one family. God is the father of this entire universe; that is why we're all brothers and sisters. We belong to one family, so we must learn to love others, and we must also learn to bear with others and be patient with them.

I'm telling you this as my children. Here in America I've witnessed that you're often impatient with each other. That's why your family life has become difficult and painful. Also, you start relationships too soon and end them too quickly. That's a big failing.

From the moment of birth, fortunate beings receive their share of love's gifts through the love that family members shower upon them. Indeed each relative helps initiate that person into the gifts of love. Without a foundation in trust, you cannot build the abode of love. When a person is born into a troubled family, however, negative character traits get tattooed all over the mind. Consequently a thirsty heart cannot take in love. A person who cannot trust his own loved ones can never trust anyone else.

A relative or family member forms an integral part of one's own self. Therefore, we relate in the same way to ourselves as we do to one another. Trust is at the heart of these interactions; in fact, the very soul of love is the trust we've learned from childhood. As long as we do not give happiness to others, we'll never find happiness ourselves. When we live together in a family, there are always differences of opinion. Be careful that those differences do not create separation between you. Whatever actions bring long-term happiness to others are religious acts. Therefore, give love to your loved ones until they're fully satisfied, and in return they'll never leave you unsatisfied.

Our close ones are thirsty for love. If we don't offer it to them, then the reservoir of our hearts will become impure and poisoned. The nectar that resides in the heart of an individual is not there for him; it's for others. As we serve others with this nectar, the flow of it continues increasing in our hearts.

Service

Service is one of the highest expressions of love. There are two places of service: one is the outer world, the other is in your meditation room. True service to the Lord merges with service to the public. In fact, the public itself is the Lord, so that by first serving the public, your mind gets prepared for higher sadhana.

While he was with us, many disciples longed to serve Guruji. Rich ladies traveled fifty miles by car just to make his food. Some cooked *dhal*, some made rice, some cooked vegetables, while others made the chapatis. Even in shining the utensils, there was a struggle. Some would get only a spoon to shine, others a cup. Washing his clothes, it was the same ritual. One lady washed one leg of his pants while another lady washed the other leg. Due to Gurudev's schedule, all the men and women had to finish their services and leave quickly, so they came half an hour early. In that way I had a chance to witness love in action on a daily basis.

Once I went to a small village where I had previously owned some land but no longer did after becoming a swami. Thus I was given an accommodation in a separate building.

One of the key figures in town visited me just before I was going to bed. He said, "I have some work to do. I'll come back in an hour and a half, and then we'll sit for satsanga. The night is ours. We can do whatever we want."

Since he knew me before I became a swami, he must have felt comfortable making this request. So he returned around two o'clock in the morning. Surprised that I was sleeping, he knocked loudly on the door and called out, "Swamiji, why are you sleeping? Didn't you remember I was coming back for satsanga?"

I guess he thought that satsanga was some kind of engine, carting people back and forth to their destinations. As in a train station, one connects with whoever comes, any time of night or day, and takes him to satsanga.

If I'd become angry with him, he'd think that I was spoiled now that I'd become a swami. Since his request was in earnest, I got up smiling. With some problems, you have to cry. With other problems, you just laugh and keep on going. So we had satsanga the rest of the night, and when it was morning, he left. In social interaction, even saints have to bear with such circumstances. Many great masters of the world have done true service to the world after attaining the highest stages of sadhana. But service is not always easy and may demand more than we expect.

One day my disciple Amrit came to me and said, choked with emotion, "Bapuji, kindly let us know if there are any short-comings in our service. We will immediately improve it." Such affectionate words can only come from a close disciple. This husband and his wife and all of his disciples have served me with total love and dedication.

Likewise the residents of Malav were also extremely kind and focused in their service. During my twelve years in Malav, there were two or three occasions when I scolded them. In spite of this, there was no decrease in their love, nor did they change their daily routine of paying their respects to me. Whenever I spoke in anger, they bowed their heads and listened to what I had to say with love.

If they spoke, they'd say: "Bapuji, we made a mistake—forgive us—we won't do it again." Their loving humility calmed me in a few minutes. Service as unflinching as that is a rare thing in this world. The dharma of service is the dharma of love; in fact, it's the very embodiment of love. In whomever love arises, divine vision also arises. Whatever service is then offered provides a direct connection to God.

Dropping Expectations

In our hands is a flower of love. We intend to offer it, but it's difficult to give it away because we want something back. Call it a

A Fool for Love

flower—or call it your heart—either way, we expect love if we're offering it to others.

Since we expect it, when the time comes to offer love, we're hesitant. Because of this hesitation we fail the test to some degree. That's because we don't know the principle of love. *Love can only be offered, not asked for in return.*

When we give love, it's true that we receive love, but it's not due to the exchange. Love's nature always looks out toward the other and not in toward itself. To enter the heart of another and forget one's ego is a form of surrender. It's said that the flower of your heart can only truly be offered to God or guru, who expect nothing. It's like offering a drop of water to the ocean.

I was in search of an individual to whom I could give my entire life, and by the grace of God, I found such a guru. After that, my unhappiness was converted into joy. Gurudev has given me the ideal of life and also the strength to materialize it. I've lived my life on the basis of that grace.

In this world many paths have been invented in order to find love and peace. The name of the beloved Lord is Peace. He's omnipresent, so He's not to be looked for. He's everywhere. All you have to do is open your eyes to see Him. But that's no easy task. The reason we don't see God is that our eyes are closed. The eye through which we see God is called the inner eye, and it's only opened through love. We can love under any circumstance; the only requirement is to keep our minds attuned to God.

The Highest Offering

A devotee had decided to seek alms in a city where everyone worshipped Lord Buddha. Begging bowl in hand, he entered one street first and spoke out loud, "Give me an offering in the name of Lord Buddha!"

Many people came out with something to offer him, but for some reason he chose not to accept anything. This troubled the people. They couldn't understand why this swami, who begged for alms on behalf of Lord Buddha, had refused their offerings.

All day long this swami moved from street to street posing the same question. People came forward with rich offerings, including diamonds, emeralds, and pearls, but his begging bowl remained empty. Leaving the city with a heavy heart, he continued his same chant, "Alms, alms. Give me an offering in the name of Lord Buddha."

After walking only a hundred steps, he heard a very faint sound, "Swami, come here please." The words came over him like nectar and at last his heart was at peace. Moving in the direction of the sound, he saw a big tree with a hollow in the trunk. Suddenly, a hand reached out of the hollow. In the hand there was a torn piece of cloth. As soon as he saw that cloth, he extended his begging bowl.

The woman offering that cloth was a great devotee of Lord Buddha. Hungry and without hope or support, she had only the dress on her body. So hiding her body in the hollow of the tree, she offered him that garment. As soon as he received it, the swami cried out, "I've received alms in the name of Lord Buddha. I've received alms in the name of Lord Buddha."

Although such a garment would not bring any money and would not be of any use, it was given in the true spirit of surrender, and the swami understood its value. The offering of one's soul is the highest offering. Whoever gives everything he has—including his happiness and joy for the sake of others—gives the supreme donation.

Pilgrim on the Path of Love

Truly the wise proclaim that love is the only path, love is the only God, and love is the only scripture.

Impress this verse upon your mind and chant it constantly if you want to realize your deepest dreams. Only love purifies the body and mind. Love is the all-seeing divine eye and the wish-fulfilling touchstone.

Every living being lives in a stream of love. Therefore let us allow someone to taste our love as we taste someone else's love. Love flowing into another's life is the source of our happiness, and love flowing into our lives is the source of their happiness. That's universal law.

As long as people focus on material objects and forget their spiritual development, they'll remain unfulfilled. Yet it's important for all of us to become realized as fully divine beings. We must develop our inner being to become love. We may beautify the world as much as we want, but without love it's like decorating a corpse. To beautify this world, we must carry out experiments in love. Only the science of love can bring unity and remove the separation among all living beings.

Love brings union by healing the split between the body, mind, and heart. United, they merge with the soul just as countless rivers and streams merge into the vast ocean. Without love, light cannot be kindled in our hearts, our homes, or in the world. Love is the only worldwide religion. Whether you're reading the scriptures of the Vedas, the Koran, or the Bible, they're meaningless without love. The only guide on the true path, and the only thing that draws another human being toward love, is God's only ambassador, and that is Love itself.

The Lord is certainly very clever, for He preserves the nectar of love in the heart of each living being. When someone opens the door of his heart to satisfy another's thirst for love, then the recipient's heart also opens. Thus by allowing the other's love to enter their hearts, they're both fulfilled.

This path of love is very ancient. When I was born I received the initiation of love. Now with that same love I initiate everyone else. Countless times I dipped into the world's highest scriptures and received only love from them. Love is my only path. In fact, I'm a pilgrim on the path of love.

Bapuji blessing a baby

Mataji applies sandlewood paste to Bapuji's forehead

CHAPTER TEN

THE LOVE OF GURU AND DISCIPLE

*Just once, cast your sweet gaze on me, my Lord. This yearning comes
not just from one but from many incarnations. You, who embody love
and inspiration, please shine your grace on me.*
(From Bapuji's bhajan of the same name, Hari Ekvara Nirakho.)

The True Disciple

Even if we could collect all the love of this world together,
it's questionable whether it would equal one ounce of
love from the guru. Whoever thinks and dwells on the
guru constantly is a true disciple. Such a person is very fortunate.
On the other hand, one who has not experienced the guru's
divinity will have a hard time experiencing the divinity of God.
Searching from one guru to the next doesn't land you the prize.

Do you think the fruit tastes you or that you taste the fruit?
There's no way you can test a guru in one or two days. If you want
to find the true guru, you will have to be in his presence, living
close by him. It takes time for love and connection to develop.
When the love between you is like that of a father and son, or
mother and daughter, then one should take *mantra diksha* (mantra
initiation). If the guru yields up knowledge all of a sudden, you
know that it's like a shopkeeper offering goods as an enticement
for you to buy.

Before you receive knowledge, however, there must be genuine love between you and the guru. When a guru sees his disciple coming from a distance, his heart jumps for joy. In the same way when a picture of the guru appears before the disciple's eyes, it fills him with love. Whoever attains the true guru has a look in his eye and special charm in his voice, because he's continuously experiencing that guru's unlimited love.

My Indian disciples may be sad that I am in America, but I came here based on the needs of my sadhana and not because I was deserting them. I can definitely say that my heart also experiences the anguish of separation from them. My heart is the same as anyone else's heart. My heart is a father's heart; that's why its nature is fatherly; moreover it's the heart of a guru, so it has the same characteristics that a guru has.

The disciple's love is not the same as the special love the guru embodies. That love is called *vastlya* or unconditional pure love. Vastlya is a mountain of love; all rivers of love originate from it. It's also an infinite ocean of love where all rivers converge. True love is always a reminder of God's love. The mutual love between guru and disciple is of a spiritual nature that originates from godly love. Its remembrance benefits both guru and disciple and helps them evolve. If that love is true, it can never be forgotten.

Legacy of a Loving Heart

When disciples come up to me bringing garlands, fruits, sandalwood incense, or offers of money or clothing, I observe their pristine feelings rather than their gifts. Only a loving heart can spark that same sentiment in another heart, just as an unlit lamp can only be lit by one already burning.

I feel the beloved Lord showering love as He stands in the disciples' tear-filled eyes and hearts when they bow to me during celebrations. Even today my heart is overwhelmed when I see an unhappy disciple or hear someone describe pain in his life. I have never had to go anywhere to study the nature of feelings, because I can see them clearly in the hearts and minds of my disciples. Feelings themselves have been my teachers.

I still remember the moment years ago when my Gurudev approached me and said, "My son, starting tomorrow you will fast for forty days and practice mantra japa." His first two words, "My son," sounded very sweet. But I wasn't sure if they could sweeten the bitterness of what was to follow. Although I had unflinching faith in sadhana, I was doubtful whether I could accomplish such a monumental task.

Expressing my fears, I repeated a traditional saying to Gurudev: "The face of the compassionate Lord does not look at the hungry person." Then I added, "But when I fast, He'll have to look at me, because I'm going to chant japa constantly. And before I chant, I'm going to call upon the Lord and *demand* that He sit with me for forty days."

Gurudev replied with a smile, "Let the Lord worry about His own helplessness. You don't need to do His worrying for Him. The purpose of that saying and your fasting are different, so don't mix them up. As a matter of fact, the word *upvas*, or fasting, means 'to sit near or dwell close to the Lord.' But it's the Lord who sits near the fasting devotee. Actually, a devotee is hungry only for love, and since the Lord loves to look with unblinking eyes at the face of his love-hungry devotee, He never leaves him alone."

Unless a person's heart is soaked in such devotion and his eyes radiate love, how can we believe him to be a true devotee? The beloved Lord has poured an ocean of love into my heart for my thousands of disciples. God has an especially gracious plan. As soon as disciples place their minds in the stream of this love like a child placing his head in his mother's lap, they immediately receive love, happiness, and peace. The pure love that develops between guru and disciple is the first step toward loving God.

I've always loved my worldly disciples as my own children, and I'm never dissatisfied with their loving service. In the same way I've never considered my renunciate disciples to be different from me. I've never kept anything secret from them, nor have I forgotten them, whether they're near or far away from me.

At the same time, I've always been careful to see that my defects do not affect them. I prefer that they stay at other places so they can do their sadhana independently. Then they're more likely to develop self-reliance. While they may lose certain benefits by not remaining close by me, at the right time I invariably call them and inspire them with appropriate teachings for their stage of sadhana. When they reach higher stages in the future, they'll understand the purpose of this.

My relationship to you is like a spiritual grandfather. My Gurudev has given initiation to me alone. Then I've initiated others with his blessings; thus they're all his disciples. I feel that those who are my disciples are my guru's disciples. Even today He exists on this earth. As long as He's here, I cannot take the position of a guru. All I can be is a disciple. Thus we're all disciples of one great master.

From Ignorance to Knowledge

When we're born we're affected by many influences from previous incarnations. The root cause of negative influences is ignorance. That ignorance is vast and cannot be removed in one lifetime. Yet we believe we're progressing from ignorance to knowledge. More often, however, we're progressing from previous ignorance to newly acquired ignorance. Although we believe we're gaining new knowledge, real knowledge doesn't begin until ignorance comes to an end.

The word *gu* means darkness and *ru* means light. Thus "guru" refers to one who leads us from darkness to light, or from ignorance to knowledge. The light from the sun, moon, and stars can remove the darkness from this entire earth. Yet they cannot remove the darkness of ignorance. Since the guru is greater than those light sources, he can remove the darkness of ignorance and replace it with the light of knowledge.

Not everything is revealed by the guru; in fact, the opposite may be true. The real source of knowledge is rooted in practice. Not long ago my disciple Vinit Muniji asked me a question. As a sadhak of many years, he practices regularly, and the question that he asked was a secret and it could not be told ahead of time, so I didn't give him an answer. Yet he is my disciple. Whatever I have is his. So I said, "My son, discover it on your own. When you find it out for yourself, there's great joy. Then through your yoga practice, you'll realize why it's a secret."

Saints are not misers. If they were truly stingy, they would withhold everything from society. But what saints know, society has little capacity to digest. So it's only revealed when your pot isn't upside down—that is, when you've practiced sufficiently so that you have a container in which to receive it.

The Soul of Prayer

In this type of sadhana there is only one desire and that is to find God. To take refuge in God means to give ourselves to him totally. At times that causes pleasure, at times great pain.

I was nineteen years old when I sat at the lotus feet of my Guru. Receiving his love, I became intoxicated. At that time I felt supreme happiness. Just as a moth willingly gives her body to the flame, I was ready to give my life to his light.

He was a *siddha* or perfect master so he knew my mind completely. One day he said to me, "My son, I appreciate very much that you love my body, and yet, I'm not this body. What you call *guru* resides in my thoughts and actions. Practice and digest my principles, and that will demonstrate your true love for me."

So you must trust in the guru's thoughts and actions, and be convinced that he is indeed your well-wisher. A true guru is always selfless, never asking anything from you. He doesn't concern himself with your prosperity, your fame, or your accomplishments. It's enough for him that you want to grow spiritually.

There's tremendous power in the name of the guru or in the name of the Lord. You might be surprised that there's power in a name, but consider the name of someone who's very rich; no one fails to notice. So if there's power in the name of a rich man, what about God?

In a devotional song that I wrote, the devotee prays, *Just once, cast your sweet gaze on me, my Lord. This yearning comes not just from one but from many incarnations. You, who embody love and inspiration, please shine your grace on me.* Then the devotee continues his plea, *I've been suffering from the poison of greed, hatred, and attachment. Please be gracious, remove this pain, and take your seat upon the throne of my heart.*

Many prayers echo this theme. Although we may pray very hard, the truth is that we cannot bring the Lord to take his place in our hearts. The Lord himself decides when to take a seat. Whoever says, "I love the Lord" only means that the Lord has graced him with his presence, not that he's doing anything.

The devotee continues in the song, *"Oh Lord, we're all unhappy and yearning to be at your feet. Where else can we go and who else can unburden us of our pain? You're our only comfort."*

Devotion finds its way into many types of prayer. But once you've meditated or shared your words of devotion, you must listen for a response and not think that your prayer is offered in emptiness. Even before it's uttered, the Lord hears your prayer. Reflect on this. When your child cries, does the child cry in a poem? No. Only the raw expression of his feeling comes through—in a sense—the child's cry is a prayer without words. That's what touches your heart. In the same way, your prayer without words immediately reaches God. You may not realize that crying is one of the highest forms of devotion. But whoever cries knows sadhana. If you cry in front of the Lord with a pure heart, other techniques pale in comparison, for in crying, all principles of yoga are included.

I'll tell you about my tears. After bowing at the lotus feet of my guru, I mentioned to him that I intended to tell him one of my secrets that day. Gurudev smiled sweetly and said, "Tell me."

"Gurudev, when I pray to God, I begin to cry," I said.

"No."

"Really, I'm crying," I told him.

"Yes, you're crying," he said, "but you're crying for your own pain. You're not crying because of separation from God."

We really know how to cry, and we cry very often at the feet of God. In fact, we cry so much we could fill our two hands with tears, but not a single drop is for the Lord. On this side, everyone is crying. However, on the other side, believe it or not, God is crying because of His separation from us!

We believe that there's joy in laughter. But there's greater joy in crying because when you cry for the Lord, that brings you to His feet. Those are not tears of sadness so much as tears that give birth to bliss. You must know that this pain is God's blessing for us. It's a tool that takes us into prayer and deep connection. In spite of having such a beautiful tool, however, we must admit our love for God is insufficient if we don't use it.

No matter what country you were born in, the soul of it is prayer. Every one of your churches and every one of your holy places consist of prayers. Prayers offered in earnest are the most miraculous tools. Traveling the path of yoga, I've completed thirty years. Although I came very close to death five times, I survived by the grace of God. To pass through such difficulties was like passing through a great fire. The tool that brought me safely through each time was prayer.

Dwell on What You Love

Find ways to increase your love for God, guru, and spiritual progress. In order to strengthen your devotion, all you have to do is knock on God's door. God will automatically open it, knowing the true feelings arising in your heart. Don't think that only you love God. God loves you very much.

It's an illusion to believe that only worshippers of God are true devotees. Devotion can also be developed through the path of wisdom or selfless service. Although all paths are identical at heart, they're different in their approach. Each one comprises a different format through which energy is channeled. The expressions may be different, but the source of each is love. Indeed it's impossible to reach the pinnacle of truth unless your path is suffused with love.

Dwell on any object for which you have intense love, and that meditation begins to draw strength and build upon itself. When you meditate on a saint, for example, imagine that you're receiving the flow of energy from all saints.

In India we direct our attention to images of the deities. That's not done for show but in a real effort to make contact with God. To experiment on your own, choose a form that pleases you.

In India a favorite image is the Lord as baby Krishna. Imagine he's right there in front of you, and you're preparing his bath. Visualize this very clearly. The bath water is scented with saffron and his clothes are neatly laid out. He's very elegant even as a baby and loves brightly colored fabrics. After dressing him, you imagine playing with him for a while, and then feeding him his favorite buttermilk. Hearing the sweet strains of his laughter, you can almost sense what it's like to hold him in your arms. By focusing on his grace and beauty, you forget yourself.

You might ask, "Will meditating like that really change my consciousness?" There's a definite change in consciousness. Ordinarily, when you sit in meditation, you start thinking about your business or your everyday experiences. When you try to remove those thoughts, more show up. Under such circumstances you might think it's better just to quit. Then another thought occurs: if you keep practicing, you should be able to attain a state of thoughtlessness. But no one has yet invented a switch to turn off thoughts, though that would certainly make it easier.

Nevertheless, there are ways to trick yourself. For example, if one set of thoughts distracts you, start an entirely new line of thoughts to replace them. Just as you do away with the impurities of your body in bathing, you do away with the mind's impurities by immersing yourself in devotion. With fewer thoughts of a worldly nature, your mind naturally becomes relaxed and surrendered.

Unfortunately most people are careless about the flow of thoughts. Instead of dwelling on what uplifts us we settle for small disturbances that attract our attention. Then unsatisfied with small disturbances, we continue collecting hourly, daily, monthly, and yearly disturbances, through focusing our thoughts in unhappy directions. It's not unlike a baby pulling his hair with his own hands and then crying out in surprise. Like the baby, we don't realize we're the source of the problem, creating our own private disturbance. Nevertheless, we have a choice to change from moment to moment, and let our thoughts dwell on God.

After teaching me various mantras, Guruji said: "Concentrate on the mantra *radha-purushottam*." In accordance with his instruction, I tried to concentrate on that mantra, but was not successful.

However, I had other remedies. Concentration depends on remembrance and remembrance depends on having an immediate vision. Since I always had an immediate vision of Guruji, by simply remembering him I became alert. The more I practiced, the more I realized that focusing on him was the most helpful way to achieve concentration. Now whenever my mind wavers, I only need to think of him and my mind calms down.

Entering the Heart of God

Since visiting Kayavarohan, I've reflected a great deal on the role of temples and religion. The temple is the head of civilization. To destroy it is tantamount to the destruction of religion and civilization. Temples are not madhouses for people worshipping stone images of God. Temples are schools of humanity, abodes of peace, lands of compromise, centers of hope, and places of inspiration and concentration. By the same token, worship of deities is not worship of mere stone images, but the worship of the unseen God. For example, when you talk on the phone, the receiver you're holding recedes into the background, and the person's voice becomes prominent. Similarly, when a devotee prays, the image recedes into the background and God assumes prominence.

Once, an expert sculptor made a beautiful image of Laxminarayan. Then it was ceremoniously installed in a temple. Within a short time hundreds of devotees began to come there for darshan. One day the sculptor arrived, saw others worshipping, but he did not bow down. That night he had a dream in which Laxminarayan appeared.

Smiling, the sculptor said, "Who are you?"

"I'm Laxminarayan."

"Laxminarayan? How can that be? It was I who made you from a marble slab."

"You're right. At that time I was only a marble image."

"And now?"

"I am God."

"Who made you God?"

"Devotees. Through their devotion they established me in the heart of God."

Since anything you dwell on expands your heart's loving capacities and calms your mind, choose whatever form resonates for you. With its mixed storehouse of thoughts, the best thing to do with the mind is to create new thoughts since then the old ones must vacate.

Because I've been doing sadhana from my childhood days and it's become the goal of my life, my thoughts have become entirely focused on God. Although I've continuously made efforts to reach the steady and unwavering stage of practice called *sthi-tapragnya* in the *Gita*, I don't consider this a perfect effort. I don't even call it penance. I merely call it prayer.

It says in the sacred *Katha Upanishad*, "The Supreme Being is not attained through speeches, sermons, intellect, or listening to scriptures. He's attained by the one whom He accepts, and He reveals His true form before him."

Daily I pray to the Supreme Being that He may condescend to accept me as I am. That prayer is my sadhana. I've lived with that prayer and earnestly wish to die with that prayer on my lips.

Kayavarohan Temple in Gujarat

Bapuji performs mudras

CHAPTER ELEVEN

INITIATING A SPIRITUAL PATH

Om namo bhagavate vasudevaya
All blessings to God, the indwelling one, who restores our divinity.
(Vishnu Mantra)

Someone once addressed Swami Ram Tirtha at the close of a lecture, "Have you just returned from America?"

"Yes, I have," he said.

Then this individual said, "I'm also thinking of going to the U.S. How expensive is it?"

"There's no expense involved," he replied.

"Well, since you're a swami, obviously someone helped you," the man said, "But how can I go to America without money?"

Swamiji replied, "Brother, you're just thinking about going to America, so there's no expense involved. The expense is incurred only when you make the journey."

It's not different on the spiritual path. As long as we think about the path to God, no expense is involved. It's only after beginning sadhana for real that we discover the cost and effort involved. When we initiate the practice of yoga sadhana, there are hurdles to overcome. After practicing for a period of time, however, the chief hurdle has to do with the fact that you can't see God. He appears as imaginary, a figment of your imagination. How can you love an imaginary God?" There is only one way out of this dilemma and that is through the experience of satsanga, which removes all difficulties.

The meaning of the word *sat* is God. The word *sanga* means "having an attachment to, or a liking for." You may have noticed how unmistakable love is when we chant and talk about God in our gatherings. If you don't feel love for God, you're missing satsanga; and as long as you're not in love with God, you haven't really begun the journey.

Determination

In beginning a spiritual practice or deepening the one that you have, you must have strong determination and a sense of purpose. You may not know how the sadhana will turn out, but you must be assured that pursuing it is essential to your wellbeing. In fact, it's essential to your life.

Ordinarily the fickle mind wavers, choosing one activity after another. We take a vow to practice something in the morning, and by evening we've broken that vow. Such inconsistency reinforces inaction and leads to despair. Therefore, scriptures have declared, "My beloved Lord lives in the palace of determination."

A story is told about a farmer named Govinda, who attended the lecture of a traveling saint and heard various people promise to give up tobacco, alcohol, or to speak the truth instead of lying. When Govinda heard these impressive vows, he approached the saint and said, "Swamiji, I'm not religious or devoted, and I rarely do anything other than farming. I don't know if I could observe a vow, but it sounds like a good idea. What should I do?"

"Take a vow that's easy to practice," replied the saint amicably.

"But I don't know which one," Govinda confessed.

"Very well, eat your meals only after you've seen someone's face," replied the saint.

Inspired, Govinda rushed home. Since it was time for his evening meal, he hurriedly looked around, but found no one at home. Looking across at his neighbor's field, he spied a donkey that the neighbors kept tethered, and he realized that that donkey would be there every day without fail. He had found his solution! Govinda went and gazed upon the donkey's face before sitting down to his evening meal.

Pleased that he was now practicing what the swami had requested, Govinda made it his business to check the field every day and to lay eyes on the donkey's face before eating. For two months he observed his vow without a problem. Then one evening, after a long day of labor, he was about to go inside when he realized that the donkey was nowhere to be found! Govinda's first reaction was anger. He was angry at his own foolishness for taking a vow, then angry with the saint for inspiring him, and finally at the donkey for having disappeared. But then a sense of determination came over him. He thought, "All my life I've never committed myself to anything. This is my chance to faithfully observe a vow."

So he went to the neighbor's house and found his son, who told him that both his parents were out gathering sand behind the house. It took just a few long strides to get to the hill where they were gathered. When he saw that the donkey was there, Govinda felt relieved. However, the donkey and his owners had their backs to him, so he approached closer, since he had vowed to eat only upon seeing the donkey's face.

As he heard their excited voices, Govinda realized something unusual was going on. In fact the neighbor and his wife had found a treasure chest buried in the field and were hugging each other in ecstasy. As soon as Govinda saw the donkey's face, he exclaimed out loud, "I saw it! I saw it!" Surprised, the neighbors turned around, and when they heard what he'd said, they imagined he was referring to the treasure. Right on the spot, they promised him a portion of it if he kept it a secret.

Govinda's heart was firmly convinced that he had received this boon only by practicing his vow. Extremely grateful, he wrapped his share of the treasure in a cloth and returned home for dinner.

Hearing this story, you're probably wondering if you take up determination as a spiritual practice whether you'll find buried treasure? My answer is "Yes." Whoever clings to a vow with solid determination invariably finds treasure, although it's not the kind that's buried in the earth. Only a person with firm determination can experience such a victory. That's because patience, tolerance, perseverance, enthusiasm, and concentration—all of which make up true determination—provide the means by which you uncover the secrets hidden in the depths of your soul.

An Extraordinary Love

A unique aspect of yoga sadhana is that the wholehearted practice of any one technique spontaneously elicits the entire spectrum of yogic techniques in a natural sequence. As a result, the initial stages of yoga prepare the groundwork for the more advanced stages.

The great unifying factor, however, is self-study, or *swadhyaya*. Self-study helps to integrate knowledge, action, and love. To attain knowledge, you must seek refuge in the scriptures. To accomplish action, you must seek refuge in the body, and to find love, seek refuge in God.

Love is born spontaneously of its own accord, and although love and knowledge may seem different, they're actually the same. Therefore, wherever you see love, knowledge is the seed lying at its root. Where you see knowledge, love or devotion lies at its root. The three streams of devotion, knowledge, and yoga have once source; wherever one is present, you'll find the other two. Thus these three principles are different wrappings for the same underlying experience, which is love.

In India, one of our foremost saints was called Saint Tulsidas. He has written the most famous explanation of the *Ramayana*. As a supreme poet, he practiced sadhana for many years and finally achieved liberation.

In his early years his love for his wife was extraordinary. If his wife went from one room to the next, he would accompany her. If she got up, he got up. If she sat down, he gazed at her face. Often she thought, "Why does he act like this?" But she loved him, and she loved being loved. Still it worried her that he might drive her crazy.

One day when Tulsidas went out to do an errand, his wife decided to take advantage of his absence to visit her mother, whom she hadn't seen for a long time. As soon as Tulsidas came home and saw the house locked, he knew where she had gone. Immediately he set out for her mother's house. In his travels he had to cross a river. Since there was no boat available, and he had no change of clothes, there was nothing to do but jump in the river fully clothed and swim across.

Soaking wet, he continued on his way. Although it was late, even that wasn't a hindrance to him. The memory of his wife's face served as a light to carry Tulsidas through the darkness. When he finally arrived at the house, he circled it two or three times, trying to figure out how to get to the second floor. By means of a tall plant, he managed to climb onto the lower roof. Grabbing something that looked like a rope, he used it to pull himself through the open window. There he found his wife sleeping in the exact place he had imagined. Slowly he approached her and sat down near her bed.

Imagining she would be extremely happy to see him, he woke her with a slight touch, but she screamed out in surprise. Seeing him, she continued screaming, for his hair was matted, his clothes were soaking wet and he looked like a madman.

"How did you get in here?" she asked, finally overcoming her initial reaction.

He smiled and said, "You left a rope hanging by the window for me to climb up. You must have known…"

"What rope?" she asked and looked outside. There she saw an enormous snake uncoiled, hanging in plain view of the window. Shocked, she returned to her bed.

Facing her husband, a stream of words came pouring from her mouth: "This body is made of skin and bones, flesh and feces. Yet you are attached to it and idolize me. If you had half the love for God that you have for me, you would have attained Him by now."

No sooner had she said this than a light went on in his mind. At once Tulsidas bowed at her feet. Tears rolled down his eyes. "Sister, you've spoken the truth. I've been a fool. I leave you as my wife now so that I may pursue the path to God. Please grant me your blessings."

After receiving her blessings, he left her by taking hold of the "snake" and climbing down.

For the next twelve years Saint Tulsidas lived in seclusion and practiced his sadhana with such intensity that he reached the feet of the Lord. It was his great devotion to his wife, however, that created the opening to embark on that difficult path.

Faith

During an extended famine, people of a small town in India found their faith sorely tested. Because of the lack of rain and loss of crops, people were disturbed and grew restless. One day the town members gathered and decided to create a special ceremony in the temple. They called everyone together to see if the prayers they offered in a large group would bring rain.

Many people began walking to the temple. As they traveled, they saw a ten-year-old boy carrying an umbrella and were surprised. "Why are you carrying an umbrella?" someone asked him.

It was his turn to be shocked. "What do you mean?" he said, "When we pray to God, He's going to make it rain, and then we'll get wet."

Although people smiled, the boy had the last laugh. Following their prayers the great heavens rumbled and rain came down in torrents. Clumping together, they lifted the boy on their shoulders as they traveled home, so his umbrella could protect everyone. Only in truth it wasn't an umbrella. It was his faith.

Faith must come from your heart. Embarking on the spiritual path, faith grows proportionate to the practices that we're doing. Seeing good results encourages us to go further. If there's any faith that's of a supreme nature, it's faith in God.

A guru and disciple traveled together in the forest and rested for a time under a tree. Awakened all of a sudden, the guru spied a great black poisonous cobra in front of him, and was scared that he'd bite his disciple. So he addressed the cobra with great respect, "Nagdev, where are you headed?"

"To drink the blood of your disciple, "Nagdev replied.

Puzzled, the guru asked, "You mean all you want is his blood?

"Yes," replied Nagdev. "If you give me his blood, that will pay off his debt from a past incarnation, and I'll be satisfied."

"Just a moment," the guru replied, as he made a little bowl of leaves. Then he took out a knife and approached the sleeping disciple. Suddenly the guru sat on his chest, and the disciple opened his eyes in fear. Seeing that it was his guru, however, he closed his eyes.

"From which part of the body do you want the blood?" the guru asked the cobra.

"From the throat."

Making a small incision in the throat, the guru caught the blood in a bowl. The disciple did not say a word. After the cobra drank the blood, he bowed to the yogi and left.

Two or three months passed, but the disciple never asked the guru about it. One day, when they were sitting together, however, the guru put his hand lovingly on his disciple's head, and asked, "My son, why didn't you ask me about that day when I put a knife to your throat."

With tears in his eyes, the disciple said, "You're my father and my mother, you're my brother, sister, guru, and friend. If there's anyone who's my true well-wisher, it's you. So when you were on my chest cutting my throat, I knew you were doing something good for me."

Now that is called faith. But it doesn't grow overnight. The disciple must develop it through practice. Faith that cannot be disturbed even under trying conditions is true faith. That's why it's said that the devotee who's not tempted by the allure of maya, or illusion, has a faith that can never be shaken.

Faith is never defeated by failure. In other words, if faith doesn't succeed with one action, it tries another; if that action fails, it finds a third. Whenever faith experiences failure, it becomes increasingly more vigilant, enthusiastic, and aware. Any true faith is invariably the grace of the Lord.

The way your life unfolds is decided according to the nature of your faith. Wherever you have faith, you begin to grow in that direction. Because of its nature, faith serves as a strong force. We tend to move in the direction where we're first attracted. If those attractions survive long enough, they turn into stronger feelings, such as admiring, enjoying, or loving. Those feelings in turn increase and soon develop into faith.

Many situations arise in life that hurt or disturb that faith. But those who are true devotees do not lose their faith, even under trying conditions. On a spiritual path the guru's instruction is always to keep the flame of your faith burning brightly, no matter what else you do.

Action

Enter the cave of your inner mind and close the doors so that disturbance can't enter. Once you learn how to withdraw your senses inward and enter within, you'll find it's very peaceful inside. In that stillness, consciousness merges with the soul and you leave disturbance far behind. However, you must choose some path of yoga in order to be free of fear and disturbance.

You'll find postures very useful. It makes no difference whether you like postures or not. We sell other goods as well. In fact, we sell whatever the customer asks for. If you say, "I don't want asanas or pranayama," we'll ask what else you want? Perhaps you want scripture or bhajans? Perhaps selfless service?

If you say, "I don't like moving my body but I love exercising my tongue." Then we'll recommend chanting *ram, ram, ram*. These goods come very cheaply. Just ask, and we'll give you whatever path you want.

Everyone wants help of some sort, and yoga's an excellent source of help. But you'll have to move into action. Learning and study are preliminary means to help inspire you and get started, but after a while they're empty if not accompanied by practice.

In order to experience contentment and to continue growing in your sadhana, you must become skillful in action. That means developing concentration, paying close attention to all aspects of the sadhana, and practicing indefatigably. Unless these actions unfold as an art form, they're incomplete and defective, and will impede further progress. When your actions become art forms, however, the doer is no longer a doer, but becomes an artist and a yogi.

When a baby's very young and before he can walk, his mother carries him around. If he were to say, "Don't carry me around; let me go to town," of course that's impossible. Likewise, those who say to God, "I don't want to do anything but let me grow fast" — are like babies. Sooner or later action is called for.

Awareness without Judgment

When physical and mental purification begins to take place through yoga sadhana, it's at that time you begin to see both your faults and good qualities very clearly. That's the sign of your spiritual progress. Whoever cannot see his faults or good qualities has not progressed on the spiritual path.

One who's wholehearted in his progress enters his meditation room and bows at the Lord's feet. As he bows down, he's filled with tears. One eye is on the Lord and the other on his own faults. He says to the Lord, "My first fault is that my mind desires the wealth of others." Then he adds, "And I'm not strongly enough drawn to the feet of God." By accepting these faults, the devotee admits to God, "My mind and all the modifications of my mind arise from you. Therefore, only you know what to do with them." One who easily sees his faults should know that the fountain of knowledge is now pouring forth in his heart.

Sometimes there's a temptation to compare your progress to others. Seeing other's faults makes it easier to accept your own. However it's a mistake to focus on other's faults. Doing so will contaminate your thoughts and affect your consciousness adversely. For example, a colander and a needle got together. When the colander saw a hole in the needle she said, "Oh my goodness, you've got a hole!" But then when she looked down at herself, she saw innumerable holes and immediately felt ashamed.

Objectivity is no easy thing. Although I've been practicing sadhana for more than thirty years, as soon as I enter my meditation room I find many weaknesses within myself. Sometimes I wonder if I've progressed at all, and that thought brings tears to my eyes. As a result it can be hard to advise my disciples on any matter because I see my own weaknesses so clearly. Once my disciple Amrit asked me what the main benefit of this sadhana was and I instantly replied, "Your mind becomes so sharp that you have constant self-analysis going on at the highest level."

Impure eyes see very far. Those looking mainly at the faults of others have such a keen ability that even if faults are hidden, they find them out. But when you turn that focus inward, it helps strengthen your practice. Instead of searching for other's faults, observe your own more clearly and take the opportunity to wipe them out as they arise.

One day a camel saw a dog walking by and commented to him, "Well, you certainly have curves in your body."

"What are you talking about?" the dog asked.

"Didn't you know your tail is curved?" replied the camel.

Looking behind him, the dog made note of that and then studied the camel very carefully. After his eyes went up eighteen times and came down eighteen times, he concluded that the accuser was the one with the most curves. In fact, it's said that the camel is unique in having eighteen curves in his body.

Resisting or struggling when we encounter our shortcomings only makes them worse. Instead of fighting faults, it helps to develop new strengths to counteract them. For example, I was sitting on my swing at the Malav Ashram after lunch one day when it suddenly dawned on me that Ayurvedic medicine advises walking one hundred paces after lunch. Since this was simple to do and I rarely stepped out of my room or exercised, I decided to give it a try. Immediately I got up and circled my meditation room seven times. After that I continued the same practice for many years and gained triple benefits: first from the walking, then from the japa I did while walking, and finally from the sacred practice of circumnavigating a place of worship seven times.

The main principle is to avoid wrestling with faults you want to remove. Fighting faults only increases the mind's disturbance. Since practicing virtues decreases mental restlessness, however, a simple way to remove a fault is to seek refuge in its opposite virtue. For example, practice silence to combat talkativeness. Exercise to combat overeating. And always remember to seek pure company and inspiration to combat the tendencies of the mind.

Satsanga

Satsanga is like a lake. You can bathe in it. By bathing in pure thoughts and good company, your thoughts and actions are then purified. As long as your thoughts and actions are impure, you cannot recognize God or guru even if they were standing right in front of you. Once you receive the guru who is showering grace upon you, there's nothing else you have to do. By the way, my name is also Kripalu, which means "merciful one."

When one is convinced that God exists and is for real, then prayers get established and *shradda*, or faith, is created in satsanga. "Sat" means God. "Sanga" means "friendship." Whatever helps you fall in love with God can indeed be called satsanga.

The most dynamic form of satsanga is the relationship between the guru and disciple, that serves as the source of growth and transformation for whoever follows the guru's teachings closely. Unfortunately the dynamics of that relationship are not well understood in the west. When you meet a true guru and steadfastly commit yourself to his teachings, your faults and impurities will gradually be removed. Of course that doesn't happen through the guru's efforts alone, but through your conscious determination to work at removing such faults. At last when those impurities are removed, however, you come to the realization that God has been with you all along.

In order to gain full advantage of satsanga, then, you must learn the difference between right and wrong company. As long as you haven't entered the company of truth, there will be no real transformation in life.

To illustrate this point, once I was giving a lecture on the *Bhagavad Gita*. After finishing the lecture I used to take a walk, just to move around. A lawyer in attendance accompanied me. After walking a short distance, three or four people who knew him came to discuss a court case. Excusing himself, he said to me, "Guruji, this is worldly talk, you won't understand it. It's like when you're talking about God, and we don't understand."

I responded, "That's not true. You can't say I don't know anything about the world. I've given it up. If I didn't know what the world was, how could I have left it? Consider that bowl of rice in your hands. If you can't distinguish the husk from the rice, you may wind up eating husks and throwing the rice away."

Likewise in true satsanga, the impurities of the mind are gradually washed away and the mind becomes pure. Only that which can change the direction of our minds has any power. By closely observing such influences, we begin to determine what's good and what's not good for us, what's true and what's a lie.

Once there was a devotee who traveled everywhere in search of Ram. No matter where he went, his poor heart cried out, "Where are you my Lord, where are you?" Then he met a saint who told him that Ram is located in your heart. Grateful for such information, he replied, "If Ram is in my heart, I intend to find him there. So he sat down under a tree and closed his eyes. He began to meditate, searching for Lord Ram. After some time he saw two glaring eyes, a huge mouth and ugly features in the face of a demon. Then he experienced lust, anger, jealousy, and fear. Frightened and dismayed, he opened his eyes and said, "If Ram is in my heart, why can't I see him?"

What he hadn't realized is that those demons dwell up front but Ram's hidden behind them. Only when you remove impurities can you reach Ram. Rather than fearing the demons, on this path you'll have to face them.

Although worn out from his search, this devotee continued asking the same question. Meeting another saint, he asked, "Where can I find Lord Ram? Do you know his address?"

The saint responded, "Yes, I do. If you go around asking everyone, you'll never find him. But when people gather together to chant and pray, that's where you'll find Ram. He dwells in satsanga." When he found his answer at last, this devotee gladly joined others to chant in satsanga where he instantly made Lord Ram's acquaintance.

The heart that becomes mellow and cries Ram has Ram in it. Those eyes through which one searches for Ram have Ram in them. Yet we must search. Only by letting go of "I and mine" and getting hold of "Thou and Thine," can we find God. That letting go is necessary in order to merge into the presence of Lord Ram, into God consciousness.

Love of God is available to everyone equally. How much you receive depends on your connection. It's similar to the conduction of electricity: whatever's connected to the source receives light. In the same way, the flow of love comes from being in the company of saints, or reading scripture that evokes their presence and good qualities. This love always flows according to your desire. But what you may not realize is that as your love for God or guru increases, love from them begins flowing towards you. And you may have thought it was a one-way street!

God Himself Takes Care of Us

Eventually we must realize what a sorry job we do trying to guide our lives by ourselves. Recognizing that there are in fact two energies available to direct the course of our lives, we have a choice. First, we can do it ourselves or secondly, we can yield to that force that works through us which is God.

When we sow a seed, it grows into a tree with a large trunk, branches, leaves, and flowers. Yet we forget the seed of our own creation. If there's any seed in this universe, it's the presence of God. Then we emerge as the branches, leaves and flowers.

In life, most of us experienced how our parents protected us when we were little. From that we can gather that a greater force protects us even when we're fully grown. Again, that force is God. God is the cause, and the whole universe is the effect.

Do you really think a flower or leaf is self-sustaining? Roots serve them both and help them grow. Our root lies in almighty God, for He's protecting the entire universe. Under these circumstances, if someone worries about anything, it's a mistake. There's nothing we need to worry about. All we need is faith and trust in God.

In a small town there was a saint who lived in a temple. He was old and very kind and loving. In order to receive food, he used to go to various towns with his begging bowl and then return to his abode. He was always given food, but one day he was given a special type of grain packed in a large bundle. Since he was old, he needed to travel by horse from town to town.

"Guruji, you can carry this package on your horse," the donor said. As the saint traveled, suddenly he thought of how selfish he'd been. Here he was sitting on this old mare, carrying an extra burden. Not only that, but also the mare was pregnant. So, in order to help her out, he took the bundle and put it on his head. Then he continued down the road.

While traveling he passed a puzzled devotee who asked, "Why are you carrying that bundle on your head?"

Eagerly the saint responded, "This mare is pregnant. I don't want her to be weighed down by such a heavy load."

Gaping at him, the devotee replied, "Guruji, you and the bundle are both on the horse."

"Oh, yes, you're right," the saint replied.

Don't you realize we do the same thing? If God Himself takes care of us, why should we worry or carry the load on our heads? Are we suddenly feeling sympathy for God?

You can say that whoever worries too much is truly crazy. It isn't necessary to reduce God's load. For that matter, it isn't necessary to worry about anything.

Bapuji in three yoga asanas

CHAPTER TWELVE

ON THE BATTLEFIELD OF YOGA

Each and every desire is the general of an army, and since we have many desires, there are millions of armies operating in this one brain, taking us in different directions. Thus, we're engaged in a full-scale battle.

Who would have imagined yoga as a battle? Since we acknowledge the meaning of "yoga" as union, it seems contradictory. Although merging or union does come about as the ultimate outcome, one must first see to the battle of opposing forces going on within. When the mind becomes resolute and stands firm, then only can you declare a victory.

In the past, religion was practiced in every aspect of life, even on the battlefield. In the famous battle of Kurukshetra in the *Gita*, two armies on a field expected to destroy one another. But even then the notion of the good fight guided the events.

In the beginning of the fight, each side acknowledged the other. If the person opposite you were older, you would first shoot an arrow at his feet as a sign of respect. If your enemy's chariot got wrecked, then you would get out and fight on foot. If someone's sword broke, his enemy would throw away his own sword and they would wrestle to the ground. That is written in scripture. Thus warriors were fighting for *vijai* — true defeat. In the past, warriors even blessed their enemies saying,

"Now we face each other. May you experience the triumph of winning."

Today's warriors are completely different, and wars happen without regard for religion or ethics. The war of the bomb is the war of the coward. I have found the modern art of war to be absurd. First of all the modern war is in no way a fight for truth. If you want to give it a name, call it an unexpected attack. It is not a technique but rather a breach of faith.

War can only be considered an art if it is approached through dharma, with just cause and the appropriate means for achieving it. Otherwise it's no better than simple cheating. In the past, in order to establish peace, wars were fought with religion as the motive. After that wars were fought for selfish motives, to establish territorial boundaries or economic advantage. A conflict fought for selfish motives is not a war; it's just a takeover. There is no honor on either side of the battlefield. Nor is people's true happiness at stake. To fight in service to humanity means removing the cause of bad feelings among others and establishing feelings of love and peace. That is an honorable war. Once you achieve it, you do away with the need to fight altogether.

The War between Mind and Prana

Just as external warfare occurs on the battlefield, there's an ongoing battle raging within any serious practitioner of yoga. At war are two types of energy: the energy of mind and that of prana. Mind is subtler and exerts a greater influence over prana, which is the grosser manifestation of energy in the human body, directly related to the breath.

When the mind becomes agitated, it throws the otherwise normal flow of prana (or breathing) into disarray. In such a state we must regulate the flow of prana by resorting to *kumbhaka* (the holding of the breath), meditating, or chanting mantra. Even witnessing beautiful scenery or taking a cold shower will do the trick.

Although prana is exceedingly powerful, in the earlier stages, the mind is more powerful than prana and can subjugate it at will. That works well for those who've resolutely committed to practice, but for whomever there is indecision, unruly prana takes over. Establishing peace of mind and balancing pranic energy thus have mutually sustaining effects upon each other. Since impatience, fear, anger, or despondency are invariably the products of untamed prana, yielding to them often encourages prana to become more fickle. Through practice and focusing your effort, however, you retain a resolute mind and balanced prana at the same time.

At different times in my sadhana I've experienced great restlessness and the gradual erosion of my ability to keep my mind composed, as it's at war with unruly prana. Regardless of the struggle, however, I know that in the end my mind will be vanquished, yet it's my mind's firm resolve that has brought me to the battlefield in the first place. The reason is simple. I've resolved not to give up my daily spiritual practice even under pain of death. Having accepted this state of surrender with great devotion, my mind does not want to desist from its natural duty. However, from time to time it does become extremely restless and vulnerable from encountering numerous obstacles. Now, having come so close to the sight of death, however, it will not break its own sacred promise.

Prana and mind are engaged in constant battle. This fratricidal warfare forms the classic battle of scripture, and Lord Krishna is its guide here as well as in the epic battle of the Mahabharata. Who would have imagined yoga as a battle? Since we acknowledge the meaning of "yoga" as union, it seems contradictory. Although merging or union does come about as the ultimate outcome, one must first see to the battle of opposing forces going on within. When the mind becomes resolute and stands firm, then only can you declare a victory.

Until you understand the fundamental issue of this strife between pranic and mental energy, you won't be able to be steadfast on the yogic path, despite Herculean efforts toward salvation. As it is, the mind is inherently capricious. From daily exposure to external activity, a steady stream of thoughts and impulses arising from passion, anger, and fear sway the mind. To make matters worse, prana often instigates the mind during yoga practice, making it even more excitable. Indeed it often drives the mind to the brink of perversity.

Through all this, the only constant is to persevere in practice. As a result of repeated confrontations with prana, your mind gradually becomes strengthened and develops the fortitude necessary to withstand the violence of prana's movement. In the end, the mind displays such amazing powers of forbearance that it remains impervious to even the most intolerable of intrusions. Only then can it truly be called "peaceful," or balanced.

How to Quiet the Mind

"My mind is so disturbed. How can I quiet it down?" This question has been with us forever. Although many unhappy people request guidance, the solution is rather simple: in order to find peace you must let go of disturbance.

Imagine that I'm drawing a line on a piece of paper. At one end is peace and at the other end is disturbance. If you say you want to move from disturbance toward peace, it seems obvious that you must first give up disturbance. Yet most of us have a hard time letting go because we insist on remaining focused on what disturbs us. We keep dwelling on the wrong end of the line.

Suppose you've become tired after standing up for hours. If you ask someone for help, he'll simply say, "Sit down. Then if you get tired, lie down. Then stand up." Where peace is concerned, however, we remain standing endlessly, holding onto the same disturbing thoughts, while clamoring for repose.

The second aphorism in Patanjali's *Yoga Sutras,* "Yogas chitta vritti narodah", says that yoga helps remove disturbances from the mind. The different aspects of the mind include reasoning, *chitta,* decision-making or intellect, *buddhi,* and the organ of action-ego, *ahankara.* Chitta compares notes on its observations and passes information on to buddhi, which decides on a course of action. Ego sends out messages regarding the decision and engages the sense organs to follow.

The impact this process creates is called *vritti.* To understand vritti, think of it as a desire. Each and every desire is the general of an army, and since we have many desires, there are millions of armies operating in this one brain, taking us in different directions. To master them all is an overwhelming task. They're so mischievous that when you try to exercise control, narodah, over one vritti, another gets out of hand. When you try to control that one, the others run away.

However, if we intervene or cut off sense stimulation, we can withdraw from the disturbance and go deep within. At that time prana begins to vibrate in harmony with the mind and the senses line up and cooperate with prana. However, if the mind is restless, prana becomes restless and the senses follow suit. So if you want to become steady, first steady your mind, which steadies prana, which in turn calms your senses. Whenever you find your mind divided, use the tools of yoga to bring about steadiness.

Imagine, for example, that you're about to do *padmasana*, the Lotus posture. Ordinarily you would extend both legs, pick up one leg and place it on the opposite thigh and then repeat on the other side without thinking. However, if you want to steady the mind through Padmasana, you'll have to perform it in a different manner. That method is called the kriya of chitta and prana. Kriya refers to an "action of the soul," which manifests primarily as breath. When you practice a movement with kriya and focused attention, prana and chitta are harmonized.

Here's how it's done. In the beginning, sit with both legs extended. Begin breathing in and out very slowly. Notice if you're in a hurry and consciously slow down. After you've taken a few deep breaths, extend your arms to grasp one foot. Again do this in an extremely slow and steady manner. Gradually bring your foot up and place it on your thigh. With such concentration, chitta and prana come fully present and as you hold the foot, all three are brought into alignment.

After placing your foot on your thigh, again become still for a moment and breathe steadily. Extend your thoughts to the other foot, and as soon as your mind is there, prana will be there. Repeat the same process, moving in slow motion. Once you've brought the foot onto the opposite thigh, pause and take in several breaths. Then allow your thoughts to focus first on one palm and then the other. If your breath is slow and your focus is deliberate, you will achieve the kriya of chitta and prana and will experience a deep and abiding peace. Such practice creates harmony of the senses, body, mind, and prana.

It's All Yoga

Although ordinarily the mind is more powerful than prana, in the *Kundalini Yoga Upanishads*, it's said that a sadhak should first of all master prana. You must master prana because although the mind is master of the physical senses, prana is master of the mind.

If mind is master of the senses and prana is master of the mind, then *laya*, subtle consciousness, is master of prana, and that laya is supported by *nada*, the deepest sound. Unless one reaches this state and has a direct experience, it's difficult to conceptualize. From prana to laya to sound, each is a more subtle extension of the energy field, gradually dissolving into the next form. Prana dissolves into life, the cause of all nature. When nada dissolves, it's called light.

This happens in stages. The vital air or *vayu* results in nada. So the vayu is the base of nada. From nada, *anahat nad*, or spontaneous heart sounds, emerge from within. From that the grosser manifestation is the word, and the next formation is the sentence. The extension of it is language. But the entire realm of prana exists behind the mind and gives life to it.

Steadiness in prana comes about through steadiness of mind. In yoga, the first task for the sadhak is to achieve concentration of mind. Because his mind has been divided among many pursuits, many different thoughts come and go, firing like rockets within a short period of time. The mind is never concentrated in one direction, and so it is necessary to first concentrate one's mind in a particular direction. To withdraw the mind from various objects or activities and focus it only on one is known as meditation.

Just before we begin any action, there is a thought generated in our minds and only then we act according to that thought. When the mind thinks and orders prana to do a particular thing, prana takes possession of the senses or the organs of the body to complete that action.

Normally, we do things in great haste. Our thoughts are so quickly generated that no sooner have we thought the thought, then our hand reaches out or we take a step forward. But to do any act as an act of meditation, we have to first concentrate our minds. Focusing deeply on what we're about to do, we ensure that our prana is also directed that way so that all our energies are focused and concentrated.

Let me give an example. Seeing a book lying in front of me, I make a decision to pick it up and put it on my lap. When I slowly lift it up and put it on my lap, I will be doing it from a meditative place. As I'm only thinking about this book and only doing what I want, my whole attention is concentrated toward that end. I'm not mindful of anyone during this experiment. Rather, it's a meditation. As I begin lifting up this book, my mind is entirely focused. I begin breathing deeply, and all that I see or feel is the sensation of this book in my hand as it's moving toward the table. An inordinate stillness sets in. Then suddenly book, hand, mind, and breath become one.

That's an example of the kriya of chitta and prana, the subtle action that brings them into alignment. If you experience unsteadiness of mind, prana, or the senses, you must practice in this way to bring them under control. Whatever you do must be done with perfect harmony and focused attention, forgetting everything else around you.

They say that whatever work you do, if you concentrate your mind, it's yoga. Regardless of whether you're worshipping God or drinking a glass of water, it's all yoga, provided you act with concentration of mind. Shri Patanjali also says that we can choose whatever we want and that will be meditation, but the type of action we choose should be *sattvic* or pure in nature so it doesn't create any disturbance in our mind.

Surrendering Does Not Mean Losing the Battle

If you dip a colander into the river, it comes up empty. The mind of a worldly person cannot hold knowledge because it's like a colander. However, when you experience in-depth pain or disappointment and see no way out, then the holes are filled, and the colander becomes solid.

As long as the door of hopelessness is closed to us, we have not truly entered the depths of yoga. That's the same door

Arjuna approached to wage war in the *Bhagavad Gita*. Finding himself completely out of options, he experienced what we now call *Arjuna Vishada Yoga*, the yoga of total disappointment.

Arjuna was the commander of the entire army and it was time to begin fighting. Facing the opposing army full of his brothers and relatives, he moaned, "If I kill them, it will be such a loss. Their wives will grieve and cry. Their children will cry. Why should this war be fought?" So he said to Lord Krishna, "Here's my bow and arrow. I give up. I don't want to fight."

There's a greater lesson to this story. Since Arjuna was filled with grief, at that time he could not access supreme knowledge. It's only when our minds are in a neutral and objective state that we're ready to receive knowledge and not when we're either grieved by failures or excited by our successes.

When an archer shoots a target, he first concentrates on one point; then he releases his arrow. In the same way, when we come to the yoga of Arjuna's total disappointment, our task is to see clearly where we must go. Although the whole world burns for us in the fire of disappointment or hopelessness, we can't see in the moment of emotion but must wait until the smoke clears. When our mind becomes empty of thought, we can shoot straight ahead, attaining the supreme goal. It's only when we become honest and simple that we're potential customers for the yoga of disappointment. Whoever arrives at that stage has truly been drawn to the feet of the Lord.

In the process of witnessing and regulating prana, a state of surrender is necessary to unfetter the mind. In the language of yoga, this is called relaxation or complete letting go. This state of surrender does not burst forth suddenly but only awakens gradually as we witness the futility of this battle. The devotee reaches such a hapless and bewildered frame of mind that he loses a sense of direction and purpose. Out of such churning of his heart, however, he suddenly discovers the light of his conscience guiding him. Through that illumination, God's grace reaches him.

Then he gives himself up to a state of complete surrender, ceasing all physical and mental efforts to fight against the natural flow of events. Allowing his life to remain afloat on the spontaneously arising ebb and flow of circumstance, he continues to be focused in the stream of activity. However, since he has inwardly dedicated the fruit of his actions to God, his actions become selfless, spontaneous offerings.

Bapuji at desk

CHAPTER THIRTEEN

MY GUIDANCE TO DISCIPLES

What you practice has the capacity to take you all the way to God. The only thing to remember is to utilize these tools of yoga with patience, purposefulness, and peace of mind. Using them diligently, your intellect and analytical power will expand. At the same time your ego will gradually dissolve.

Below I offer you the message that my Gurudev gave to me for the purpose of God-realization. The following list includes a summary of his guidelines for yoga sadhana, intended for serious practitioners on this path.

Only those devotees with unshakable love for their guru can cross the ocean of *samskaras* and attain the supreme love of God. Serve the true teacher with purity, faith, and joy in your heart. One who is trying to reach God-Consciousness believing that the guru's guidance is not necessary is a victim of his own vanity, and one who disrespects the guru likewise disrespects religion and God.

1. Love all living beings, do not hate anyone.

2. Speak the truth pleasantly without causing upset to the listener. Talk less and keep silence where the situation demands.

3. Do not steal or hide the truth.

4. After mantra initiation, observe celibacy for fifteen months. During this period, married people should practice self-restraint as much as possible.

5. Initiates should have one pure and moderate meal a day with milk in the morning and evening. Do not eat meat. Do not use liquor, marijuana, tobacco, coffee, tea, or other stimulants.

6. The initiate should observe seven days a month as fast days. This should be done for fifteen months, although it's best if these seven fasts can be observed throughout life.

7. If possible, take cold baths three times a day. Carefully maintain the purity and piety of the body. Never sleep during the day. Be in bed by ten o'clock at night and rise at four o'clock in the morning.

8. To rid oneself of *rajoguna* (restless activity) and *tamoguna* (inertia or laziness) and to maintain good health, practice yoga asanas thirty minutes each morning, afternoon, and evening. This also makes the practice of celibacy easier and makes one fit to practice pranayama.

9. Practice pranayama each day in the morning, afternoon and evening. There are three kinds of pranayama. The first kind (anuloma vilom) should be done fifteen minutes. Repeat the Ram mantra for five minutes for the second pranayama, and for the third the Guru Mantra is repeated mentally.

10. The initiate should repeat ten rosaries (each rosary has 108 beads) of the Guru mantra each day. This number should be increased on fast days. During holy times, fasting should be observed and 125,000 Mantras repeated.

11. Repeat any of the following mantras to help purify the mind and restrain the senses.

shri krishna govinda hare murare
he natha narayana vasudeva

hare rama hare rama rama rama hare hare
hare krishna hare krishna krishna krishna, hare hare.

hama raghava rama raghava rama raghava raksha mam
krishna keshava krishna keshava krishna keshava pahi mam

hari hari bol hari hari bol
mukunda madhava govinda bol

12. As a source of self-study, contemplate the meaning of Shri Gnaneshvar's *Bhagavad Gita*. Memorize lines 54 to 72 of the second chapter of the *Bhagavad Gita*. Chapters 12, 15, and 16 should also be memorized and recited every day. Recite *Brahmacharya Bhavani* (treatise on celibacy) every morning. Practice bhajans, and read and contemplate good books every day. Never stop listening to the messages of pious saints.

13. Practice four types of meditation, and utilize more often the one that suits you the most. Increase meditation a few minutes at a time a total of fifteen minutes each month. By the end of fifteen months, you should be able to sit for three hours, steady and straight in one asana.

14. Read this guide every Thursday.

The next sections elaborate on some of these disciplines.

Brahmacharya

In order to build a dam, you must begin with the foundation. First collect whatever materials are necessary and then build from the ground up. In the same way, brahmacharya is a foundational practice. The great power to be attained through a spiritual path is only available through celibacy and the restraint of sexual energy.

Indian scriptures say that without brahmacharya it's impossible to attain the Lord. Why is that so? If you consider that the word *Brahma* is God, and *charya* is "the motion that takes you toward God," then, you have a succinct definition of the path. In order to go toward God, you must practice brahmacharya. It's the engine that propels the train forward, and abstinence from sexual activity is what stokes the engine.

Many people have mistaken ideas about brahmacharya, believing it either has no value or that it's impossible to practice. It's always been surrounded by a certain amount of conflict and controversy. For scientists, the belief that one can never control the sex urge (and thus effectively practice brahmacharya) has influenced people in their practice of yoga. However, there are deeper principles at work.

Iron is heavier than water, so it cannot float. It will sink. This reflects an unchanging principle of physics. However, a thousand tons of iron can be loaded on a ship and transported across the earth. This too reflects a principle of physics. Thus brahmacharya operates through both material and spiritual principles. While it's difficult to transform the energy of sex, it's not impossible. And when you take up depth sadhana, it sustains and gives life to your practice.

Celibacy is the best austerity; all other austerities are of a lower order. Whoever masters his genitals is not an ordinary person but a saint. Yogis are well aware that passion is the cause of creation, so passion is at the root of every human being.

There are two kinds of passion arising in everyone's body: physical-spiritual and mental-sensual. Physical passion is a result of prana. The awakening of passion in a child's body is the result of prana; it's not a conscious phenomenon. The passion born of prana is described as spiritual because it has the potential to be transformed; its equivalent is the awakened kundalini energy rising upward through the *sushumna* or central channel. In the *Bhagavad Gita* this spiritual passion born of prana is described as being favorable to dharma: "In beings, I am the passion which is not contrary to dharma."

Ordinarily the awakening of passion in a man or woman is due to external stimulation and is of the mental-sensual type. Due to their impurities, however, people rarely transform their sexual energies, as they are busy acting upon these urges. However, yogis derive great benefits from channeling this energy.

When you take up brahmacharya, your body becomes light and your mind remains steady. With such tranquility and stillness you can see the root cause of problems and clear away pain and suffering. However you must engage in practice in order to understand the benefits.

In the final analysis, brahmacharya can only be known through experimentation and practice. It's hard to grasp its effects as a mere concept. While this subject is profound, brahmacharya becomes easier in proportion to how much you love it. Your love in turn gets strengthened in proportion to your practice.

Many people follow *vam marga*, or the left-handed path, indulging in sex, alcohol, or other types of stimulation, and consider that to be a form of yoga. That's an illusion. Illusions occur in yoga especially before achieving the final states of consciousness and although they appear to be true, they lead to wrong practice. Those who practice vam marga have misunderstood the ancient scriptures. Even if they're scholars, they're fools, for spiritual progress is not possible without celibacy.

The more you understand the value of celibacy, the easier it gets. When someone drinks too much water, he must use the bathroom more often. When someone lives a stimulating life, the sexual urges become stronger. Just as urine and feces are naturally present in the body, so sex is also a natural force to be dealt with.

However, a yogi or yogini can attain the same state of consciousness as a young child. Very young children have little desire for sex. After many years of sadhana, energy patterns change in the yogi, and there's no longer great disturbance through sexual urges. Those who reach that state of consciousness are considered to be great masters and are called *urdvaretas*. Dadaji, my Guru, was urdvaretas and reached the highest.

When one becomes urdvaretas, the semen or body fluids are transformed. That's the beginning of a complex process of attaining what's called the divine body. Just as in the child's body, the production of sexual energy mixes directly with the blood, in that state the yogi becomes childlike and his semen so superfine that it immediately mixes with his blood. So the downward passage of sexual energies is closed off, and the sex center itself becomes transformed. When that happens there is so much power in a person's eyes that his eyes alone can remove the lust of others.

This process works in the same way for women as it does for men. Whether you're in the body of a male or female, it all goes back to prakriti, which is the universal principle of nature. Only the soul remains as *purusha* or pure spirit. Male or female—it makes no difference. When purifying, both men and women have to work through the principle of nature.

Although there may be some outward differences in the sadhana of men and women, inwardly the basic principles remain the same. Imagine rainwater falling on an apple tree or an orange tree. Both trees receive nourishment at the roots. Still the fruit of each tree is different and the juice of each fruit is different. But in the end everything results from the transformation of that same water in the tree.

In much the same way, male and female hormones and sexual fluids are the embodiment of atman or the soul. Nourished through sadhana, they form the root of the transformational process. Therefore brahmacharya is a universal practice that's equally beneficial for men and for women.

When you begin brahmacharya, there are simple techniques that support the practice. Let go of any activities that stimulate the senses, such as watching movies or television, taking alcohol, tobacco, or other substances. Eat properly and get sufficient rest so you can direct your life toward spiritual pursuits in a more focused manner. Practice provides its own feedback, for as you observe restraint, it helps you identify areas of excess in other parts of your life. Then it's time to simplify.

The most important thing, however, is learning to channel love. Direct the energy of love to others just as you would to a brother, sister, father, or mother and it strengthens your practice. When a sister places her head on her brother's heart, it's as if they've merged into the ocean of love.

With this practice, a young man speaking to a young woman feels as if he's talking to his sister. When she responds to him as if she were his daughter or sister, that creates a channel for love's higher expression and tensions are immediately resolved. The feeling that the whole world is one family can be properly understood, then, through channeling love to others exactly as you would to your own family members.

Although many think brahmacharya is difficult, truly speaking, it's not. In fact, if you keep your mind filled with pure thoughts, it can be a joy. Experiment and expand your expressions of love, as brother to sister or parent to child with everyone, and that will help purify your mind. Then observe continuously and keenly whether your lifestyle creates alertness and joy. If those conditions are fulfilled, your progress will be easy.

The key to all of this is careful self-observation. I constantly analyze my feelings and intentions and ask, "Is this based in cowardice? Is there some hidden fear? Some unknown weakness?" Truly the highest quality of a spiritual seeker is objective self-awareness without criticism. For a yogi it's indispensable. To whatever extent you master the art of self-observation, to that extent you will be successful. Above all, remember that brahmacharya consists of actions that bring you closer to God. If you want the highest treasure in life, you must be prepared to pay the price.

Mitahar

In order to be successful in yoga, one needs strong prana. You can develop prana according to your capacity and inclination using the tools of yoga. For instance, with the various practices, prana can be increased through your eyes, your ears, your tongue, your skin, or through any of the five senses. Increased through pranayama or breathing exercises, for example, prana moves at the speed of a jet plane. But not everyone can digest that speed so it is better to grow slowly and steadily.

Among the many tools to increase prana, moderation in diet is the most important. *Mit* means "moderate" and *ahar* means food. Thus the word *mitahar* reflects how we should eat — not too much and not too little. The true practice of mitahar involves eating only what is necessary for the body.

Most people misunderstand the notion of mitahar and consider the portions of food they choose to be well regulated. Rarely is that the case, however. When you have not exercised and you're not hungry, you must eat less than usual. When you've physically exerted yourself and thus have greater hunger, on the other hand, if you take only a fixed amount, it will be less than you need.

Your appetite also increases or decreases according to your emotional state, for the body and mind are intricately related. So the presence of joy, fear, anger, or hurt affect the choice of foods you eat and may set you up for some kind of imbalance. In fact, diet is a maze in which even the most intelligent person gets lost. Human beings may stay even-minded while performing their work, but when they sit down to eat, they turn into demons.

A moderate diet requires restraint, while abstinence from food requires suppression. It's often more difficult to moderate what you eat than it is to abstain altogether. However, sooner or later one must eat. Mitahar varies according to each person's need. For example, a child needs to eat more often. An old man with weaker digestive power needs to eat less. When an elephant decides on moderation, the proportions will look a lot different from those of a mouse.

In the *Bhagavad Gita*, Lord Krishna uses the word *uktahar* to mean "moderate, appropriate, and well restrained." I consider this an excellent word to describe moderation in diet. Yet how can we determine what is moderate? The best thing is to eat only the amount of food that promotes physical well-being and mental alertness. If you feel sluggish, irritable, or uncomfortable after a meal, then you know you've not eaten moderately. You can master this art if you eat with precise moderation for one month. Also fast one day a week on fruit juice, whey, or green mung bean broth. Avoid whatever foods are disagreeable to your system. Such discrimination not only prevents disease and protects your health, but also adds years to your life and a greater inclination to do sadhana.

Chitta vritti narodah means, "stopping the modifications of the mind." It's one of the foundations of Patanjali's Yoga Sutras. However, any practice is meaningless if we lose ourselves at mealtimes. And that's what happens to us — we just surrender ourselves to food. Thus great yogis lose their connection to yoga, and the wisest people become fools at the table.

In India moderation in diet is considered an important part of spiritual life and many experiments in diet have been conducted there. A religion that has not given any thought to diet cannot survive. In India the three major religions are sanatana dharma, Jain dharma, and Boddhi dharma. Born and raised together, they are all interrelated and have carried out many experiments in diet. Sanatana dharma places great faith in moderation in diet. Jain dharma lays more stress on fasting. In fact, if fasting were not woven into the structure of most religions, there would be more disease and premature death than there is in the world today.

If a person practices true moderation in diet, there is no need for fasting. But for the average person, these rules are useful, for periodic fasting helps control the impulse to overeat. I ask my disciples to follow fasting practices a total of seven times per month and I myself have practiced this way for many years. It's necessary because my disciples prepare all different kinds of food. Without seven fasts a month, I'd get sick. Although I eat with great care and understanding, if I were to eat everything placed in front of me, yoga would get mad and run away, and only the food in my belly would remain.

Mantra

Mantra is the sum of all doctors and the real medicine for humanity.

One of the most important tools in the path of yoga is the practice of mantra, the repetition of potent Sanskrit syllables for enlightenment. Although one can interpret the literal meaning of a mantra, since it is comprised of letters and words, the mantra's sound itself is as important as the meaning. Repeating mantra strengthens one's willpower and purifies the mind. At the same time it bestows good health, fame, wealth, and longevity. In short, repeating mantra is a unique way to attain the main goals in life.

Each of us is deeply affected by the vibration of sound. To illustrate, once there was a great athlete who could lift several hundred pounds, throw a discus, and wrestle like a madman. One day someone was abusive toward him, and he yelled back, "Whom do you think you're talking to? I could twist you and throw you away like a piece of straw."

While he was shouting, a saint happened to pass by and overheard him.

Approaching him with great love, he said, "Can you pick up heavy stones and throw them?

The athlete said "yes."

"Well then, why not pick up this abuse and throw it away? What's a few words compared to your size and strength?"

We're all affected by sounds of different types. Mantra is a very specific type of sound; you could call it divine sound. In India we refer to sound as nad, the unstruck sound, which is on its way to some form of expression. The many stages associated with the creation of sound progress through spoken language (uttering sounds assigned a certain meaning) to a subtler form of language involved in telling the truth. Truth telling creates a higher and stronger vibration than ordinary language. When you tell the truth, there's no pollution, only purity of expression.

The next form of language is the language of God, involving only the highest principles expressed by saints and scripture. Mantra, a series of syllables that may be sung or chanted, is a language that takes you beyond thought to the source of life itself.

When a yogi meditates, the yogic fire induces all kinds of utterances, referred to as *anahat nad*, to usher from his mouth. These sounds arise spontaneously and automatically during yoga practice. All the divine mantras also manifested through anahat nad. For example, the mantra *Om namo bhagavate vasude-vaya*, which has been the mantra passed on through this lineage, was not written by any person; it evolved through anahat nad. Since the sound came from a divine source, it's not only considered a mantra but also a form of the Lord Himself.

A mantra set to music is called a dhun and during kirtan or devotional chanting there are many dhuns sung and occasionally bhajans or hymns to God. During kirtan the entire mind enters into the wave of rhythm and becomes one-pointed, focused on repetition of the mantra. This chanting has an intoxicating effect. For example, the Ram dhun I've chanted is the outcome of anahat nad. Many years ago, when I was sitting in meditation, the tune for this Ram dhun emerged. I did not plan it or arrange a specific melody; it came forth spontaneously during meditation practice.

Whoever meditates deeply on mantra winds up receiving God's word. That person is directly tuned into cosmic consciousness. That's because mantras chanted to a deity are considered to be the subtle body of that deity and contain his energy. Repeating mantra thus purifies a seeker's mind and enhances his purity, restraint, and concentration. When such a yogi arrives at the source of all languages through mantra, he becomes one with God.

Study and Scripture

Nowadays we buy insurance in order to secure our future life. With many vehicles traveling on our streets, there are frequent collisions or accidents. Likewise, a human being wandering through his life often becomes the victim of many accidents in thought, speech, or conduct.

Spiritual practice helps clear the path of conduct. And self-study supported by the reading of scriptures and holy works helps purify speech and thought. Self-study, or *swadhyaya*, is defined as "listening to, contemplating, and practicing the principles of the scriptures. By listening to the truth, the seeker's mind becomes less restless and more discriminating. In addition his intellect and ego become purified and refined.

Although the purpose of study is to help answer the fundamental questions—"Who am I? "What is God?" and "Who created the universe?"—the reading of scripture can only provide partial insight. The real answers emerge only from direct experience and perception of the truth as a result of practice. Thus, the sadhak must continually strike a balance between the practice of yoga and the deep contemplation of scripture. At the moment when his experience matches the scriptures, however, his joy becomes boundless, for that is how their secrets are revealed.

In my thirty years of yoga sadhana I read the *Vedas*, the *Puranas*, the *Darshanas*, and *Upanishads* and tried to understand them to the best of my ability. I read their verses not once or twice, but hundreds of times. With each reading I received new insights. In scriptures there is the saying, *Sa vidya ya vimuktaye*, which means, "That which liberates us from bondage is knowledge." And so whoever has a fierce desire for liberation also fiercely desires knowledge.

Both the practice of yoga and the yoga scriptures are full of secrets. The meaning of a particular scripture is understood differently by those in different stages of sadhana. Unveiling key principles, and the ups and downs encountered in yoga practice, the various stages of sadhana are fully outlined in these texts.

Continual absorption in the scriptures combined with self-study is important in developing a yoga practice. The sadhana takes us to new states of awareness, and the scriptures illuminate and reinforce our attempts at practice. Yet the scriptures' true and complete meaning can only be perceived after the yogi attains the final stages of sadhana. Then he may be considered a *purna* or perfected yogi.

Impressed by seeing my guru's many powers, I once exclaimed, "Gurudev, you are a purna yogi and great accomplished master!" to which he burst out laughing.

I said, "Why are you laughing? Aren't you a perfect master?"

"No. According to the Indian scriptures, I haven't fulfilled the qualifications."

"What are those qualifications?" I asked him, astounded.

"Only when the disciple of the perfect master's disciple becomes perfect can that accomplished master be called perfect. When you become perfected in practice, and a disciple of yours becomes perfect, only then can it be established that I'm perfect."

"That will come only by your grace," I told him.

Though he's not present with me in physical form, Gurudev's teachings are available and through constant practice I keep his memory alive. The disciple who cannot understand the value of yogic knowledge or who does not practice sadhana can never understand the importance of having a guru or access to knowledge. Traveling speedily on the earth, sailing on water, or flying through the sky are all possible with modern vehicles. Similarly, the journey within the self can be speedily completed only through the sadguru.

Patience

Patience is a key virtue on the path of yoga. It often eludes us because of its simplicity, yet it forms the foundation of a true yogi's practice. A brief anecdote illustrates the point: Two small children approach a gardener sowing seeds in his garden. When they ask him what he's doing, he says, "I'm planting seeds." "What happens when you do that?" the children ask.

"Flowers and trees grow as a result."

Hearing that, the children get excited. "Give us some seeds," they say, and then armed with several packets they run back home. Following the gardener's instructions, they dig up some earth and plant the seeds in front of their house. They pour water over them and smooth the earth firmly. Then they walk around and come back after a few minutes. Digging up the seeds, they see that nothing has grown, so they return them to the soil. This time they take a walk for two or three hours and return. Digging up the seeds once more, they are disappointed not to find anything. So they return to the gardener and ask him why nothing has grown.

"Why, dear children, you must be patient. Things don't sprout overnight. They take time to grow."

We are not much different from these children. To do sadhana we must realize the path cannot be completed in a few minutes; it may take lifetimes. Anything worth doing will take time to cultivate and time to practice. Most of all it will take time for its effects to blossom within us and to be revealed. The same is true in loving others; patience is needed. There's no overnight miracle when it comes to establishing relationships. As a matter of fact, love and patience are inseparable.

Suppose I want to throw a stone a hundred feet; with a strong arm I can do that. But if I want to throw a stone from India to America, I won't succeed. Likewise if your love goes only so far, you must cultivate patience, which extends the pathway your love can travel. Although you love others, you may feel that they do not accept your love. This is where you need to have patience, which grows subtly beneath the surface. That patience eventually creates trust and faith in another's heart and then love blooms on its own.

They say that there's no such word as impossible in your dictionary. Everything can be done in America, and sometimes even by yesterday. Nowadays if you sow seeds in the morning, by the afternoon you expect fruits to appear. But that's unrealistic. Things that are truly of merit require time and patience in order to be fulfilled.

The Mahasamadhi Shrine at Malav

CHAPTER FOURTEEN

THE SADHANA OF LIBERATION

Om tryambakam yajamahe
sugandhim pushti-vardanam
urvarukam iva bandanan
mrit yor mukshiya mamritat
Protect me, dear Lord Shiva, o three-eyed one.
Bless me with health and immortality,
And as a cucumber is cut from the vine,
Release me from the clutches of death.
The Mahamrityunjaya Mantra
(The Great Death-defying mantra)

The Foremost Principle

Yoga is certainly a science, but it's a mystical science. We can attain it only through the medium of our bodies and minds practicing sadhana for many years without fail. It won't help to become impatient or hasty. Our sadhana is that of *moksha* (liberation). We're not those who toil for *dharma* (duty), *artha* (wealth), or *kama* (desire). Ours is not the worldly path but the path of renunciation and sacrifice. In fact, we have to sacrifice everything and become dispossessed.

The first and most necessary rule in the sadhana of liberation is that external activities must cease. It's absolutely impossible to pursue sadhana in a place where external disturbances distract you. That's the first and foremost principle, and there's no room for any compromise in it.

Ordinary worldly people consider liberation to be a great pain, for to attain it they have to give up wealth, wife, fame, son, daughter, husband, or worldly gain. Since that kind of renunciation is experienced as painful or unnecessary, few are willing to go through it in order to obtain the ultimate happiness. In essence people turn their backs on depth sadhana, saying, "Right now we can't climb this mountain of liberation. Give us a little rock of happiness, and that'll be enough."

Each person must then evaluate and make the decision on his own to take up depth sadhana. According to the scriptures, only a yogi for whom yoga sadhana is his whole life can be considered steadfast. Renouncing public contact to live in seclusion, such a yogi does not concern himself with respect, praise, or criticism, To practice silence, one must avoid audiences. Therefore seclusion is the best choice. This is one example of how you must renounce conditions of the past in order to create conditions more favorable to your sadhana.

At one point my disciple Amrit asked me, "Bapuji, doesn't the contemplation of scriptures and the writing of articles get in the way of your sadhana? Won't you have to renounce those activities later on?"

I replied, "Yes, I eagerly look forward to that occasion. Sadhana has two main facets: scriptural study and yoga practice. Since they complement each other, both are necessary. After spending many years in seclusion, however, I've learned that once your practice is done, if you don't pursue activities conducive to sadhana, your mind begins to run back toward worldly pursuits."

Music, literature, and yoga sadhana have taken every minute, day, month and year of my life. They've been ocean-like to me; rarely have I surfaced from their depths. None of the world's joys or sorrows distracts me from intense absorption. On those rare occasions when I've met with disturbances, I've only spotted them on the surface, looked briefly, and then retired again into the depths of that ocean. Thus, through music, scriptural contemplation, and spiritual writings I've been able to forget the world easily. Likewise, whoever wants to stay in continuous seclusion must have engrossing activities like these, or he'll never be able to handle the secluded life.

In fact the sadhak must burn with ardor. The task of changing his personality is so arduous that he could never cope with it if he did not burn with ardor. With burning idealism he must drive the pole of decisiveness deep into the ground of his life. Anyone who commits himself to developing just one genuine life-building principle will in fact gather all the rest by means of this sadhana.

Above all, what sustains depth practitioners is our connection to God. We must live considering God to be our only support. Here we have to surrender even the siddhis, or powers, and *sampattis*, or wealth, that we might achieve through other means. The real siddhi for an aspirant of liberation is freedom from worldly bondage. Material powers can be put to use, provided that that does not come in the way of attaining liberation and contributes towards the welfare of the world.

Silence

Hand in hand with the practice of sadhana is the importance of silence. I cannot emphasize it enough. Silence teaches us contemplation, while talking confers indiscretion and unsteadiness. They say that this little elf of a tongue is a giant to control, and I believe that it's true, whether with food consumption or conversation. Silence has constantly kept me awake and aware and has blessed me with the habit of self-observation. Whenever I engage in behavior that I consider improper, my mind is afflicted with great pain. If I don't spot the mistake right away, it stands before me when I meditate and calls for immediate correction. The more I practice silence, the more subtle are the behaviors that crop up in meditation. If such subtleties spring to my awareness during self-observation, it can only be due to the Lord's grace.

Thought, which precedes speech, is subtle, covert, and unverbalized, whereas speech is overt, gross, and verbalized thought. When you observe silence, even more thoughts are generated. It's as if the mind speaks on behalf of your tongue and then listens to itself on behalf of your ears. Likewise, when you practice meditation, more thoughts arise and you become acutely aware of the mind's propensity to think.

The more you practice silence, seclusion, and meditation, the more introspective you become. With more practice you naturally progress from introspection to self-observation. Only self-observation enables you to clearly see your virtues and vices. As you progress in internal purification, your affinity for virtues increases and your affinity for vices decreases. Whoever cannot see his true self in the reflection of his sadhana cannot become a true sadhak.

Silence with discrimination is like a wish-fulfilling tree or a touchstone; it has the power to transform an ordinary seeker into an accomplished master. Through years of practice, silence has brought me everything worth having, and most importantly, it has enabled me to practice yoga sadhana steadily.

Sadhana Addict

I've done sadhana continuously for thirty years without the slightest lapse. Yet I'm not proud of it, because I don't believe that doing such lengthy sadhana is any indication of greatness. However, since I'm doing my sadhana honestly and liberation is the only aim of my life, I'm content. Because it's true that some sadhaks take much less time completing their sadhana, I've often wondered why it's taken me so long. I know the completion of the full cycle requires many births, and even if it's completed in the hundredth year of one's life, it's considered early. Still I've wondered if my progress might have been delayed in some way. I first discovered my answer in various yogic scriptures. The texts mention that a sadhak should continuously practice sahit kumbhaka until he's able to master keval kumbhaka.

(Editor's note: *sahit kumbhaka* means "interrupted holding" such as in *anuloma vilom*. One practices sahit kumbhaka until keval or kevalam kumbhaka is achieved. Kevalam means "only retention," in which there's as much as three hours between one inhalation and the next exhalation.)

I practiced sahit kumbhaka only five months in the beginning of my yoga practice. After that I gave it up. During the first five years of yoga practice, I felt that I should reinstate sahit kumbhaka, and so I again took up its practice. But once more

I gave it up after a few weeks because I didn't like doing anything willfully. The key yoga instruction I'd received from Gurudev had to do with anuloma vilom; once I began pranayama, I entered into meditation automatically. So I returned to that sadhana. Needless to say for the past seventeen years I never willfully practiced sahit kumbhaka again.

The yogic scriptures say that while awaiting the attainment of samadhi, one is incomplete. It's only when you become so engrossed in yoga sadhana that you forget even your desire for the goal that you achieve samadhi and become a true yogi.

As I am a seeker of liberation, my aim is to be void of mind. Even scriptures state that the mind is the root of both bondage and liberation. That is, the passionate mind creates bondage while the dispassionate mind achieves liberation.

This stage of sahaj yoga that I'm pursuing is extremely difficult. In the initial stage of yoga, the yogi restrains his sense organs by removing control over his body. As their functions subside, these organs become inactive. In turn, that triggers the next stage, or restraint of the mind, or chitta. When the yogi releases control of his mind, prana is strengthened and the chitta becomes restless. As a result he experiences nonattachment to the fullest capacity, absorbed completely in his practice. Any remaining chitta is free of desires; his actions are then guided by prana, or in the language of bhakti yoga, by the Lord himself.

The great sage Patanjali calls *ishwara pranidhana*, the path of complete surrender to God, the quickest. In searching for a deeper understanding of my sadhana, I derived great solace from that statement. Trying my level best to refrain from touring, public contacts, wealth, or fame, at the same time I've always been careful to maintain the continuity of my sadhana. Now I'm no longer impatient. Surrendering my entire life to the Lord, I don't care whether I attain samadhi in this life or the next one. I just enjoy my sadhana and that's why I'm doing it. Truthfully you could call me a "sadhana addict."

Surrender to God

Sometimes a sadhak will pray to God, "Look how difficult my life is. How can I possibly surrender to you? If I could dedicate two or three actions, that'd be fine. But the scriptures say to dedicate *all* my actions to you. Don't you think that's going overboard?"

There's a fine line between actions dedicated to God and those dedicated to oneself. Only those actions performed in order to achieve the Lord or to purify body and mind can be considered dedicated to the Lord. Reading scripture, listening to bhajans, or considering the words of a saint or holy person are actions dedicated to God. Anything performed as an offering releases the sadhak from the bondage of the world. On the other hand, those actions performed for pleasure, fame, or wealth bind him to the world.

The moment an action is performed with attachment, the sense of doership and the desire for results inevitably arise. By maintaining the role of witness to our actions, however, we can act without attachment to the results. That's surrender to God. In the *Bhagavad Gita* Lord Krishna clarifies the type of actions to be performed when he instructs Arjuna to become free of all attachments and perform his actions for the sake of *yajna*, or a sacrificial offering to God.

Once we have truly offered our lives to God, we can step out of the way for His work to be done. We should willingly accept whatever He gives us whether it's happiness or unhappiness, because it's always in our best interest. Some cry, "O God, why are you giving me so much pain?" yet you never hear anyone complaining, "O God, why do you give me so much happiness?" So the first principle in surrender must be letting go of any conditions we hold for our happiness.

In order to surrender fully, the sadhak must lovingly dedicate his life to the Lord and take refuge only in Him. In the course of his yoga sadhana he comes to realize the Lord's domain and power through direct personal experience.

However, there's some confusion about this notion of surrender. If you don't know whom you're surrendering to, how can you do it? A simple example will suffice. If you're traveling and must first cross a river, you'll need the help of a boat. We can say that you've surrendered to the boat only after taking your seat in it. But is it possible to surrender without getting in? Before surrendering on a spiritual path, it's necessary to make contact with God. Therefore, to surrender you must know the God to whom you're surrendering. But this is not something you know by thinking about it. It's a matter of direct experience.

Love must first arise in your heart before you can surrender to God. In order to generate love, the seeker must move close to a saint, a sadguru, or a true scripture. Only a lit lamp can light an unlit lamp. Then that love generates a force that continues to lead you in the direction of dedication and service. Everything happens naturally so you feel as if you don't have to do anything willfully; God takes care of it all. That's true surrender. Yet this deep state of grace is not easy to understand and may take years of practice before you actually experience it.

For example, I gave lectures on the *Bhagavad Gita* addressing the subject of surrender for many years. Yet at the time I didn't understand it. I didn't even know I didn't understand it. It was only when I entered true yoga sadhana that I understood the nature of *sharanagati*, or surrender to God.

Although you need the mind to perform good and bad actions, the Lord says give up all actions performed through the mind. That means giving up the cycle of karma. When there is no good or bad karma left, then what's left is called the kriya of prana. That means however prana guides you, you live according to its guidance. That's known as sahaj or spontaneous yoga, also called kundalini yoga. To take away the mind's control over the body and surrender to the workings of prana is the kriya of prana.

When a person performs any actions prompted by desire, he believes that he's the doer of every action. His desire for the fruits of action is the cause of bondage.

However, there's no possibility of going without action. So wherever there's a mind, an actor is behind it performing actions. Only when prana acts alone is there no one behind it. Ego's not present. Behind prana, the prana of all pranas is in control, which is the Source.

At the earlier stage we surrender to prana in the form of vayu, (air or breath), working through the body, but as we progress further, we surrender to the prana from which this body receives its energy, which is the Source. Action happening through the Source is called "karma sannyas" — otherwise known as giving up attachment through surrender to prana. To submit to prana is the same as seeking refuge in God, for the prana is actually the envoy, or energy that brings us closer.

Once a great learned man from Poona came to see me. He was ninety years old and was considered an authority on many different subjects. When offered a seat, he declined and instead sat on the floor in front of me, saying, "I haven't come as a learned man, Bapuji; I've come as a disciple. Although I've studied and taught scriptures, there's still one question that remains unanswered. My question is this: Does one find liberation through karma or through surrender? If you can be liberated through karma, then why must you surrender and what is the need for God? On the other hand, if you can find liberation through surrender to God, then why perform action?"

Although this was a complex question, he had searched deeply, so I could also respond at the level of his inquiry. I told him that the real name for karma is surrender. Immediately he bowed down, and his eyes filled with tears.

I continued, "They are not two. In fact, they are one. There is action in surrender and surrender in action. Whatever actions you perform are offered to God himself, and that spirit of surrender brings ultimate freedom. Lord Krishna says give up all karmas, good and bad, and surrender your life to prana. That will bring you close to Him. Whenever an individual surrenders to prana, his actions are directed by God alone." This gentleman was greatly satisfied with my answer and offered his pranams before leaving.

"Whatever My Lord directs me to do through my body, mind, or intellect, or through my consciousness, I will do. It's all His wish." Those are the true words of a devotee. In other words, he's gotten rid of all desires except attaining the Lord, so the Lord himself takes up the burden of his actions. That's a true state of grace.

I was blessed at last to know this experience of surrender intimately. For many years I had been practicing sadhana faithfully and was often transported into states of bliss. One night, nearly beside myself with God-intoxication, I ran out of my hut and jumped into the Narmada River. Since it was monsoon season, the river was flooded and moving very swiftly. After struggling for some time, I felt myself overpowered by the river's pull. I became afraid I would drown. Still I kept on swimming. All at once I heard a voice call out to me, "Stop swimming." Yet I kept on trying, imagining I could somehow escape. Again the voice cried out, "Stop swimming." The voice was unmistakable; it was Dadaji, instructing me to give up.

At that moment I let go and felt my body floating downstream without any effort. It was God's grace carrying me. Spontaneously, a prayer emerged from within me as I sang, *Om namah shivaya gurave sacchidananda murtaye namastasmai namastasmai namastasmai, namo namaha.* I surrender to you, Lord Shiva, my Guru, in the form of bliss, consciousness, and truth. To you I bow, to you I bow, to you I bow."

Although I was facing death, I continued to chant that prayer. Several miles downstream I was finally pulled from the river. Many good townspeople had followed along and there was a great commotion. To my surprise a large number of peacocks gathered in a circle around me, as if to protect me. It was unusual to see such sacred birds gather in a deliberate fashion. At the same time one cow separated from her herd and sat by me to offer comfort. Dazed and spent, I would not have gone anywhere if it weren't for one of my sly disciples who all of a sudden said to me, "Gurudev, it's your sadhana time now." Slowly and obediently I allowed myself to be taken back to my hut.

Kundalini Awakening

In every branch of sanatana dharma, kundalini shaktipat initiation can be given to the disciple by sight, by word, by touch, or by the guru's will. Lord Brahmeshvar is the original propagator of this path. If someone considers a great yogi to be his guru and cannot reach him physically, with his faith, he can still receive initiation and his kundalini will be awakened.

After deep study of and practice of *dhyana*, or meditation, japa, and yoga, kundalini can be awakened according to the guru's guidance. Even without a guru, if a person practices pranayama, meditation, japa, and other yogic practices according to the scriptures, kundalini can be awakened. That happens by the grace of God.

This path is filled with infinite problems and difficulties, however. If the sadhak cannot recognize and understand the meaning of awakened kundalini experiences, they may frighten him. Shocked by the unruly nature of kundalini, most people give up. However, those fortunate to have the guru's guidance will be able to persevere. They will understand that what's happening to them is part of a deep purification and initiatory process and will have enough faith and steadfastness to move through the difficulties.

If the siddhi yogi desires, he can give shaktipat to hundreds and thousands of disciples at a time, but the tradition in India is only to give shaktipat initiation to the few who deserve it. That does not mean that the undeserving ones receive no benefit.

The grace of the guru is very much like rain; it falls without distinction as to time or place, so everyone benefits. But due to differences in growth and readiness, some people benefit fully and progress quickly while others receive partial benefit and progress more slowly.

Because I was concerned about people's level of readiness and preparation, for many years I hesitated before giving shaktipat diksha. I wanted to be a true yogi and I wanted my disciples to be true yogis. Not everyone was prepared to receive this initiation. Yet many people clamored for it. Because I felt such love for my children I wound up giving shaktipat anyway. Afterwards I discovered that only Rajarshri Muni was able to keep up the practices. I consider the love I feel for my disciples to be of a higher nature but still it is an attachment, so I cannot be proud of anything at this time.

For many years I studied the scriptures and compared the experiences I was having as a result of my sadhana. I never believed anything except if it happened to emerge from my own direct experience, but later I compared it with the *Shastras* and yoga scriptures because there was no one I could consult at my stage of practice. I have meditated and surrendered my life to the Lord with such intense sadhana but still the senses are strong and problems arise. This is no ordinary pursuit. There are so many obstacles that it's easy to give up.

When kundalini awakens, the aspirant can easily get frightened. Kundalini works in the most unusual ways. It can be violent or unpredictable as it carries out its work of purification. All of this is difficult to understand unless you have had some direct experience. Although its outward appearance may be frightful, the heart of kundalini is full of love. Only the true yogi recognizes it for what it is and accepts its actions, for in the final analysis, it leaves nothing untouched or untransformed. Kundalini is the force that creates the universe; it has the power to maintain or destroy this world. If you want to know what it is in its most basic form, kundalini is nothing less than God.

Divine Body

Established in 1974, the temple in Gujarat has been called Kayavarohan, which is also the name given to the town. The word *kayavarohan* is composed of two words in Sanskrit: *kaya*, which means "the body," and *avarohan*, which means, "to descend." So Kayavarohan means, "to descend into the body." Thus, it refers to the process by which the Lord descends into the body of a yogi to manifest a divine body, and also the means by which Lord Lakulish descended into the jyotirlinga at Kayavarohan.

Whoever attains the divine body is a complete or perfect yogi. Through the practice of yoga, one's body undergoes various stages of purification, as the yogic fire removes old impurities and a divine body is formed. This is not an overnight event; it takes years of diligent practice. The ordinary body gradually sloughs off its lower elements and begins to take on a divine semblance.

After years of practice, there are various mantras that flow from the yogi's mouth while in samadhi and he hears various subtle sounds. This nad (sound) sadhana continues for many years. Eventually he is granted the rare fortune of drinking the divine nectar while in samadhi. The yogic scriptures say, "The Lord embodies the nectar of immortality." In addition, the scriptures call this nectar by many different names, including "Ram nectar," "Hari nectar, "Brahma nectar, and "Soma nectar" or the "nectar of immortality."

When the devotee in the advanced stages of *nada* yoga is chanting the mantra *Om* or *ram*, nectar is secreted from the opening situated at the "tenth door." Located at the base of the soft palate on the roof of the mouth, the tenth door can only be accessed by the tongue in *khechari mudra*. It is this secretion that causes the yogi's body to evolve into a divine body and bestows the wisdom of ultimate truth along with supreme nonattachment.

The practice of khechari mudra is an important milestone for a yogi. However, attaining it doesn't mean the yogi is complete. It takes a great deal of time and practice for the purification that enables a yogi to complete the cycle of yoga. In fact only once in 2000 years does a yogi complete these stages, including khechari mudra. Of these I mention Gnaneshvar, who wrote a brilliant commentary on the *Bhagavad Gita* in that exalted state, and Chaitanya Mahaprabhu.

During prolonged yoga sadhana and when practicing khechari mudra, my body would become ice cold. I often warned my nephew Dinesh and other devotees, "Anytime you find that I'm not coming out of sadhana or I'm in this cold death-like state, don't think I'm dead. And certainly don't take me to be cremated. It's the effect of the yoga sadhana."

Sometimes I was unable to stand up because the activity of the prana was so strong in certain parts of the body. Then I needed the help of kind disciples. Dinesh in fact called me a "center of gravity" doll when he helped move me to my sitting room. I'd have to be careful, for if I moved, my prana would shoot right up to the crown chakra and I'd immediately go back into samadhi.

Thus this practice has profound effects. One enters altered states of consciousness for hours on end. Devotees can only experience this nectar of immortality when the prana and *apana* (prana that has a downward pull within the body) unite and flow together and the khechari mudra is sufficiently potent. This cannot be accelerated or brought about through will. After years of practice, however, the body will be transformed.

Meanwhile there are different stages of concentration as the yogi progresses toward completion. Entering the state of samadhi, he may be eating, walking, or performing any action, but he is constantly in samadhi. This is known as sahaj or natural samadhi. However, he becomes fully established in samadhi only when his life energy, which is within, becomes steady and remains within. When his energy reaches the seventh chakra, known as the thousand-petaled lotus, at such times the yogi enters into samadhi very much like a child in the mother's womb. There is no breath and no signs of life. If doctors were called in, they would firmly agree that this person is dead. But such a yogi is not dead; he has achieved immortality. In that state, whenever he decides, he can return.

This is the supreme-most science of the world and yet it is hardly known or understood outside of India. Intent upon liberation, the yogi must pursue this sadhana diligently and with great focus and concentration. Such a person does not come into society to serve others. Must the sun leave the sky to enter your home? Thousands of miles away, it gives light to everyone. In the same way, no matter where he is on earth, this yogi gives the world what it needs without moving an inch.

Siddhis

Nowadays you find many clever people posing as saints and doing things considered as miracles by the common people. Although these cunning yogis are only performing magic tricks, since they're wearing the mask of saints, many people believe them to be gods possessed with supernatural powers.

When miracles occur, they have distinct characteristics and are often referred to as "siddhis" or supernatural powers. There are three aspects to a siddhi: the first is the presence of shakti or the power of God. The second is the power of the saint performing the miracle, and the third is the faith of the people. Without shakti, there's no possibility of performing a single miracle. Of the remaining two, the faith of the people is more powerful; in fact, if people have strong faith in a person, even without divine powers, a miracle can be created. However, the people do not know that this miracle is the result of their faith.

Saints who practice devotion to God place importance on right conduct and pure thought and therefore are not attracted to miracles. When astonishing events do happen, they may describe them as the divine play of God or miracles of divine power. However, miracles are related entirely to the possession of siddhis. According to ancient scripture, only yogis were the originators of miracles because only yogis had done the requisite sadhana. Just as when gold is melted in a fire and takes on the appearance and qualities of that fire, so also in samadhi a yogi takes on the appearance and qualities of God.

At the Summit Station ashram, Amrit took me one day to the lake and said, "In winter when it's bitter cold, this lake freezes and residents walk on it." So now I ask you, aren't ashram disciples the same as yogis who walk on water? Many people travel long distances in ships built by science. Isn't that a miracle? Yet even after witnessing a submarine drop beneath the surface, you still want to see yogis walk on water!

One who has become proficient in yoga is called a siddhi yogi and is capable of performing unusual feats. A siddhi yogi can overhear conversations from a long distance without the help of any instruments. This is known as "clairaudience." Although the invention of the radio has turned the art of distant listening into an ordinary matter, would you call this invention ordinary? Siddhi yogis can also see objects and living beings thousands of miles away. This is known as "clairvoyance." With the invention of television, however, science has made far off seeing ordinary. Still this power can be derived from long practice of yoga sadhana. At the same time, the siddhis of these yogis should be used for God's purposes only.

In the later stages of yoga, after years of practice, certain siddhis may appear. In fact, there are six well-known qualities or siddhis associated with being God-like:

·*Virya*: to be urdvaretas or in complete control of sexual energies.

·*Jnana*: To attain direct spiritual knowledge or omniscience.

·*Vairagya*: Complete and ultimate detachment from worldly pleasures.

·*Yasha*: Divine glory.

·*Shri*: Divine wealth.

·*Aishvarya*: Divine peace and happiness.

When a yogi abandons worldly activities and engages in intense sadhana, at some point he attains urdvaretas, reversing the flow of sexual fluids upward through the central canal or sushumna nadi by means of khechari mudra. Attaining final samadhi, he then achieves the divine body with the above characteristics. In other words, he becomes God-like. During this transformation, after the first five chakras have been totally purified, he achieves what is called *sabij*, or samadhi with seed. The seed refers to the presence of thought, though greatly purified. He receives omniscience and omnipotence through the attainment of sabij samadhi. Following purification of the final two chakras, however, he attains *nirbija* samadhi (without seed), where thought is no longer present. He has then achieved complete detachment from worldly and sensual pleasures and is a purna yogi, a liberated soul.

Since he's completed both sabij and nirbija samadhi, he attains all eight supernatural powers, which include the ability to be as small as he wants (*anima*) and the ability to become as large as he wants (*mahima*). He can also be as heavy (*garima*) or as light (*laghima*) as he wants and has the ability to fly.

No scientist believes in such things. We cannot conceive of siddhis or spiritual powers from our normal state of consciousness; in fact they seem unreal. How can a body with solid bones suddenly become as light as cotton or reduced to the size of an atom?

Scientists will continue to be nonbelievers until such time as a yogi emerges in possession of these full spiritual powers. However, as I described earlier, no true yogi wants to show off his siddhis; in fact, he didn't ask for them in the first place, nor does he want them. It's the greatest irony of all—just when God supplies him with miraculous powers, he also takes away his appetite for anything supernatural. God's very clever. Thus, one who approaches yoga sadhana with the hope of developing siddhis goes nowhere. These are a byproduct but not the final destination of yoga. What a yogi truly longs for is moksha or liberation.

Pilgrimage town of Rishikesh

Pilgrimage town of Hardwar

Bapuji descending steps at Kayavarohan Temple

CHAPTER FIFTEEN

THE FINAL VICTORY

Liberation means the total eradication of suffering. It is attained only through discriminate knowledge. That is the moment the darkness of ignorance fades and the light of knowledge shines. Only a rare yogi receives its benefit; nevertheless, every human being is invariably blessed with a divine ray of knowledge at some point in his life. While ordinary knowledge confers no blissful experience, extraordinary knowledge brings divine bliss. Indeed, that is called the grace of the Lord. Such bliss comes only with genuine experience, and does not lose its effect for as long as one lives.

Moksha: Liberation

Moksha is for saints or great masters because they feel the pain of their bondage to life. Strangely enough, the average person doesn't feel that bondage. Actually there are two kinds of bondage: in one, we accept bondage consciously; in another, it's forced upon us. This can be compared to entering a room. If you lock it from the inside, then you feel comfortable. But if somebody locks you in from the outside, you feel trapped. So what's imposed upon you brings unhappiness whereas what you accept does not.

Moksha occurs in several different stages. After attaining complete control over the physical senses, the activity for controlling the subtle senses begins. As a result of that, your mind slowly becomes extinguished. That is samadhi and can be divided into its subtle parts. Karma yoga begins from the *muladhara* chakra (basal plexus) and ends with the *vishuddha* chakra (the throat). Jnana yoga begins from *ajna* chakra (the forehead) and ends with *sahasrara* chakra (the crown). Then mind becomes non-mind and is extinguished. As sugar melts and completely disappears into heated milk, the mind, which is created out of nature, again returns to nature. That is the path of liberation.

While moksha takes you toward God and gives you everlasting peace, happiness, and freedom from suffering, in traveling the path of moksha you must be prepared to experience separation from God, the very opposite of what you hoped to achieve. Until the final meeting you'll suffer pain and shed many tears for the Beloved. Few realize that this is actually a practice of yoga. The state of separation from God is a very special condition called the yoga of separation — or *Viyoga*. That means "meeting in separation." However, when devotees first experience it, they don't consider it a good thing because of the tremendous pain involved.

Imagine a river divided by two riverbanks. On the worldly side, there's a big crowd of people. On the opposite bank, an individual stands alone seeking liberation. While others chat and enjoy the scenery, he remains quiet and observes the moon spreading its cool light everywhere. In spite of that coolness, his heart is burning. Because he experiences deep separation from God, he receives no coolness or relief. Even when night is gone and the entire sky is filled with light, the pain of suffering remains with him. In that condition, day and night are indistinguishable. Unable to sleep at night, the devotee cannot stay awake during the day. The joyous union he experienced in an earlier stage of yoga is gone. Nevertheless at this stage the value of separation is greater than the value of union.

In *sanyoga*, or union, the Beloved is very close to you. As a result, your mind remains balanced, peaceful, and quiet. If the Beloved goes from one room to the next, there's no pain of separation. During its opposite stage, viyoga, there is separation, but within that, a special meeting happens. In truth, there's not even a moment's separation, because the Beloved is constantly in your heart. He's not separated from your thoughts, your heart, your memory, or your whole being. In fact, separation from the Beloved should be considered the highest yoga, because it keeps you the closest to Him.

Suffering from the pain of separation, you cannot cross the river. At such a time, however, the grace of God descends upon you in the form of imagination, and your mind receives some solace. "Suppose I have two wings; then, if I fly, I'll reach my Beloved," you think. As a result of imagining this with deep devotion, your heart quiets down, your tears stop, and once again you enjoy the bliss of union.

Losing It All

The port of sadhana is very small and there's only one entrance. Smart people miss it but those with faith enter. Yet even after entering it's not possible to go far. It takes great determination and one-pointedness.

One of the characters from the *Mahabharata*, Dharmaraja, was a gambler. While gambling he began losing things one by one but was intent upon continuing the game. Eventually he lost his home, his servants, and finally even his wife.

This parable illustrates the true approach to liberation. Since yoga is the game of losing everything, it's only if you're prepared to sacrifice like Dharmaraja that you can pursue this path. You must learn to surrender body, mind, senses, and prana. In much the same way, I have surrendered everything I consider to be mine. Now I want nothing.

Even while being a renunciate, you take your desires and cravings to the forest. There's no escaping past karma. Yet you give up your claims to the past. To be a sadhu is to belong to God. It means being a practitioner on a path, decreasing vices and increasing virtues. That can be done anywhere.

My guru once said. "Your boat should be in the water, but without water in your boat." In other words, be in the world, but drop worldly impressions. However much we think of ourselves, that's how much the world is in us. To the extent we're devoted to God — that's our point of deliverance.

Struggle

Our lives flow between birth and death and the experience of many struggles. Life itself is a struggle. This world in fact is a battlefield like that of Kurukshetra in the *Bhagavad Gita*. Since we live in an unbearable age of darkness, known as the "Kali Yuga," we can't tell which direction struggle will be coming from. So whoever's born into this world must be a warrior.

Although our struggles invariably lead to pain, we forget that we're struggling because we have so many remedies for the pain. In fact, everything we do in the waking state whether we're sitting, walking, or eating, in the end winds up being a remedy for some kind of pain or discomfort.

When we consider the nature of our struggles, we may think them to be cruel or depict them like horrible demons. Yet the true nature of struggle is not evil. It's really an angel in disguise, bringing good to everyone. Struggle keeps us from becoming lazy. It keeps us active and aware, and bestows the kind of knowledge that can't be obtained from any other teacher. Struggle is thus the prana or animating force of our lives. Leading us from darkness to light, from ignorance to knowledge, and from death to immortality, struggle is a skillful sculptor who carves a beautiful statue out of an ugly rock.

We may not be able to receive struggle with love, but we should never turn it away. That would be turning away from the grace of God. We may retreat for a while though, recognizing that there may be some helplessness in doing so, but there's no absence of bravery in it. In the end we must face these struggles. It's better to struggle bravely than to give in out of fear, for this is not a battle with an enemy but a struggle with a friend, out of love.

Struggle provides us with the opportunity to practice self-discipline. Then when we've persevered and fulfilled all the requirements of that discipline, struggle lays attainment at our feet in the form of different siddhis or powers and silently walks away. A yogi who's won the great struggle experiences indescribable bliss. Ecstatic, he looks around and finds God standing beside him. Although he embraces God, he then remembers to turn and pranam at the feet of his struggle. With a pure heart he prays, "Oh great benefactor! So often I fought or turned away from you, but you ignored my ill will and placed me at the feet of almighty God. Without your help this would have been impossible. I bow to you, dear angel of struggle, may you triumph everywhere."

How Long Must We Wait?

Despite all the pitfalls of sadhana, we must remain firm that we'll achieve our deepest longing and our goal. Why be disappointed or entertain thoughts of failure? An ancient tale provides hints for this path.

Considered to be the highest teacher of bhakti, Narad Muni, sage of the celestial realm, is the originator of devotional songs, bhajans, and the means for expressing love for God. One day Narad Muni was passing through the woods where a yogi was meditating.

Very pleased to see him, the yogi inquired, "Muniji, you've blessed me by giving me your darshan. I'm hoping you'll find something out for me, since you dwell at the feet of the Lord. I've been wanting to know this for a long time. Will you ask God when I'll attain the highest?"

"Yes, I'll ask your question," Narad replied.

Traveling further, Narad saw another yogi meditating. When he approached him, this yogi bowed at his feet, express joy in seeing him, and asked the same question.

"I'll get your answer when I return to the feet of the Lord," Narad told him. Then he left. After a year or more, Narad Muni returned and visited the first yogi who received him with great reverence and said, "Did you remember my question?"

"Yes," said Narad.

"What did God say?"

He said, "It will take you as many years to reach the highest as there are leaves on this tree."

Overcome with joy, the yogi stood up and danced around the tree. "I can't believe it. I can't believe it." Then he added, "The number of years means nothing. The good news is that I will definitely achieve liberation."

From there Narad went to the second yogi who also received him with love. Narad let him know that he had asked God the question.

"What did God say?"

God said, "It will take twenty-five years."

Although the first yogi had as many years left as the leaves on a tree, still he danced with joy. Yet the second one cried like a baby. Who knows how much time it will take any of us? That's beside the point. To attain the Lord's vision is an overwhelming need; nothing else holds a candle to it. Disappointment arises in those who have not felt the need strongly enough. Regardless of obstacles, then, hold to your purpose. If the need is real, you must indeed fulfill it.

Dejected, the yogi began crying. "I can't believe it. That's such a long time. When will I ever know God?"

Bapuji standing with crowd

Disciples share Arti

PART THREE

DISCIPLES EXPLORE THE MEANING OF SADHANA

If the tree is known by its fruit, then the real test of Bapuji's love comes through the experience of his disciples, for we are the bearers of his legacy. We carry the teachings of sanatana dharma to several continents and many different countries.

In the following chapters, by reconstructing experiences and insights that flowed from our time with Bapuji, we expand our understanding of his extraordinary contributions in the field of yoga and in the transformation of our lives.

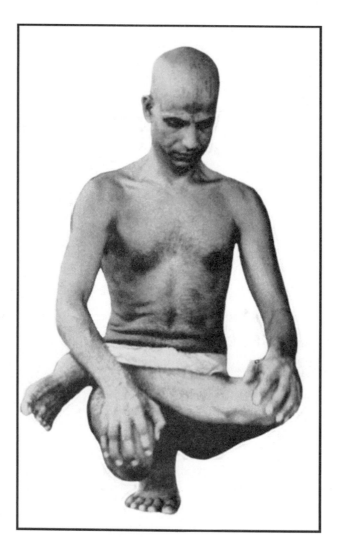

Pandangushthasana

CHAPTER SIXTEEN

BAPUJI'S KUNDALINI YOGA PRACTICE
AS TOLD BY YOGANAND MICHAEL CARROLL

Although Bapuji did not formally teach the components of sahaj yoga, the closest thing to an experience with him takes place in Yoganand's Advanced Kripalu Yoga classes. In this chapter Yoganand's treatise on Bapuji's yoga sadhana gives a greater context to this practice, describes its history and roots in ancient India, and provides a framework for advanced practice.

To gain a broader perspective of Bapuji's sadhana, we must first understand its roots within the context of the ancient yogic tradition of India. By studying how the ancients focused attention and worked to raise energy, we sense its power to transform consciousness, awakening the dormant potentials of the kundalini shakti.

I first became absorbed in depth practices while living at Kripalu Center in Pennsylvania in the 1980's. After several disciples had returned from a pilgrimage to India, I was able to get hold of a series of eighteen postures they had retrieved from Rajarshi Muni, one of Bapuji's chief disciples. Muniji had outlined the use of eighteen specific postures along with breath retention, yogic locks, and visual focusing as the keys to raising kundalini energy. Having already experimented with postures and with anuloma vilom (alternate nostril breathing) for anywhere from four to eight hours a day, I was convinced of the power of yogic practices and had already witnessed various subtle forms of the awakened energy.

The benefits and risks associated with advanced practices have not been thoroughly studied or documented. This is in large part because few people have practiced them. It is also because advanced techniques work multiple areas of the body at once, sometimes intensively, and it's impossible to explain their effects through logical principles alone. Many of the effects of depth practice are nonphysical, occurring on the mental, emotional, or spiritual levels.

Although these depth practices require great focus and concentration and are not appropriate for beginning hatha yoga students, it's very helpful to understand their broader context. When we know where the path ultimately leads us, we can have a more informed practice at each stage of development.

The Tradition

Although this yoga is not for everyone, it exists for all time as the ultimate tool of liberation. In India it was taught for many centuries as part of the mystery school tradition. Knowledge of postures, pranayama and advanced practices were essentially passed on in secret form through several levels of initiation. There were many layers of practice, some of which were even contradictory, and all of which led to different states of enlightenment. Yogis kept their practices secret (so as not to harm the unsuspecting or untrustworthy) and often wrote their texts in a way that would be hard to understand for the uninitiated. The *Hatha Yoga Pradipika*, for example, written in the 14th century, has strange descriptions of postures and scrambles the order of many of the practices so that it's impossible to make sense of them.

In India Pashupat yoga was a mystery tradition associated with the deity of Lord Shiva. Referring to the animal self, the Pashupat path literally means to descend or go down into the animal self (within the body). One who is a Pashupati has mastered the animal self.

In theory we have many parts of the animal self from which we are walled off because they threaten or terrify us. Enormous layers of grief, rage, unrestrained sexuality, or violence dwell within that walled-off self. When we engage in depth practices, those energies begin manifesting and we have no choice but to confront them. In the beginning stages of yoga there are many restraints and observances that are taught (*yamas and niyamas*) in order to contain those energies. As we advance on the path, however, we purposefully add locks, mudras, and kumbhaka (breath retention) to heighten the energy charge. As a result, the animal self begins to assert itself even more forcefully into our experience.

For the Pashupats that was equivalent to going into battle; the Pashupats wanted to find the animal self, and like Shiva, ride it without fear. As a result many of their practices seemed wild or unruly to those who were uninitiated. Translated for modern-day practitioners, depth practice requires us to see our conditioning and experience the intensity of whatever anger, sex, or fear may be present without acting upon it or dissipating the charge. When we can witness sensation with self-acceptance, then the experience is transformed into pure energy and we integrate yet another aspect of the animal self into our being.

For thirty years Bapuji practiced a blend of sahaj or kundalini yoga on the mat and the resulting Pashupat yoga off the mat, ten hours a day without fail. He did spontaneous postures, kumbhakas, mudras, and holdings, and then sat and allowed the awakened energy to move through him. The effect of these practices was to cut all external supports to *ahankara* (self) and allow the awakened energy to be freed. Often he would chant, dance, or go into ecstatic trance following his immersion in yoga. The key principle transmitted by his guru was surrender; to be willing to surrender continually to the workings of the energy was Bapuji's greatest source of transformation.

Relationship between Energy and Ahankara (Self)

The main purpose of such intense practice is undoubtedly to raise energy, at the same time increasing sensitivity and strengthening the container of body and mind to accommodate the increased levels of energy. But paradoxically, the self is then dissolved in the overwhelming flood of energies that are unleashed.

In yogic tradition the self is referred to as *ahankara* — literally the "shape of the self." Loosely translated as ego, the ahankara is our everyday perception and sense of identity as well as the organ of everyday action. We build it just like birds weave a nest, taking things from our surroundings, only it's more likely to be beliefs and ideas creating our sense of self, rather than physical structures.

It's important to recognize the relationship between the ahankara and our energy level. Each of us learns to function at a particular level of energy. When the energy gets lower than that, ahankara falls apart; it also gets uncomfortable with greater amounts of energy than we're accustomed to. In times like that, we invariably do something to dump the energy. Most of the time we're not aware when we're eating chocolate, smoking a cigarette, or taking a drink, that we're trying to modulate our energy levels. However, ancient yogis grasped the intrinsic relationship between ahankara and energy and tried purposefully to raise the energy through their practices, deliberately creating a disturbance. What they discovered was that for every increase in energy there was a correspondingly different perception. Thus when we raise the energy, we shift our perception of the self.

They also discovered that with profound shifts in energy, ahankara dissolves, and for brief moments we access a place of transcendence, oneness, and peace. Every time we return from such states, we reassemble or reintegrate at a different level.

Hungry for freedom, yogis wanted to expand and take in everything, exploring perceptions and dealing with problems that arose at all energy levels. What got in the way, however, was the presence of the censor — the part within us that blocks or negates experience. With intense practice there are some things that are so charged that it won't allow us to see or experience them directly. In order to experience them, we have to override the censor, but we can't do that through the power of the mind alone. However, if we create a strong enough flow of energy, it floods the ahankara and overrides the censor, accessing those deeper streams of experience. That is the essence of kundalini practice. After strenuous practice of postures, kumbhakas, mudras, and locks, we sit back and watch the energy flow.

The Stages of Practice

For simplicity sake this practice is divided into five stages, however only stages one through three are practiced voluntarily. The final stages flow spontaneously such that effort dissolves into surrender. Practices are graduated in intensity and depth in order to help us build strength and withstand the increased flow of energy.

1. In stage one it is recommended that you do pranayama for one month.

2. When the energy remains balanced, then go on to stage two, in which you do asanas with normal breathing. This stage lasts approximately three to six months, if one has had prior experience with yoga.

3. In stage three you begin doing asanas with kumbhaka, or breath retention.

4. In stage four asanas are done with spontaneous kumbhaka.

5. Finally you progress to the point where both asanas and kumbhaka are done spontaneously (It's difficult to estimate timelines, as this will flow from the depths of your practice.)

Advanced yoga practices were traditionally taught only after a certain level of proficiency had been attained with the basic postures and pranayams. Through these techniques, a practitioner gained suppleness and strength, and acquired the awareness needed to practice advanced techniques safely.

The Eighteen Key Postures

The eighteen postures listed below form a sequence that depth yoga practitioners can master through time. These are not meant for beginning yoga students. When you become proficient in performing these postures, they are then combined with a different set of locks, visual focus or *drishti*, and either internal or external kumbhaka, a series of practices that will be described in detail and that greatly intensify the effect of the postures themselves.

1. Akarna Dhanurasana: Seated Bow Pulling Posture
2. Ardha Pavanamuktasana: Half Wind Relieving Posture
3. Baddha Trikonasana: Bound Triangle Posture
4. Bakasana: Crane Posture
5. Bhujangasana: Serpent Posture
6. Bhunamanasana: Bowing to the Earth Posture
7. Ekapada Bhunamanasana: Head to One Foot Posture
8. Kokilasana: Cuckoo Posture
9. Maha Mudra: Great Secret Posture
10. Padmadolasana: Lotus Swing Posture
11. Padma Matsyasana: Lotus Fish Posture
12. Parvatasana: Seated Mountain Posture
13. Supta Vajrasana: Reclining Diamond Posture
14. Tolangulasana: Balancing on Fingers Posture
15. Ustrasana: Camel Posture
16. Uttanapadmasana: Upward Stretch in Lotus Posture
17. Utthita Vajrasana: Lifted Diamond Posture
18. Urdvapadmasana: Raised Lotus Posture

Explanation of Locks in Yoga Practice

The three locks: *mulabandha, uddiyana bandha* and *jalandhara bandha* are done in a specific way for the specific purpose of generating strong sensation in the body, so the mind is absorbed. The ancients believed that an energy center exists in the pelvis that when activated can surge through the body and flood the body with energy. In the beginning we must build strength so that the energy won't overpower us and we can hold it inside and not act on it. Ancient yogis believed that the way we activated these energies was to lock the door to the pelvis and trunk (through the locks) and to restrict the breathing (through the kumbhakas).

Through shallow breathing and guarded or habitual posture, the ahankara maintains its fort-like dominance over prana. To build a channel through the restrictive ahankara means bringing aliveness back to the chest, belly, and pelvis. Locks are very specific keys to opening those doors. Combined with breath retention, they provide great intensity and activation of energy. Imagine holding your breath for a short while; then lengthen the amount of time of the holding until you reach a point of crisis. Just before that point the thought occurs, "Oh my God, I'm going to die." By momentarily stopping the breath, we intensify the concentration of energy. Restricting prana on a physical level, we intensify its effects on a psycho-spiritual level. Learning each of the locks and kumbhakas is a gradual process; always proceed in such a way that the mind is easily engaged and the intensity increased proportionate to what you can tolerate.

The mulabandha or root lock is achieved by pulling upward on the whole pelvic floor. If done appropriately, you cannot breathe while holding it. Mulabandha generates strong sensation in the pelvis and can be done on either the "in" or "out-breath." The uddiyana bandha or stomach lock is done only on the out-breath; after you exhale you generate a strong upward pull through the abdominal viscera and hold. Jalandhara bandha is a closing off of the throat by half swallowing and then compressing the chin against the chest. Locks cannot be done in back bends, standing, or twisting postures.

Asana, pranayama, locks, and kumbhakas all work to increase energy and heighten sensation. If we can make sensation strong enough, then the external world disappears. Ancient yogis wanted to generate sensation inside the body and make it so strong that it automatically absorbed our attention. It was then no longer an act of will to keep an internal attention, but a spontaneous absorption directed by the flow of prana.

Explanation of Mudras and Drishti

Another part of the ancient practice is called "mudra" — a secret or hidden doorway. Mudras are doorways to places inside where blissful sensation can be generated. Although we have not been trained to hold a powerful charge within our bodies but rather to dissipate it, when we close our eyes and sit with pure energy, we forget our bodies and the world outside. We are reduced to a flow of energy. When a mudra becomes strong, *pratyahar* (sense withdrawal) happens. Of the ten mudras referred to in the *Hatha Yoga Pradipika*, only three can be done willfully; the other seven arise spontaneously as you continue with depth practices.

When practicing mudras or locks, if you close your eyes and let your gaze wander, it will automatically go to the place in the body where there is the most energy. That is the practice of drishti, which means "to see or be present through one's gaze." Ancient yogis used drishti as a compass pointing us to the place where the energy was the strongest in the body. If you keep your eyes soft, energy accumulates, and then your eyes will follow as it moves through the body. If energy is concentrated in the lower part of the body, your gaze will center on the tip of your nose. If in the upper body, eyes move to the third eye point or the crown. The will is not controlling this practice; again, it is generated through the movement of prana.

To work with the powerful energies of kundalini, then, one must increase sensitivity, strengthen the container, and watch the ahankara dissolve. This is no easy task. Particularly difficult is the mastery of the sexual force. When sexual energy became very strong, yogis increased the kumbhakas and mudras. Starting in the genitals, the energy would then rise up and be felt in different places in the body.

Wherever the sexual energy goes, it creates an enormous level of absorption. The ten mudras outlined in the *Hatha Yoga Pradipika* refer to ten places in the body where the sexual energy can go and provide intense absorption, much deeper than any ordinary practice of meditation. Yogis wanted to bring that same absorption from the genitals to the crown chakra and create what might be called a cosmic orgasm. In that process ahankara gets blown to bits.

To walk around with that kind of charge requires extraordinary discipline and at the same time great surrender. We must continue to build ahankara to withstand the force of energy and the nature of the various manifestations, understanding the more than 84,000 postures to which the ancient yogis referred. In Pashupat yoga this translates into a huge and endless variety of internal experiences, as many as there are creatures on the earth, which we must be willing to face when they surface. It is no wonder that Shiva, the supreme Pashupati, wore coiled serpents for necklaces, sat on the rug of a tamed tiger, and had a bull facing him in an attitude of worship.

Once awakened, kundalini is the strongest energy we will ever experience. It works like a deep cleansing and therapeutic agent, sweeping away impurities and transforming animal tendencies into divine potential. Through depth practices we first develop will, and then greater attunement or sensitivity as we hold a greater charge in the body. Finally it is the ability to surrender to the overpowering workings of the energy that takes us to the highest stages of sadhana. There is no limit to where we travel and what we can experience. It must be obvious by now that this path is not for everyone. To practice with such intensity one must be a fool, as Bapuji said—ready not only to face death, but if need be, to willingly place our heads into death's gaping mouth.

with Ma Om Shanti

with Yogeshwar Muni

with Rajarshi Muni

with Vinit Muni and Yogi Amrit Desai

Bapuji with Disciples

CHAPTER SEVENTEEN

CAPTURING THE HEART AND SOUL OF SAHAJ YOGA

Gurur brahma
gurur vishnur
gurur devo maheshvarah,
guruh sakshat param brahma,
tasmai shri gurave namaha

The Guru is Brahma; the guru is Vishnu
The Divine guru is Mahesvar (Shiva)
The guru is the highest form of God
To that guru I offer my full heart in surrender.

(Ancient Sanskrit Prayer)

In this chapter various disciples, who were initiated by Bapuji and chose to follow a path of sahaj or spontaneous yoga, offer commentary and illuminate Bapuji's guidance as experienced directly through practice. The initiatory experience, a very powerful time of receiving the wisdom and shakti of this lineage, is also described in depth.

Choose Nothing Less Than the Divine Body

Having received shaktipat initiation from Bapuji, I began having many different experiences related to the awakening of kundalini. On the 19th of February of 1971, I was initiated into sannyas.

On the morning of my initiation my head was shaven clean. After bathing, I was directed to the idol of Lord Lakulish (Dadaji) to pay my respects. Then at 10:15 AM, Bapuji took me into his meditation room where I worshipped him by bowing at his feet. First he gave me the sacred mantra *Om namah shivaya*. Then he performed the necessary purification rites for me. Finally he gave me saffron clothes and instructed me to put them on.

He said, "Son, henceforth this body of yours will be known as Rajarshi Muni. Be a true yogi and do not be satisfied with any attainment less than the divine body."

Then he conferred the most secret shaktipat initiation, instructing me to sit in siddhasana and meditate. When I became introverted, Bapuji touched my chest near the heart region. Instantly I experienced a jolt as if from a live wire. Losing awareness of the outer world, I experienced a flash of light in the recesses of my heart.

After a few minutes the radiant form of Bapuji appeared in my meditation, blessing me. Without any movement of his limbs, this subtle form began gliding toward me, and my eyes automatically gazed at his feet with great reverence.

After that image disappeared, there was darkness and then a sudden bright light akin to the moon, which gave birth to the statue of Lord Lakulish. For a while I experienced divine bliss, as I worshipped him in meditation.

Suddenly the staff that had been held in the statue's left hand exploded, causing a huge flash. A long, luminous weapon emerged from the staff and shot to the sky with great velocity. Terrified by this explosion, which felt like it was happening in my own body, I began to tremble and perspire.

The sky was covered with smoke as if it had been set ablaze. With this sudden change in the atmosphere my uneasiness mounted. Before my amazement could subside there was another explosion. The fruit in the statue's right hand exploded and countless seeds erupted from it like lustrous stars. In no time they were lost in the smoky sky. I was highly uncomfortable and the mental tension was unbearable.

Meanwhile out of his matted hair jets of water spouted up like a gigantic fountain. These innumerable jets of liquid hurled high into the sky, reaching the layer of smoke. As the water mixed with the hot smoke a terrible hurricane manifested. In a few moments there was lightning and thunder and a heavy downpour.

Everything was enveloped in darkness for a few minutes and I couldn't see anything. It seemed as if a deluge of water might submerge the earth and that my limbs were melting away. I experienced a gradual draining of my strength and vitality.

Gradually a soft light appeared and though the idol of Lord Lakulish had disappeared, I heard a voice speaking in an unintelligible language. Looking around, I could see no one.

Meanwhile the radiant form of Bapuji appeared before me once again, and smiling, he placed his hand on my head. That touch had a miraculous impact as the nerve centers in my brain became activated. Immediately I understood every word of that voice speaking an unintelligible language and realized it was samadhi bhasa (language of the transcendental state).

That mysterious voice then proceeded to explain the entire chain of extraordinary experiences I had just passed through. Afterwards I understood the hidden secret of yoga.

When my meditation came to an end, I was so exhilarated that I didn't want to open my eyes. I realized that out of his great compassion, Bapuji had opened my inner eye and blessed me with the ability to discern samadhi bhasa.

Recalling the stanza of one of Bapuji's popular bhajans, I now understood the true import of *guru kripa*, or guru's grace:

"Oh guru! Open my eye to the inner sight.

I surrender to you, Oh Ocean of love!

Illuminate the path of my life with your holy light,

Oh guru! Open my eye to the inner sight."

Tears of joy gushed from my eyes at the thought of Bapuji's selfless grace. That marvelous experience led me to realize that Truth, or Reality can only be recognized through inner vision and never with the physical eyes. Inner vision is indispensable on a path of yoga; it's like a boat that carries one across the ocean of phenomenal existence. Without it, yoga practice is bound to remain fruitless.

Putting his merciful hand over my head, Bapuji blessed me.

"Son," he said, "The secret mystery of yoga I demonstrated to you today through shaktipat is the same mystery passed from guru to disciple in our lineage, which was founded by the godly sage Atri. This is the real initiation into both yoga and sannyas. In this initiation adopting saffron clothes is not important, but passing the secret of yoga to the disciple is. The future of your yoga practice will now be free of all obstacles, and you'll be able to proceed on the complete path of yoga."

This is the true shaktipat initiation, different from the shaktipat given during seminars, in which special techniques of relaxation are taught for the release of prana. Here the guru subtly enters the body of a disciple and unfolds his inner vision. It's only after this initiation that a disciple's intellect gains the capacity for extrasensory perception and the ability to comprehend the mysterious experiences of yoga.

Later I asked Bapuji, "This human body that's made up of five destructible elements—earth, water, fire, air, and ether—how can it become immortal?" I wanted to know if the release of prana brought about these changes.

He answered,"No, the mere release of prana cannot do so. However, prana is an important instrument for the spontaneous manifestation of khechari mudra, which in turn eventually leads to a transformation of the body. With the aid of khechari mudra, a yogi is able to sip the nectar that trickles from the brain. This nectar has the power to dissolve the existing molecules of his body and replace them with new indestructible ones. In this manner the divine body is formed."

Swami Rajarshi Muni

Bapuji—Keeper of My Heart

I'd been searching for a long time, visiting many gurus. However, I often saw through them, taking note of their attachments and lust for women, fame or money. When a dear friend of mine who was dying begged me to see Bapuji, I decided to go just as a favor to her.

When we arrived at one of his seminars, I stood at the back and watched what was going on. Surrounded by women who were donating to the temple at Kayavarohan, Bapuji actually had money in his hands. That made me very skeptical since saints don't usually handle money in India.

Nevertheless I continued going to darshan, standing in the back watching him. Soon I noticed him watching me as well. With most other saints and gurus, I was able to discern their innermost secrets—not so with Bapuji.

In not too long a time I realized I was seeing the real thing. I also realized it was my own attachment to women, fame, and money that had prejudiced my mind earlier. But there was definitely something different about him that warranted further investigation.

I continued seeing him in darshan. Evidently he was transmitting a lot of shakti for I felt something happening in my sadhana and my practice became more focused. In one particular seminar, Bapuji asked people to write down their experiences but I was so absorbed in meditation that I couldn't move.

All of a sudden, in my inner vision I saw Bapuji coming toward me with an unlit candle in his hand. When Bapuji took that candle and held it next to his heart, it burst into flame. Coming close to me, he waved the candle in front of my heart and I saw it burst into flame as well. Then I merged with the flame. From then on I knew that Bapuji was the true guru and keeper of my heart and that the only thing left for me to do was to turn my life over to him.

Not long after I experienced that awakening, I left my job in a big company and dedicated my life to yoga. I was fortunate not only to receive my sannyas initiation from Bapuji and the name Vinit Muni, but also to be able to accompany him to America where I could meet his western disciples and experience their great love for him.

It was not always easy to serve Bapuji, especially since my knowledge of English was limited. Nevertheless, I made a bold attempt. I remember laughing with the disciples when we were packed into Nandanvan, the barn at Summit Station. It was pouring rain, and I got elected to translate Bapuji's speech since Amritji was away. However, I could hardly hear what Bapuji was saying because the barn was noisy and the rain was so loud.

Finally I made sense out of things. Bapuji was teaching from one of his bhajans. He said, "Don't be like the dirty bees that fly back and forth..." However, I didn't know how to translate a certain word, so he smacked me on the head.

Smiling, Mataji supplied the word, and I repeated, "Don't be like the dirty bees that fly from one dung heap to the next," and he bopped me again as we all burst out laughing.

Bapuji always knew when we made mistakes translating him, even though he didn't know English. That was not a problem since he tuned into the vibration of the words and immediately knew their meaning. He also knew how to make fun of everything: he made fun of our foolishness, his foolishness, and the strange job of translating from one language to another. In fact, when we couldn't come up with the right word, he'd say it louder and then shrug his shoulders, telling us "Mango means mango." In other words, get to know the thing itself; don't get lost in words.

Swami Vinit Muni

Change of Life Baby

For five years I cried daily for Bapuji to come to me. In January of 1978 I received a letter from Vinit Muni on Bapuji's behalf with specific instructions for my practice. Even more importantly, the letter said Bapuji was coming to Nebraska.

I had been practicing yoga for twenty years. While at the Sumneytown ashram in 1973, I experienced a major kundalini awakening and had memories of going back to the beginning of my time on this planet. Spontaneous asanas that I would never have attempted on my own occurred, and I learned to walk all over again. When I saw Bapuji in person in 1977 it was a true spiritual homecoming.

On April 3, 1978 Bapuji and Vinit Muni's plane landed in Omaha with a brief layover. I met Bapuji and Muniji as they stepped off the plane. There was a small gathering for Bapuji at a darshan room at the airport. Two days later I drove to Columbus and spent time with Bapuji at the home of Ramesh, Neeta, and Susmita Panchal. Urmila Desai and Vinit Muniji were there and we all had special darshans with Bapuji.

On the 120-mile trip back to Omaha, it started to rain, and I began to sob. Even though I felt grateful to be with Bapuji, it was extremely painful to leave him. Struggling with the rain and lack of visibility, I decided to return to Columbus.

Observing the pujas for Bapuji was wonderful, but when it came time for me to leave the next morning, my disappointment knew no bounds. I confided to Muniji how I'd hoped for mantra initiation. Muniji then replied, "But Bapuji hasn't given mantra diksha for years."

"Well, then what do people do?" I asked.

"Bapuji instructs them to go to one of his sons and take mantra from them" he replied.

Startled, I said "Like you? Muniji, you're my brother. How can I take mantra initiation from a brother?"

Muniji replied, "Okay, here's what you need to do. Bapuji takes his 'coffee break' at two o'clock. When he comes out, repeat the following words to him." He outlined a plan, which sounded good to me.

Bapuji had gone into the next room for his break a little early, so I waited outside his door, consciously breathing slowly and mentally practicing Muniji's suggested phrase. However, when I saw Bapuji I could only jabber these words, "Bapuji, I want to do japa but I can't do japa because I haven't had proper mantra initiation. Since you're my father, you have to give it to me!" Bapuji spoke no English, and of course I knew that, but it never crossed my mind that we didn't speak the same language.

Instead of sounding calm and serene, I must have sounded hysterical. Bapuji glanced at Urmila who explained what I'd said. Then he motioned for me to come before him.

Instructing me in japa techniques, he said the first word of the mantra and

I repeated it. He then repeated the mantra ten times and I repeated it each time after him. Fascinated, I watched as he kept track of the rounds on his hands in the same manner that I had learned in yogic counting.

At the end of the initiation when I pranamed, it was like someone had gently pulled my feet out from under me. As I lay flat on the floor, I took full advantage of this once in a lifetime chance to pour my love into Bapuji as I bathed his feet with my tears. It was the most auspicious event of my life.

Upon arising, I noticed that Muniji had entered the room. He then translated Bapuji's instructions for me. Bapuji wrote *bhav* in Gujarati and pointed to himself and to me. Muniji translated that Bapuji had a deep love for me.

Then he wrote something else. Muniji said, "The yogic powers are not toys to play with."

Because I was unable to be with him, Bapuji gave me a technique to merge with him. The mantra that he gave me was the seed mantra for accessing his divine energy. I was instructed to repeat this mantra fifty malas a day. A mala is similar to a rosary with 108 beads. This practice continued without fail for five years. I kept count of fifty malas a day, the rest of the time it played in my mind.

From that point on, immersion in yoga and the chanting of mantra was automatic. If you've ever detasseled corn, you can understand the experience of reciting mantra. All day long you walk the fields seeing the corn and all night long as you rest, you continue walking the fields, pulling tassels. It was the same with mantra practice.

Receiving mantra diksha meant total acceptance as Bapuji's yogic daughter and was essential for my sadhana. Without any effort on my part, the mantra played in me continuously. Since a mantra holds the vibration of the Lord, it was like having continuous darshan through every thought, memory, and every moment of my life, past and present.

Later Vinit Muniji told me that Bapuji had arranged this trip to America so that he could initiate me. He had said that he would not travel because it would interrupt his sadhana, yet he came for me. I am so blessed that this compassionate Master would shower his blessings upon me. The very next time Bapuji sat for meditation after giving me mantra diksha he entered a state of *nirvakalpa* samadhi (where there is no breath, heartbeat, or brain waves). He had been striving to achieve this for many years. What luck I had to be initiated at this most auspicious time in his sadhana.

My entire life and sadhana have been devoted to Bapuji and I am very humbled

to have received his darshan and to be his "change of life" baby—the only female disciple to be initiated directly by him in the U.S.

Leela Bruner

Living in Guru's Grace

After all these years, the most important thing for me is having been in Bapuji's presence and having known the power and energy of his love. That is foundational to my growth. From 1973 when I first met him in meditation to the time I spent with him in India and America (1974-1981) until the present, his influence has remained constant. Although I studied many traditions and forms of yoga, just when I felt I'd synthesized the best way to achieve bliss without a guru, I met Bapuji. His powerful energy blasted right through my willful paradigm, and my life changed forever. Nowadays teaching hatha yoga Kripalu-style at Philadelphia University, and in corporate settings, night schools, and other venues, including the staff of the *Philadelphia Inquirer*, I continue to feel his influence.

When I went to the dedication of the Kayavarohan Temple in India in 1974, I was fortunate to bow at Bapuji's feet and to receive his blessings. After so many years of passionate seeking and experimentation, I returned to the simplicity of what I'd known as a child. In a private initiation Bapuji gave me the Sanskrit name, Hare Sharana, which means "surrender to God." Over a period of several months I practiced sahaj yoga in his ashram, building up to six hours daily. In this special meditation I would surrender to the flow of yogic phenomena, including spontaneous postures, breathing exercises, mudras, mantra, and primal sound. When my energy flagged or the weather became intolerable, I took refuge in Bapuji's bhajans and even received a music lesson from him.

Many of Bapuji's bhajans expressed his struggles and feelings of failure on the path. These spoke to my condition as well. One in particular, *"Tari icha ti badhutai"* helped me through a dark night in the monsoon season. The words "All things that happen, Lord, happen by your grace…" helped ease me through the transition of leaving India because my visa had expired. Just before leaving, I went to Bapuji with piles of prayer beads for him to bless. He laughed and said, "You're not taking malas home; you're taking home your devotion.

I asked him if I needed another initiation or more advanced training before I left, and he said, "No, I gave you shaktipat, which is the best initiation. Now you have everything you need for your life. On this path nothing is to be begged for; everything is to be offered up."

I felt that what he was saying was that whatever I needed would always be provided by God.

He added, "Love and serve them as I have loved and served you."

"Stay with me, Bapuji," was my immediate response, and he answered, "I'm with you always."

For the next year I was fortunate to live with my parents, who gave me their blessings to continue my sadhana. Their suburban home was a peaceful place to do yoga and meditate, and I received help from unexpected quarters whenever I got stuck. In fact one day I looked out from my window and saw my mother struggling to uproot a tree that was killing her garden. Inspired, I went outside, picked up an axe, and started hacking away at the roots like a warrior. When I returned to my meditation, a more advanced energy process began spontaneously "uprooting" things inside, just as I'd been uprooting the tree outside. It was liberating to rediscover service as an essential principle that Bapuji taught, which could be integrated along with love and surrender.

In 1976 I learned that Bapuji might go into seclusion and not be available for darshan, so I returned to India. I met up with Amrit and Krishnapriya, and they asked me if I thought Bapuji would accept an invitation to come to the United States. Uncharacteristically, I responded, "If you ask with that much love, how could he refuse?"

Something made me say that. Yet I see in retrospect that it was part of God's plan. In fact we were fortunate to welcome Bapuji onto American soil the very next year in 1977.

Like that experience, there are many other instances where the unexpected turns into the workings of God's plan. I am in awe of my yoga students, for example, who as beginners often become my gurus. When they receive Bapuji's energy through the medium of my classes, they often reflect his teachings back to me. I keep learning and growing even more while serving the guru in them. While compassion for my students and diligence in my daily practice help me refine my teaching, I never forget that I am first and foremost a student and disciple of my guru. The best lesson is to remember who's in charge. Then when I dive into meditation and connect with the power of devotion, I'm living in Guru's grace.

Hare Sharana H. Zandler

The Meaning of Liberation

When I first saw Bapuji, I realized instantly that he was a true yogi. Although I had traveled extensively in India and visited many ashrams, for the most part I wasn't impressed. The only yogi I met whom I wanted to spend time with before Bapuji was Ananda Mayi and she wasn't offering formal teachings. I felt I needed that. Although I tend to be more of a jnana yogi, when I first met Bapuji I burst out crying. I stayed five days in his ashram and was initiated into sahaj or natural yoga. Since then I've practiced eight hours a day for 30 years.

What stood out for me was Bapuji's story about wandering naked into the Narmada River and floating downstream. Bapuji didn't know how to swim and feared he was going to drown. Upon hearing Dadaji's voice, he went into the fish pose and then leaned back in the water and floated safely downstream.

I realized his story has an esoteric meaning. In order to do yoga you must essentially throw yourself into the river of prana and let yourself be carried by prana's natural flow to liberation. Surrendering to that shakti takes on the power of a life and death experience. In fact they say that the fixed price for siddha yoga is your life.

After I left Kayavarohan and returned to America I realized that Bapuji had given me a new sense of direction in life. When

I returned to India six months later, he said, "You should understand that one meaning of atman is the 'sexual seed.' Mastery of that is the key that opens the pathway to liberation." If you look up the meaning of brahmacharya, it means "moving with God or walking with God."

So that became an important focus. While visiting India for the third time, I sat with Bapuji as he attempted to explain shakti-pat. Since I could not entirely grasp the idea of shakti transmission, he patiently explained it several different ways, drawing from Patanjali's sutras. Suddenly a light went on in my head. Catching that, he immediately slapped his thigh and burst out laughing. In fact he laughed so hard he fell over. I loved seeing how lighthearted he was and how much joy he derived from my learning process. Of course disciples helped him right himself but his laughter continued.

My dreams of Bapuji were not ordinary dreams but very real. They were generated from the special realm of spirit called siddha-lokha. In the most vivid one I was walking through a forest to a Shiva temple and Bapuji was sitting on the porch. The whole atmosphere was filled with golden light. Although I wanted to approach him, there were poisonous snakes surrounding the porch so I hesitated.

"Are you afraid of the snakes?" he asked.

I said, "No."

He then replied, "You shouldn't lie." Then he began laughing and I confided the truth to him. He said that snakes represent desires and that rather than be afraid of them, we should detach from whatever causes those desires. With that realization the dream vanished. Yet I'm convinced it wasn't a dream but a visitation.

Bapuji's great contribution to the world has been to revitalize the path of liberation. For many people it never even occurred as a possibility. However, the divine body is not a fairy tale, it's a real state. I've seen evidence. Although I'm seventy-three, as a result of sadhana I'm regaining the strength I had at forty-five. Before I embarked on this spiritual path, I thought the purpose of life was to be successful and a good communicator.

After meeting Bapuji I realized it was to achieve liberation. It's easy to toss around a term like that, but sitting in his presence, I realized liberation was a complete and total state of absorption in the truth—not as a concept but as a living experience. This doesn't mean abstracted from the world or from your body but realizing life's truth within and through your body. Then through this path the world itself is transformed.

Yogeshwar Muni

The Narmada River in Gujarat

Bapuji teaching

CHAPTER EIGHTEEN

DISCIPLE STORIES AND RECOLLECTIONS OF BAPUJI

There's no doubt that Bapuji has had a widespread and long-lasting influence in those of us fortunate enough to have known him or practiced his teachings. In the following series of reflections, affirmations, and anecdotes, we discover particular ways our worldview and actions shifted or evolved from the lessons learned at his feet.

Vivekanand Richard Michaels shares, "When I consider Bapuji's influence in my life, the image that comes to mind is throwing indigo dye into a big container of water. Once the dye is mixed in, you can't separate it from the water. Nor can you say that one part of the water is saturated while another is not. That's how Bapuji's affected me; his influence runs through my entire life and worldview. It's impossible to separate what's his and not his."

Although what Vivekanand says is true, it's still helpful to sift through stories and experiences, determining what has been transformed in the alchemy of Bapuji's presence and his teachings. Therefore we focus attention both on our present activities and their inspiration in the past to discover his imprint in our lives.

Indelible Proof of his Presence

Before Bapuji even set foot in the States, I had indelible proof of his presence and his knowledge of me.

In the fall of 1973 I was completing the design of Muktidham, the meditation hut situated in the woods overlooking the lower Sumneytown ashram. As an architect, I had overseen the design and construction of this project, and Yogi Amrit Desai told me that I would be in charge of the ashram when he began his three-month seclusion in Muktidham that winter.

Meanwhile, I was also busy teaching yoga classes five days a week and traveling as far as Harrisburg, a good hour and a half away, to do so. Living alone on the upper floor of Ananda Kutir, I had made a firm resolve to recite one round of japa every night before bed.

Then one day, Leah, a visiting disciple, approached me on the path to Muktidham. She was quite a visionary and depth practitioner, and I was surprised when she said to me,"Manishi (my name at the time), Bapuji came to me in a vision the other day and asked me to relay this message to you — "

I was listening intently, as she spoke.

"He said, 'Tell Manishi he doesn't need to sit for japa each night before bed. At this point in his sadhana the most important practice must be karma yoga.'"

Since I lived alone in Ananda Kutir, there was no way anyone could know about my practice, least of all Leah Holton, who lived outside Philadelphia and only visited on occasional weekends.

This information confirmed that Bapuji's knowledge and awareness weren't bound by time, space, or other constraints, and I sensed then that his energies were universally available and accessible, based on our connection.

Nowadays my main sadhana is meditation. Along with formal sitting, I've also developed the practice of paying attention to my body, my emotions, and my intuition. Learning to be available for what intuition tells me has been an important development, for no matter what thought pops in or what the source is, I can feel the rightness of the guidance. Through Bapuji's influence, I've learned to test it out against experience.

I continue to receive help and inspiration from nonphysical sources, and Bapuji is central to that. Although I don't usually sit in front of his picture and ask him what to do as I used to in the past, I sometimes ask Bapuji for a sign to reassure me of his presence and support.

Several months ago I realized I was late for an appointment in Boston, a two and a half-hour drive from the Berkshires. Feeling somewhat mischievous, I asked Bapuji for help not only to get me there on time, but also to find a parking space and even have time to eat. That's a large order when you're headed for Harvard Square. In the past year, traveling to that same location, I've often had to circle for an hour before finding a place to park my car.

Although I left rather late, I arrived in a ridiculously short time, and just as I approached the building, a UPS truck pulled out revealing a magical parking space for me. Then, unbelievably, there was 45 minutes left on the parking meter, exactly the amount of time I needed to eat and visit my favorite Harvard bookstore.

Though this may seem insignificant in terms of Bapuji's influence, it was a good reminder for me, helping me move out of ordinary thinking into expanded consciousness for help and guidance. I notice that whenever I ask Bapuji for help, no matter how urgent or insignificant the matter, something shifts perceptually within me and the possibilities for change then become boundless.

Vivekanand Richard Michaels

Uniting People in Peace

After all these years, I feel my sadhana has blended into the seva I'm now doing at the UN. Currently I'm working on a project to introduce yoga and meditation to the UN staff. It's already in the system; there's a meditation room set up in the General Assembly building where we meet and meditate on a monthly basis.

My work is to unite people around the world in a celebration of real and lasting peace, embodied in the phrase Bapuji often repeated, vasudhaiva kutumbakam, the whole world is one family.

A great transformation occurred for me as I spent time in Bapuji's physical presence. There was some alchemy between us I can't describe, but since he was the embodiment of love, I too became more loving. In fact I grew into my Sanskrit name, Premdas, which means "servant of love."

I believe that Kripalu Center was my training ground and now I'm in the game. For me that game is doing peace work and bringing what I learned at the ashram into a larger arena. I still long for a solid, spiritual community as a support to this work. Yet it seems to me there's a Kripalu renaissance in the air, helping those who wish to re-energize their connection to Bapuji and this path to do so.

Although now my inner process has more to do with letting go of external forms of God and diving deeper into my inner being, I believe we're being called to reorganize in a new way, while retaining the spiritual focus we once had. No space exists between the past and present nor is anyone gone from us. In fact, all the masters are here, helping us move forward with our individual missions of peace and love.

Premdas Michael Johnson

I Turned to Bapuji in My Heart

On September 17, 2001, I sat in a circle of 55 survivors of 9/11. I was called to New York City to help these tender souls integrate the horrors of what they saw, and the trauma of what they had escaped. How could I do it? No one with any amount of training had ever been prepared for something like this.

It was Bapuji I turned to in my heart. I had seen him countless times do one simple thing: receive others with a heart of compassion, willing to be touched by the suffering before him. I began that circle by first looking around. I consciously looked to the heart of each person: top level executive, janitors, young corporate assistants, and secretaries. I sat in the "world family" — so tragically wounded just days before. I knew I had to meet each person in their suffering, to not look away. I had to go beyond my awkwardness of "what to do," and create a listening far bigger than what any one of us could singly provide another. My job was to show up, to be willing to answer the call to service unlike anything I had ever done before or since. This was not a time to be faint of heart, despite my fear. I was called and answering was choiceless.

I knew Bapuji had surmounted great challenges in his life of service. Not only was his heart big enough and soft enough to meet suffering, but his teachings were passionate about the healing of society, the meeting of strangers as our own family members. The biggest challenge I'd ever faced in my life of service was before me, and I knew Divine Love had to guide the way. I leaned back and in, into an invisible, upholding grace, a grace Bapuji spoke of constantly, a grace I believe in and rely on to this day.

I took a breath and opened that circle with prayer. I knew each person had to first feel safe, for "safety" had just been smashed into slivers of glass and choking particles of dust. Towering structures had just turned to sand; where else were we to go for a sense of safety than to God? It was from that place of safety and attunement, compassion and community, that each person began to release in words, the fear and trembling that lived in their heart. My role was to bear witness, to do so with love and compassion, but even more so, with willingness, willingness to enter their suffering with them. We cried one another's tears, cheered one another's' courage, grieved one another's loss, trembled together in the shock of it all. And we did so — together. A world family linked in love, drawing strength on a force beyond ourselves. I could not have met the call that day, nor the ones in the weeks that followed, without the living example of Bapuji in my heart.

Vidya Carolyn Dell'uomo

Legacy of Love

Although I work as a holistic physician in New York City, I don't have the same focus in yoga sadhana that I used to when I lived in the Pennsylvania ashram. I don't believe that yoga is necessarily the best thing for me, but I'm continually searching for answers and am content with not knowing. Experiencing different paths, I find what calls to me next.

Yet there's no doubt that Bapuji's legacy was the legacy of love. That was his great gift and I find that there's no acceptable excuse for not being able to love fully. It's always an option. I remember learning from one of his darshans that love is a practice and that it has many facets to it. You could practice being more loving by standing in front of a mirror and talking to someone in a kinder fashion. I tried that practice and had great luck with it. I still use it today when I feel on the verge of saying something hurtful or unkind. I go back to the mirror and practice sweeter forms of expression. Just catching myself before I actually speak in itself is a practice. The overall effect, though, has been to help me be more aware of my communications in general and my specific intentions with each person in particular. It's helpful to know you can actually carry out experiments in love.

Bapuji's commitment to love under all circumstances was unshakable. He taught me to practice putting into play whatever principles I wanted to deeply experience in my life. That was a great lesson. Although my life as a New York City physician has taken a different turn, its essence remains forever about love, service, and gratitude.

Chidanand Ron Dushkin, M.D.

The Power of Yoga

If I'd never met Bapuji, I'd eat, drink, and live a normal life. Or perhaps I'd be dead. It's hard to say, but most importantly Bapuji opened me to a deeper understanding of my purpose in life and to the fact that there were more options available than I'd ever dreamed of. Now I feel his presence every minute that I'm alive, and he's changed me forever inside and out.

All I have to do is think of Bapuji and my personality automatically changes. The other day it was freezing cold here in my studio and I wanted to cancel my yoga class. Then I immediately thought of Bapuji and knew it wasn't the right thing to do. So I held the class. As soon as I began teaching, my body became supple and my mind calm. It's as if he infused my spirit with his presence.

That happens whenever I think of him, whether I'm stressed out or angry, or simply ignorant of what to do next. Any little problem or question that I turn over to him is invariably resolved in an uncanny manner.

Although I'm 47 and run a business in England, I was born in Surat, in the state of Gujarat in India. For many years I practiced yoga and planned to be a monk. Living in a monastery, I studied with Bapuji and learned what it meant to be a sadhak.

Although later on I studied Iyengar, Ashtanga, and various other styles of yoga, no one ever taught yoga like Bapuji. In regular hatha yoga you learn how to lengthen the spine and stretch toward your knees while holding Paschimotanasana; with Bapuji you practice bandhas, drishti and long holding. Even a simple posture like Vajrasana becomes transformative using his methodology. And most important is the predominance given to the breath.

Nowadays people lack the patience to breathe properly, but I remember Bapuji's insistence on starting with pranayama. Without it, you may as well just do physical exercise, for you won't receive the benefits of the postures nor access their hidden depths.

Although the time I had with Bapuji was short, since he left in the late seventies to go to America, he often demonstrated the power of yoga in my presence. He allowed me to observe him as he assumed different states. Along with other students, we carried out different experiments. My favorite was to wrap him in cold soaking wet towels while he sat on the floor in Paschimotanasana. No sooner would we wrap him up than we'd see steam coming off his back and in minutes the towels would be bone dry. He demonstrated this so we would understand the heat generated from tapas or austerities.

Teaching us that human life depends not on the number of years you live but on the number of breaths you breathe, Bapuji demonstrated many yogic powers. Not only could he stop his breath but also his heart from beating. Gathering us together, he'd say, "It's two o'clock. I will stop my heart momentarily, so please observe closely but do nothing. I'll be back with you at 2:05 PM."

Then we'd gather excitedly as he lay down on the floor. There were doctors and medical people among his students and everyone paid close attention. I'd put my hand near his nose and mouth but could feel no breath and others checked his wrist but there was no pulse. Truly he was like a dead body.

Promptly at 2:05 he would open his eyes and resume breathing. Then his characteristic humor would return and he'd encourage us to deepen our own yoga practice. It wasn't that he was showing off; he just wanted us to know how far yoga could take us.

Ashok Naik

A Loving Grandfather

In the early seventies I sent this letter to Bapuji:

Dear Bapuji, If words were adequate, I would send you all there are in the world; but they are not. No words can express my love for you. I'll remain forever at your feet. One prayer I pray, one wish I wish – that I may love you and be guided by you till the Lord receives me home again. In love and devotion, Jyoti

That was the letter of a twenty-year-old, smitten by her grandfather guru. I still feel the same feelings reflected in that young letter. Even though it's thirty years later and I'm working as a relationship counselor and social worker, I can see how Bapuji's teachings shaped my life and opened me to a future focused in loving others and loving myself.

Personally I felt very loved by Bapuji. He always called me by name, and every time I went to *vandana* (our worship ceremony), he made a face and then bopped me on the head.

It amazed me how close to Jesus Bapuji was. He spoke about him as if he knew him personally. When he came to America, he studied the Bible and the life of Jesus and then wrote a book entitled *The Passion of Christ*.

One Christmas we gathered in Sumneytown to receive Christmas blessings. Since Bapuji was not up to traveling because of the intensity of his sadhana, we received permission to go up to Muktidham and wish him a Merry Christmas.

None of us questioned for a moment putting on saris or dhotis and trekking up to the house in the freezing rain and cold. (Admittedly we did have on long johns underneath our ceremonial clothes.)

Bapuji was there to receive it all. When he appeared we sang "Jai Bapuji," to the tune of "Joy to the World" and in that moment we were mere children chanting carols to our beloved grandfather. He received us with such a great outpouring of love it was incredible.

His love was always there as a palpable presence. In fact my greatest regret was not sufficiently focusing my energies on him. I was young and so engrossed in the petty squabbles of being a disciple that I scarcely recognized his miraculous love, let alone basked in it. I sat in Bapuji's presence for four and a quarter years and though I know he reached me at the deepest levels of my being, it was hard to feel his reality close to me or translate his teachings into action.

Although it was difficult to get to know him, I suppose that that's part of his mystery. He could be as close and loving as a grandfather and at the same time because of his sadhana, as distant as a saint. In either case, however, his love was unmistakable.

Jyoti Kate Feldman

A Cure for Depression

Watching Bapuji be fully present to whatever experience he was in, whether it was writing on a chalkboard, eating a meal, or singing a dhun inspired me to be as present as I could be to each day of my life. But first and foremost I must be the best human being I can be so I can wholeheartedly practice sadhana and open more deeply to spirit. His teachings and his life brought the yogic scriptures alive for me.

I always felt that I was Bapuji's disciple more than Amrit's. I was planning to go to India after finishing medical school in 1977, but when Bapuji came to the states I remained here, and his guidance became a powerful force in my life. The first time I had knowledge of him was in 1970. He came into my dreams two nights in a row when I was depressed after my high school love left me. In each dream I needed to pass some kind of test. One was a test of courage to save my ex-girlfriend from severe pain. The other was to choose between love or wealth, fame, and prestige. I managed to save my friend and I chose love above the other considerations, and after a display of flowers and celestial bells appeared, Bapuji put a garland around my neck. When I awoke, my depression was gone!

In 1976 when I attended the opening of the Summit Station ashram, I had another dream of him. Laughing, he reminded me that the picture of the bald man in the main chapel and the man who tested me before were one and the same. In 1980 when I decided to move to Kripalu Center, he encouraged me not to stray from that commitment.

When I left Kripalu in 1995 I went into a deep depression and my world fell apart. However, Bapuji was with me every night in meditation encouraging me to be with the pain and meditate even if all I saw was darkness. I followed his guidance. After months of darkness, one night the clouds lifted and I reconnected with my inner light in meditation. I would never have persisted in these practices if he hadn't visited me in his subtle form.

He inspired me to create my own yoga teacher training after I could no longer work at Kripalu Center. In fact, in meditation he kept saying, "You are with me and I am Kripalu, not a building or an organization." So I created my own course putting everything in it about yoga that I loved. In meditation he suggested I call it "Prana yoga," as its true purpose was to contact and let go into the movements of prana and to focus on an active form of postures. He said if an Indian man like him could have touched so many people in America simply through doing sadhana, then certainly as an American physician I could touch people's lives by offering yoga training. Through his advice, inspiration, and example, I created Prana yoga, which after seven years has over 200 teachers in the New York City area alone.

Finally, I hold the experience of love in the highest regard. I learned from Bapuji to consider love the most important blessing of this life and to nurture it at all costs. I practice this with my girlfriend from Iceland and with my seventeen-year-old daughter Kelly, and even though there are many challenges, I have no regrets. I know that nurturing those I love to the best of my ability is truly the highest sadhana.

Prabhakar Jeff Migdow, M.D.

Sadhana is its Own Reward

I'm writing this in my Manhattan apartment in 2004, nearly 28 years since first meeting Bapuji. Much has happened since then, but still I have his photos and books on my shelves, and, above all, what he embodied in my heart.

I had moved to the ashram in my teens and had read the miraculous tales of his life with his guru. I saw him as a great living saint, not unlike those I read about in the *Autobiography of a Yogi*. I assumed Bapuji would be a yogi of miraculous powers, with transcendental — or even omniscient — vision. But when he arrived in the United States, in the spring of the following year, there were no supernatural events that I could detect. Bapuji spoke little of miracles or even esoteric yoga practices.

I was disappointed by this lack of intriguing mysticism. Instead, Bapuji told quaint stories emphasizing such simple moral practices as truthfulness, selfless service, or loving-kindness. Within the first year of Bapuji's stay, however, I adjusted to his apparent lack of metaphysical glamour and became more receptive to the great loving Presence that animated him.

One morning Bapuji gave a talk about the importance of chanting mantra. His eyes twinkled when he explained that when you chant the name of Ram the impurities go out on the "Ra," and when you close your mouth on the "mmm," the impurities cannot get back in! Everyone laughed, but the teaching carved an impression on my mind.

A few days later I sat in my office where I did bookkeeping. I'd become aware, day by day, of how overwhelmed I was, not only by the external details of my job, but also by the internal confusion of my mind. It was a dusty blur filled with doubts, dreams, imagined slights, and retorts, fears, and worries. When at last something broke down inside me, I dropped to the floor and crouched in a fetal position. I began repeating, "I can't stand the craziness of my mind, I can't stand the craziness of my mind." Then I remembered Bapuji's words: "Chant the name of Ram."

From that moment I began to repeat "Ram" constantly, and even wrote it down every chance I got.

After a few days of this practice I was amazed by the clarity I experienced. As a result, I decided to repeat my guru mantra — *Om namo bhagavate vasudevaya* — the mantra Dadaji gave to Bapuji to initiate all devotees in his lineage. Inspired by Bapuji, I was fierce in my chanting practice. Within a short time, my mind was far clearer, more peaceful, and brighter then I could have imagined. And some unexpected boons were in store: within a month the shakti from my mantra practice became so strong that I moved spontaneously into automatic asanas, pranayamas, and mantras — mystical stuff indeed!

Thus, through the grace of Bapuji's teaching, I did touch the magical realm I'd been seeking. But by that time I was not so impressed with such external manifestations, other than as a sign that some grace and purification were working in me. Instead I realized that sadhana is its own reward.

Shivanand Thomas Amelio

He Saved My Life

I am absolutely sure that Bapuji saved my life. I mean that literally and figuratively. Back in March of 1975, I was experiencing a mysterious illness. I regarded it as a "purification by fire," and surely that's what it was. Headaches, body aches, and fever depleted my strength and drove me into delirium and a near-death experience.

Just before heading for the hospital, in a few moments of lucidity I sat with Gita for prayer and visualization. At that time I saw, felt, and instinctively knew that I was held in Bapuji's presence. It was a sensation like being enveloped and held in big white wings of love. Although I moved in and out of consciousness, during that whole time I rested in those arms of love, secure in the knowledge that I was safe, protected, and at peace.

I came back to life *full* of life, feeling the ever-present sense of Bapuji holding me and filling my heart, my thoughts and my being with his love. As I recovered, I listened to Bapuji chanting the prayer, *karpuragaurum karunavataram...* That is still my favorite prayer. Even now it carries me to that place of deep peace and love.

I sat many times in the meditation room on the second floor of the Sumneytown ashram. What was at first a photograph on the altar became a real live being, for Bapuji and I had developed a living, breathing *relationship*. It changed my life and turned me inside out.

Even in the hospital people noticed. As people in hospitals often do, they would glance at me as they walked past my door. Then they would do a double take, saying, "What are you doing here? You look *radiant*."

When I told them I had nearly died from an illness, they shook their heads in disbelief.

"Radiant" was the word I heard over and over. Even Yogi Desai used it when he came to see me. Friends at the ashram said it, and I felt it. I knew I was alive from within, and that this near-death was really a close encounter with the Divine. In fact it was my spiritual awakening.

When Bapuji came to Sumneytown in 1977, I went to his darshan as often as I could. I brought my children, grateful that they too could receive his blessing and experience his presence.

Although I loved his storytelling and the lilt of his head when he spoke, I especially loved his dancing. Bapuji gave us all an invitation to know God through dancing, or was it "to know dancing through God?" At any rate, his words about music, dance, and God have been an inspiration to me and form the heart of what I share with others as an instructor of yoga and dance.

Purnima Connie Miller

A Living Teacher

Twenty-three years after Bapuji's passing, I learn more from looking at his photograph than from the talks of interesting, living teachers. His wisdom comes through every gesture and every word that he uttered. In fact my entire professional life has been dedicated to researching what I experienced when I received his darshan.

I was fortunate to be in his presence while he visited the U.S. Through the transmission of shaktipat , Bapuji evoked in me what he referred to as "bodily-spiritual passion." I can only describe it like a series of labor contractions giving rise to a yoga practice far beyond the instructions of any yoga teacher. For example, while chanting with him, I experienced strong jolting, internal contractions known as bandhas throughout my body before I even knew what to call them. For decades, in practice I suddenly cried out, laughed or uttered gibberish-like mantras known as anahat nad and would then move almost surreally into postures that I was otherwise incapable of doing.

The lack of any Western psychology to adequately explain these experiences led me to complete a Ph.D. dissertation in which I interviewed many advanced yoga practitioners on this path. Later that research became two books: *Eros, Consciousness, and Kundalini,* and *Words from the Soul: Time/East/West Spirituality and Psychotherapeutic Narrative.* My research into these esoteric aspects of yoga and tantra has led to more than thirty conference presentations in the US, Europe, and India, where I am frequently invited to give talks on kundalini yoga.

Bapuji's tearful story of Buddha's first encounter with aging, witnessing an old man teetering on his cane, opened my eyes at the age of twenty-six to the poignancy of the human condition. As a therapist I learned that a subtle, poignant moment often has more power than a dramatic catharsis. Once this took the form of my demanding county funds for real silverware and not plastic, for a Christmas dinner I had planned for the indigent, mentally ill in Atlantic City, New Jersey. Another time, I asked an incarcerated youth to thank his father for a cigarette he had just received, triggering tears of closeness between them.

Applying the powers of apology, forgiveness, and admiration in even the most desperate situations works miracles. Although it may sound trite to heal highly abusive marriages "with love," that's exactly what I've found works, based in Bapuji's urgings to cultivate nonviolence and love, especially within the family. It's been the basis of the spiritually redemptive marriage counseling I've done for the past thirty years.

I remembered Bapuji's early struggles and attempts at suicide and began to look at my patients with severe cases of depression or psychosis through a different lens. In fact I even came to see psychosis as acute loneliness, rather than as a mere psychiatric disorder. Just as Bapuji was touched by a stranger in his darkest moment, there was also healing and integration for my patients once we touched down into the deeper issues of loneliness affecting them. Whether in my work bringing yoga into youth prisons, or flophouses for the homeless or mentally-ill, or in counseling couples striving to save their marriages, Bapuji strengthened my ability to see beauty and poetry in the struggles people face on a daily basis.

There's no part of my life that remains untouched by Bapuji's influence. His demonstration that a yogi of unparalleled dedication could also be a playful, joking, and loving grandfather who delights in telling stories to help us with various concerns of life, freed me from assuming a stilted spiritual life. For example I have taught yoga classes wearing a rubber Halloween mask. But, more to the point, he was so easy to love because he himself had so much love for others.

Above all, Bapuji was explicit that he would continue sadhana until his death, never assuming that he would retire after attaining some "final enlightenment." For him, spiritual growth was total and lifelong. Witnessing that type of commitment and his unparalleled high standards in approaching any practice—whether that of yoga, absolute truth, or enlightenment, inspired me the most.

Piyush Stuart Sovatsky

A Strong Foundation

I think the single most profound and lasting experience with Bapuji is that I had the experience of being fully and completely *loved* by him. There was nothing in the way—just pure, simple, deep flowing love. The only other time that I felt anything similar to that was at my father's death. In the day or so before he passed, he was able to look at me with such presence and unfetteredness that it was the same experience as being with Bapuji. I had never felt my own father's love that intensely and it was a tremendous gift to receive that before he died. But it was a familiar feeling, because I'd had it with Bapuji. It was indeed a blessing, as most people never get to feel that level of connection and acceptance.

I always felt so blessed that I played the harmonium — as I could sit up close and tune into Bapuji in a different way than just chanting along. I was fortunate to be able to lead chanting during darshans or ceremonies while he was with us. Often in group darshans he singled me out and bestowed extra love and care. I don't really understand why he gave me personalized attention, but once he told me that he had a sister named Bhanu. Perhaps that was the reason. Having his personal acknowledgement was unbelievable. It impacted me in a very deep way — getting what all of us desire — to be noticed. It was deeply fulfilling.

Although I did not serve him on a daily basis like Shila or other sisters, I had more contact with Ashutosh Muni, one of his close disciples. Through him, I learned more about who Bapuji was and how others close to him experienced him. Although I no longer keep an altar, I have Bapuji's photos in an album. But several times a year I have a dream in which Bapuji appears. It's always so wonderful; it's often humorous, and usually we're relating on a very friendly, personal basis.

I've had two dreams of dying/letting go and both times he was right there at the moment of transition. Both times I didn't die. But both dreams were very profound, in terms of my ability to let go and trust in the transition. In the dream I felt I could do that because either Bapuji appeared, or I was asking him how to let go in those final moments. It makes me feel much less apprehensive about death because I'm certain he'll be there with me.

Above all, Bapuji gave me an incredibly strong foundation of love and support on which to base my life. I know that I am loved and that allows me to move through my life without the desperate need to search for that experience. At this point his love is part of my being and it will never leave me.

Bhanu Harrison

Bapuji's Healing Powers

I grew up in India in the state of Gujarat and my mother was a devoted follower of Bapuji. For many years she loved and served him; thus he became the guru of our family and we were all devoted to him as well. I was lucky to be able to visit him and occasionally serve him in some fashion.

By the time I was seventeen, I had developed a severe speech problem; whenever I spoke I stuttered. I had been to see many people, but no one had a remedy to improve my speech. Needless to say, it was quite a hardship, especially since I felt I could never talk to girls with such halting speech.

Finally in desperation I went to Bapuji and with the usual temerity of youth insisted that he do something about it. He smiled and gave me his blessings. Then he said that in six months it would be taken care of. I went back to my studies, and six months later, to my amazement I discovered that I had no problem speaking whatsoever. And I've never had a problem since.

Bapuji never boasted about his healing powers, but they were at work all the time. Usually he remained behind the scenes and would never take credit for them. But for years people filed past him and he would give them mantras or recommend certain simple foods to eat. Then they'd find themselves cured. It worked like clockwork. In fact, just being in his presence was in itself a kind of cure.

Kirit Shah

Answer to a Prayer

As a devout American Catholic teenager with a deep spiritual bent, inspired by mysticism and the lives of saints (whom I believed could only be Christian), I used to cry that I was born too late and would, therefore, never have a chance to meet or know a real saint.

I had left the Catholic Church when I was 28 and spent the next ten years as an agnostic. When my teenage daughter was hit by a car in 1979 and lay in a hospital in New Jersey seriously wounded, however, I found myself in deep crisis. Sitting by her hospital bed late one night, I prayed the deepest prayer of my life. *"Dear God, Whoever you are, Whatever you are, with or without form, please hear me."*

I continued with my prayer, *"There are only a few things I know to be true, and these I know deep inside me. I know that there's Wisdom behind this creation; and I know that behind this Wisdom there's Love. Above all, I know that this Love gives meaning to everything. Although I haven't lived a spirit-centered life for many years and have cut myself off from that love, I want to be tapped into that Source again. Please show me how I can be a spiritual person again. Please give me a teacher, someone to show me the way."*

At the time I offered that prayer, I had no image of the kind of teacher I was asking for, and I was certainly not thinking that I wanted a Hindu guru! Five thousand miles and forty-eight hours following that prayer I was taken to my first satsanga ever in Alaska. When I saw a photo of Bapuji on the wall, I was drawn to Him like a magnet. I knew that I knew Him, but couldn't remember where we'd met. Within minutes I had a profound shakti experience and was told that He was the saint I'd been longing to know all those years.

I took His photo home and began praying to Him day and night, saying, *"Bapuji, You are the One. Although I know you're my Master, please give me a sign to confirm that it's true."* Bapuji made me wait for my sign for five months until Easter of 1980. Again while attending satsanga in Alaska, I had profound shakti experiences in which I recognized Him from before time began. I knew Him as my own Divine Self. I was One with Him. I also understood that through lifetimes of ignorance and error, I had forgotten.

Although I was in agony that I could ever have forgotten, I was in ecstasy that I was now remembering! Five months after first learning about Bapuji, a firm prayer arose in my heart. I told Bapuji that I must see Him and be with Him. At 3 AM on Easter morning, 1980, Bapuji came to me in a vision. Standing before me, He said, *"I am yours and you are mine. Do not worry for I will always be with you."*

A few hours after that, Shanti, whom I did not yet know well, approached me and said, "I was out in the woods meditating today, and Bapuji told me to give this to you." Then she handed me a check for $500 to cover airfare to see Bapuji!

On the airplane traveling from Alaska to Philadelphia to see Bapuji for the first time, there was a tremendous battle going on within me between my heart and my head. My mind would say, "What are you doing?"

My heart answered, "I'm going to see my beloved Master, Whom I haven't seen for lifetimes!"

My head would say, "Are you kidding? Do you really think that little old man from India is going to know you?"

My heart answered, "Of course He knows me! He said that I am His and He is mine!"

When the glorious day arrived on Guru Purnima in 1980, I first saw my Beloved Master walking down the front path of the little house where He was staying in Summit Station. I was overwhelmed with awe, love, and shakti when He approached me and blessed me. Touching my head, He spoke to me through the third eye and said: *"It is all true; it is not your imagination; it is all true."* From that moment I knew that I was forever in the hands of this great saint.

How can I describe His effect on me? The first time I touched His Holy Feet, I felt that a complete metabolic change had taken place within me. In fact, although I had been eating meat up until that day, touching His Feet made me an instant vegetarian. On the way home to Alaska, I tried eating a small bite of turkey in a chef salad and became violently ill. Then I heard a voice saying, "No more meat," and so it has been for the last twenty-four years!

For me Bapuji was the Ideal Saint—totally loving and compassionate, yet at the same time completely humble. Although He had a marvelous sense of humor and could turn a phrase beautifully, He was much more than we could see or know. He was truly a great and powerful yogi.

Eighteen months after meeting him face-to-face, Bapuji left His body. This was a terrible time for me. I had moved into the Pennsylvania ashram, but by 1989. having spent nine months in India over the course of seven years, I left the American ashram for good and received *sannyasta diksha* or initiation in Bapuji's lineage in Kayavarohan.

After that I spent eight years as a wandering *sadhika* or spiritual pilgrim with no income or fixed abode. I was totally in Bapuji's hands. He taught me to ask no one but Him for what I needed, and He provided so well that I never went without food or shelter. I spent two and a quarter years in India either wandering on pilgrimage or living in ashrams doing sadhana. Much to my surprise, in 1997 through my mother's request, I heard Bapuji calling me to return to Ohio and take care of her. Since she's not been well and needs twenty-four hour care, I've been doing mother seva ever since.

Nowadays there's only one thing I really know and that is this, I belong to Bapuji; He is my All in All. Although I don't know what He plans for me from one day to the next, I am totally in His Hands.

Swamini Umamaiya Udasin

The Battlefield of Yoga

Although I had had a hard time reconciling the battlefield scene in the Bhagavad Gita with the principles of nonviolence I learned in yoga, Bapuji explained that the story was an allegory for the spiritual quest. He said that Arjuna's enemies were not his physical relatives but his own desires, which he needed to overcome. Rather than an external battle, Kurukshetra was the internal battle every seeker must wage on behalf of his sadhana. I could certainly relate to that.

I first met Bapuji on a pilgrimage to India in 1974 for the opening of the temple at Kayavarohan. My first impression was of a great loving soul. His head bobbed in ecstasy as one by one we bowed down before him and received his blessings. Intuitively I knew then and there that he was everything I had hoped for in a saint or a guru.

By the time I visited the Summit Station ashram in Pennsylvania, I was afraid that I was losing my wife to yoga and to Bapuji, such was the intensity of her devotion. Offering pranams to Bapuji with a heavy heart, I was already grieving the imagined loss of my wife.

When we returned to our seats, however, Bapuji's opening remark was, "If you don't trust your own Guru, why not find another one?" I was shocked. That statement felt as if it were directed to me alone.

In my mind I responded to him, "Bapuji, I could never have anyone but you." I decided then and there that I'd better trust my guru. Afterward my worries entirely disappeared.

To my knowledge, Dadaji never told Bapuji that he would attain his divine body in this lifetime. He told him that his special grace was that he would become the foremost yogi in the world. Dadaji certainly delivered on his promise.

When one looks at the complete commitment Bapuji gave to his sadhana and to his unrelenting quest for perfection, I think of him as all the more remarkable. Undoubtedly Bapuji was the foremost yogi of his time.

Bapuji once told us that saints never make predictions on their own but that sometimes God speaks through them, foretelling future events. However these are spontaneous utterances that originate from God himself.

I recall one such prediction that fell from Bapuji's lips at Summit Station. Seemingly out of nowhere he told us that in approximately a hundred years America would have its own "divine body yogi."

Who knows? Perhaps we may all return to witness this miracle...

Sandip Kumar Dennis Konchak

Yogi Amrit and Urmila Desai

CHAPTER NINETEEN

FINAL REFLECTIONS ON SERVING BAPUJI AND SELF-REALIZATION

As many of us awaited his arrival in the States in 1977, we felt that this was no commonplace event; as a matter of fact, it seemed miraculous to have Bapuji join us. There was a tremendous surge of energy and excitement in the air. Great expectations gave way to the realities of Bapuji's sadhana and seclusion, and the special Sundays when he granted us darshan. As life unfolded, we witnessed everything from the sublime to the ridiculous, from serious contemplation to times of his teasing or our torpor. But above all, in his presence we got to experience a true pilgrim of love.

Preparing for His Arrival

I was the lucky one to receive the phone call at 2 o'clock in the morning one winter night: it was Krishnapriya on the other end, calling from India to let us know that Bapuji was coming to America. Already friends had gathered in the hall as I divulged the news and there were whoops and hollers.

Best of all, when I called Manishi in Kripalu Bhavan to inform him Bapuji was coming, he said,"Yeah—and when's Dadaji coming?"

Walking around Summit Station the next morning, it suddenly dawned on us that we were in no way prepared to receive Bapuji; the retreat was half-built and still carried its original farm-like facade. There was enormous work to do and scarcely two months before his arrival.

Besides the external work, I immediately chided myself on my progress in sadhana. I felt that I would have to get absolutely pure and work out all of my karma before Bapuji came. How else would I be eligible for his darshan?

No one could have imagined the transformation of Rajeshwari, that ugly building on a bare lot that had once been a shooting gallery. However, we worked long hours painting, refurbishing, and decorating, staying up hours past satsanga and in the end it finally looked like a home for a king, as its name implied.

Then we planted gardens, fixed up the grounds, painted interiors, and focused attention on the biggest project on hand: the completion of Sadhana Mandir, the temple dedicated in Bapuji's honor.

I remember Krishnapriya recounting some confusion about a telegram from India. Originally she heard Gurudev say, "Finish Sadhana Mandir."

Considering the scope of the task, however, she told us he'd really meant, "Finish your sadhana, my dear."

At any rate, the night before Bapuji's arrival, they lowered the roof into place and rushed to clear the grounds around Sadhana Mandir. The rest of us scrambled into our places as well, dressed in white (and with paint-stains surreptitiously spotting hands and faces), offering him our flowers.

Sukanya Christine Warren

Learning How to Serve Bapuji

When Bapuji first came here, I had no idea how to serve him because I had never done that before in India. But everything worked out fine. When he was seated, I could tell if the light was too bright, or it was too hot or cold in his room, and I would adjust the temperature. After serving him all the time, I began to know when he needed his glasses or a drink of water. Toward the end of his time here I even knew what he wanted to eat before mealtime. Upon serving him, he would often say, "That's exactly what I wanted." I guess when you think about someone all the time, you get tuned in to their thoughts. I felt like he was my father, and that the sweetest thing in the world would be to serve him as I would my own father.

Once he said to me, "I'm sixty-eight years old and this is the first time in my whole life that I'm experiencing such bliss in my sadhana, and that too in Muktidham and in your house. So you must be my incarnation daughter."

Then he told me that we would be together again some day. I consider that the treasure of my sadhana. In fact I didn't need to sit and chant or do japa; while he was with us, I thought of him every minute of the day and serving him was my sadhana.

Bapuji would often tell us little stories to amuse us when Gurudev and I were in darshan with him. Because I wanted to keep track of these stories, I kept a pen and pad available to jot down notes from his stories. After I'd left, he would take the notebook and make corrections if I hadn't gotten things right.

Invariably he spoke to inanimate objects as if they were alive. One day he talked to a radish on his plate and asked if it came from India or from America.

At another time while trying to get a new pen to write, he told us about his conversation:

"I said to the pen, 'Why aren't you working?' The pen replied, 'Because, you don't know how to write, stupid.' Trying again, I still couldn't get it to write. So I said, 'I'm not stupid; you're the one who's stupid because your sister, the other pen writes perfectly.'"

That's how he talked to things around him. Usually he had two or three pens around him, so if one wasn't working, he'd use another one. One time he handed me a pen and said, "I like that pen so much that if you ever want to call on me, just meditate on that pen. Then I'll come, wherever I am." I still have that pen on my altar.

After Bapuji took his final samadhi, I was planning to go to India for the ceremonies and had my visa and ticket ready. Suddenly I thought, "What's the point of going?" I knew I'd have to see my parents and friends and those who knew Bapuji. Even though my heart was burning with grief, I'd have to smile and talk to everyone—which felt like a big pretense. So I decided to stay here and do japa instead.

For fifteen days that's all I did other than go to the bathroom, eat, or sleep. I couldn't even cook an Indian meal for myself because every time I started cooking, I would think of Bapuji and start crying. The final night I stayed up till midnight chanting mantra and it seemed as if the whole room was filled with Bapuji's presence. As I got up to go to bed, I turned out the light. Then I thought, "If Bapuji comes through, he won't be able to see in the dark," so I quickly turned the light back on. Then of course I remembered.

Mataji Urmila Desai

His Mischief

Late in February we had a four foot snowfall in Sumneytown. I was working with some of the brothers to clear the footpath up to Muktidham so that Mataji could walk easily, carrying Bapuji's morning meal. Whenever Bapuji was in Sumneytown, he stayed in that cottage overlooking the ashram.

That particular morning Mataji seemed so cold, wearing only a sari and a little shawl, trudging up that steep hill. Meanwhile Mangesh and I were working madly to clear a path. We'd been shoveling and clearing since five o'clock in the morning.

Finally we were down to brooms. As we swept the snow away, more snow fell, until finally we were standing in front of his door, Mataji was moving back and forth to keep warm. Even with an umbrella held over her, she had a huge mound of snow on the side of her head. Snow continued falling and we kept sweeping.

Finally the curtain to the meditation room moved, and Bapuji looked out the window. With eyes wide open, he popped his head out the door, amazed at the huge amount of snow. I'll never forget the look on his face. It was the delight of a child, the surprise of an adult, and his own brand of mischief all mixed in together as he welcomed this trio bringing him his morning meal.

Yogindra Richard Cleaver

The Stirrings of Shakti

Bapuji seemed like a very sweet old man, but to tell you the truth, I didn't sense anything unusual or different about him, and so I couldn't relate to all the hype and commotion about his being here or his sublime spiritual presence.

Then one day I was asked to record one of his speeches. It must have been Guru Purnima, but I forget which year. At any rate, since my seva was connected to A/V, I was the logical candidate.

Here was the scenario: Bapuji would read his entire Guru Purnima speech and then we'd record it so that Gurudev could have it translated well in advance of the event. That way he'd be able to read right along and translate from the Gujarati in the appropriate places. So I set up the equipment, gave Bapuji the mike, and then watched the controls as he began reading...and reading. It seemed like hours that I sat there listening to him.

Once he left, however, I remained in the room and closed my eyes for a few minutes. Suddenly I felt my consciousness shift and the stirrings of shakti move through my body. It was wild. After the intensity was over, I got up, took a walk and had no idea what to do with myself, I was so high. So I did the only thing I knew to bring my energy back to earth — I went and ate a big meal.

Snehadip Douglas Anzalone

Lessons in Perfection

Washing, ironing, and serving his meals, I was very fortunate to be able to serve Bapuji directly. In fact Vinit Muni once reminded me that people travel hundreds of miles in India just to be able to do what I'm doing.

So I felt very blessed. After the Indian woman who'd been serving him left, I was privileged to serve him right in his house. Mataji took me to Rajeshwari and introduced me to him.

Immediately he began chanting in a dreamy voice, "Ansuya, Ansuya, Ansuya." I was setting up the table where'd he be eating, and he continued to chant, "Ansuya, Ansuya, Ansuya" while sitting on his swing. It was music to my ears.

After lecturing each day that summer, Bapuji went back into silence and I missed hearing his lullaby of my name. However, one day I got to drive him from the main temple back to his house, and when Gurudev introduced him to me again, not realizing Bapuji knew my name, Bapuji spoke out loud.

He said, "Ansuya is the great, great grandmother of Lord Lakulish" and I thought to myself, "Wow, I'm their grandmother, what a piece of luck!"

When Bapuji first came here, we wanted him to taste different American foods, so we made him pizza and hoagies and we even rushed ice cream up to his house, before it melted. Although he tasted a little of everything, the only thing he really liked was toast.

If you ever want to take lessons in perfection, serving Bapuji is an ideal place to begin. Every day we'd go up at exactly the same time and every day Bapuji would open his door at exactly the same time. Then we'd serve him his morning meal, make the bed, and quickly clean and replace soiled laundry with clean clothes. It happened like clockwork.

Once I gave Muniji my mala to have it blessed by Bapuji but then I got caught up serving the meal and doing the wash, so I forgot about it. When I brought him his food, he said, "Come here."

Removing my mala from his altar, Bapuji put it around my neck. That was totally unexpected. I can still see him standing in front of me with that broad smile on his face, blessing me.

It's hard to believe how often I got to serve and interact with him, especially because at the time I was shy. Nevertheless, I kept a secret box of Bapuji's things that we'd collected when we were cleaning. I'd distribute his old toothbrush or used-up soap to various disciples, who'd be ecstatic to have something he touched directly. If there were a little bit of oil leftover from his bottle of bath oil, I'd give that away too. It sounds crazy to collect these things, but whoever witnessed his extreme love and gentleness wanted to be as close as possible or at least have some souvenir of his presence.

When I served him, I tried to make everything look beautiful and appealing. Thus if I gave him a drink, I'd put it on a tray with a flower and a lovely napkin. At one point Bapuji wrote something on his chalkboard that Gurudev translated.

This is what he wrote to me:

"Ansuya offered me this drink and along with it a beautiful flower in a vase. Because of that gesture, the drink became sweeter and more divine. I kept drinking the drink, seeing Ansuyabhen standing there. So I drank not only the drink but also the pure love she offered along with it."

Ansuya Helaine Wolfe

Puja to the Doorknob

One time Saguna called me to Muktidham to fix a doorknob on the bathroom door. It had fallen off and although Saguna kept sticking it back on, it wasn't screwed in tightly enough so it kept falling off.

Since I worked in maintenance, I grabbed my tools and went up to the house. Immediately Saguna said, "You have to do this really fast because it's almost time for his sadhana." That made me nervous. However, I looked at the doorknob and the issue was pretty simple. Two parts that had separated needed to be fastened back together.

I worked on them to get them just right and when I pushed the doorknob in, it fell off again. Twenty times I tried to complete this simple task but still it didn't work. Then I felt desperate, knowing Bapuji's meal was soon over and it would be time for his meditation.

All of a sudden Bapuji called Saguna and me into his room, and we bowed before him. He wrote on his slate that he'd had trouble with the doorknob before, and he thought that if Saguna could put it back together, then so could he. So he tried to repair it but he couldn't. Then he said, "I surrendered and bowed down to the doorknob."

I visualized him there in the house by himself bowing to the doorknob. Although he laughed and made fun of it, I was so blown away by the story that when I went back to the door I was still thinking of him bowing down. My heart was lightened up. Without even thinking about it, I quickly put the bolts back in and tightened the doorknob. Needless to say, it worked perfectly.

Parmanand Jack Buckley

Bapuji and the Children

Bapuji dearly loved the children at the ashram. Although I was a single mom at the time, I felt that Bapuji was Mala's parent and guardian as well, always looking out for her.

Every Sunday we went to darshan in the meditation room, and Mala, who was four at the time, brought her dolls to be blessed. She would stand at the door and very solemnly raise her doll up to him when Bapuji entered the room. He always patted the doll on the head and pranamed. Whether she brought rabbits, teddy bears, or other toys, he blessed them all.

Nevertheless I advised her not to be attached to this little ceremony, and she would say to me, "I know, Mom." Still she waited at the door week after week. As soon as Bapuji saw her, he'd welcome her into his arms and hug her tightly.

One Christmas Bapuji walked up the stairs and saw Mala standing there as usual. Reaching into his pocket, he pulled out a chocolate Santa Claus for her to eat, and she was delighted. He always found ways to surprise her and show her how special she was, like saving extra prasad candies and handing her two instead of one during darshan.

I came to rely on their connection as a source of strength for us both.

When she was seven, she went to visit her father and stepmother for a long weekend. She called me the day she was due to return home, and asked if she could stay and live with them. I honored her need to be with her father and gave him legal custody, since she was moving to Canada. After a few months, however, she became very unhappy and wanted to come back to live with me in the ashram. Her father said "No."

That night I prayed to Bapuji with all my heart. I felt helpless. The next day would be Bapuji's farewell darshan before returning to India. Just before darshan, I spoke with Mala. She said she'd been crying in school every day. She cried on the phone asking me to help her to come back.

When I bowed down in darshan, I held onto Bapuji's feet and wept. It was the most real experience I've ever had praying for help. When I looked up at him, he acknowledged me deeply.

The very next day Mala's father called and said that he needed her to return to the ashram and live with me. On the previous night, her stepmother, who for several weeks had been ill and unable to attend to Mala's needs, had a tubal pregnancy burst at midnight. She was unaware that she was pregnant; however, when the fallopian tube burst, her life was saved. Since she needed time to recover, Mala returned to the ashram just as Bapuji was leaving for India.

I felt certain that Bapuji had intervened for the good of all involved.

In 1995, when Mala was 22 years old, she accompanied my husband Paritosh and me to Dadaji's temple in Kayavarohan and to Bapuji's Mahasamadhi site and ashram in Malav. When we sat in his meditation room in Malav, Mala was moved to tears. She said to me, "I remember how much he loved me."

Rambha Suzanne DeWees

A New Possibility

On June 15, 1978 I moved to Pennsylvania and was sent to the Retreat at Summit Station. Soon I was put to work taping lectures, including Bapuji's talks, and coordinating the transcribers who typed his messages onto paper. It was a magical time. Bapuji alternated between the Sumneytown and Summit Station ashrams, which were about an hour apart.

I remember driving him from the lower to the upper part of the Sumneytown ashram. That was a ritual that followed his Sunday afternoon darshans; each week one of us disciples was selected to drive the short distance.

As soon as he was situated in the front seat of the car, he peered out through the windshield, apparently fixated on something entrancing. He looked around with such God-intoxication, you might think he was stoned.

Over and over, gazing out the window he said, "*Prabhu, Prabhu*" (God, God). I could tell that he was definitely seeing something that we weren't seeing. This visceral experience of someone else's perception of God was so real and palpable that I was stunned. That's what I wanted, and there he was sitting in the car right next to me. I'll never forget it as long as I live.

Another memorable experience was watching him doing mudras, dance-like postures, at the back of Rajeshwari. This elegant home had once been a shooting gallery when Summit Station was a carnival site. That he lived in such a place was itself a contradiction.

However in keeping with that tradition, his performance of trance-like mudras and postures was full of primal force, and we could feel a tendency in our own bodies to do similar movements. Something had taken over this elderly gentleman and was showing itself through movement.

I was entranced and deeply moved. Invited down as part of an A/V team, I felt it to be a rare privilege to witness this side of the master and to feel the effects of being in the presence of his samadhi.

It was most important to be present to the state of consciousness which

Bapuji so naturally and easily maintained as a result of his sadhana. That itself taught us. For how can anyone know such states of mind, apart from direct experience? Although the divine shakti is present, albeit largely blocked in us all, most of us have an approach-avoidance to a deeper relationship with It, to complete merging into God.

From his unblocked example, however, Bapuji helped free us up, while in his presence, to at least a glimpse of what is possible, of what is our true natural state, and for that I'm eternally grateful to him.

Gitanand Gray Ward

The Reality of Sadhana

I first met Bapuji when he came to Kayavarohan West in California in mid-1977. He arrived with Vinit Muni and Amrit Desai at the San Francisco Airport and we did arati for him in the arrival lounge. The first darshan was in a yoga center in Berkeley with about 150 people. I also attended a semi-private darshan with Bapuji where we discussed sadhana. Later he settled in at the center my teacher Yogeshwar founded on a 600-acre property in the Napa Valley. Sitting there surrounded by people, I felt his presence and spirit fill the entire room.

When he arrived, Bapuji moved into an isolated building with no lawn in the back yard. Many of us had worked night and day to transform this former spa into an ashram. At some point during his stay, a lawn was delivered, rolled up in strips on the back of a truck. It was immediately set in place. I later heard that Bapuji had watched this process and had commented, "Only in America!"

I was never interested in the Indian trappings nor did I yearn to become a yogi; I was interested only in the truth. Although it was hard to wade through the garlands, beads, and bald heads of that culture, still I could discern that Bapuji was a serious truth-seeker and not a charlatan. I saw that sadhana was real for him and it was about love, not as a belief or a personality trait but as a living, breathing, cellular reality. What affected me most was that he had truly devoted his life to this path and had done it in a mature way, not as a fad or passing fancy.

I was already drawing closer to sadhana as a way of life. Meeting Bapuji had the subtle effect of validating my intuitions about that. His presence and words were a kind of blessing over our grand experiment to do sadhana in the west.

By 1979 I had devoted myself full time to sahaja yoga, taking renunciate vows. Yogeshwar guided me in how to enter this depth practice and it was an extremely rich period in my life. I experienced to my core that the sadhana is real. However, after two years I had gone too deeply for my overall spiritual development to sustain. Sadhana challenges you wherever you are. It eventually demands your life.

In this period I went to see Bapuji again in Pennsylvania. It seemed to me that he was an adult doing adult sadhana while the rest of us were very far from this, almost like children. Seeing Bapuji again I could sense the depths he had been involved with for so many years. It was sobering for me. I had the distinct feeling that some day I would have to deal with this yoga on an adult basis but that the time had not arrived. More preparation would have to take place, more balance, more self-knowing, more life experience.

I renounced my fixed ideas about renunciation in that period, although not the core intention. It was as if my period of experimenting and basic education was over and now I could set out on my real path. I realized it was not appropriate to use intensive meditation physics just to go deeply into spiritual experiences. That was a part of the process but not the point. The same was true with the guru. I also realized that the Indian cultural style of religion was not the essence of the matter for me. I experienced my real sadhana as becoming something beyond all that, a kind of pure journey of divine relationship based in the true Self.

After Bapuji died I went to India to visit his tomb, or Mahasamadhi, in Malav. On this trip I had a surprise meeting with Rajarshi Muni, one of Bapuji's disciples, who described the nature of his sadhana and spiritual experiences with me at length. He practiced heavy sadhana but with a different take on almost everything. Finally coming out into the light of day, my mind was blown because I saw there was no one way or set of concepts that we all had to march down, even within the same lineage. What remained for me was just me and reality.

When I returned home, I felt internally liberated from something. It was as if I had known all along that the realization of my Self has nothing to do with following ideas or walking in the footsteps of others, even gurus. Ideas and gurus are important but they cannot do your sadhana for you. I had really been initiated into surrender, not a system or a culture. Visiting Bapuji even after he died had somehow generated this essential lesson for me: that my sadhana is between me and God.

In the early days, the fact that Bapuji didn't speak English enabled my relationship with him to exist in a purified environment. All I could hear was his deep gentle voice speaking and then wait for the translation. I would get his soul in that interval more than if he had addressed us in English. I remember being moved by the fact that he never appeared to be using his position or his powers for any personal agenda. He was really just into sadhana and teaching. And loving people. His presence and his memory rest very purely in my heart now. I still talk to him and pray to him from time to time.

Skanda Lawrence Noyes

Reverence for Life

I had the privilege of sitting at Bapuji's feet while he gave numerous lectures and group darshans in our two Pennsylvania ashrams in the late seventies. At each darshan, hundreds of people came up to Bapuji, two at a time, to offer their pranams. One day, watching these loving grandchildren approach him on their knees for his blessings, Bapuji picked up his slate and wrote to me, "Do you see God in their eyes?"

Responding to the vibrations of the group at another large darshan, Bapuji wrote on his slate to me, "We have all been together before. These are the old souls who have come back to us. We are all connected."

Once when I was sitting with him, Bapuji picked up a flower a devotee had offered him, turned it this way and that, marveling at its perfection. With an expression of wonder on his face he said to me, "Look what God has done."

Bapuji regarded all living things, including plants and flowers, as expressions of divine energy. He worshipped nature as a direct representation of God. One day I was driving him from Summit Station to Sumneytown in Pennsylvania. On the way I pointed out a scenic river to him. He turned in his seat in the car and pranamed with great reverence. To him the river was a sacred expression of God.

Bapuji had very few items in his personal possession while he lived in Muktidham. He had some scriptures, paper, pens, and a slate for writing, as well as a few articles of clothing. Yet he used everything with great awareness, never wasting anything and keeping each item orderly and clean. He did not treat things that way as a formality but because in his heart he truly felt everything as an expression of divine energy.

To Bapuji a pen was not just a pen but familiar enough to be called "sister pen." His watch was "brother watch." He treated every object with love.

On Bapuji's final day in America before returning to India, I went to Muktidham to pick him up for the drive to the airport. It was a poignant moment in the ashram; our beloved Bapuji was leaving and we sensed we might never see him again. With a quiet dignity Bapuji walked out of Muktidham, the meditation cabin that his been his home and place of sadhana for the past four and a quarter years.

Turning to face the building, slowly and deliberately he put his hands together at heart level and offered his farewell pranam to Muktidham. Then he lay down on the ground in full prostration, stretching his arms over his head in a gesture of deepest reverence. To Bapuji, Muktidham was not a building but an embodiment of the divine energies that had guided his life. He said goodbye to his American home with the same love and feeling as to a devoted friend.

Yogi Amrit Desai

Bapuji performs mudras

Bapuji's Farewell Darshan: Sunday 9/27/81

My beloved children, do not give up virtuous conduct and self-discipline even in the face of death. Keep unflinching faith in the holy lotus feet of the Lord and continue to practice mantra japa, bhajans, chanting his name, meditation, pranayama, postures, fasting, moderation in diet, observing holy vows, and the study of scripture. I extend my blessings to you all.

Your loving Grandfather, Kripalu

Bapuji in prayer

Bapuji offering pranamas to Dadaji

Closing Prayer from Bapuji's Bhajan

My Beloved Guru

Guru mara antarani ankha ughado re
Guru, grant me my inner heart's vision.

Sharane avyo swami snehana sagaraJivana pantha ujalo re.
O Lord, the ocean of love, I've come to your feet.
Please illuminate the path of my life.

Charmachaksu to ye akhanda andhapo
Prabhuno pantha ajanyo.
Pale pale hun gada gada kanthe
Premathi karato pokaro re.
I am totally blind, despite having eyes.
The path to the Divine is unknown to me.
I'm crying for help in every moment.

Akhi ye avaninan tirathoman bhatakyo
Nadie nadiman hun nahyo.
Mandire mandire dipa jalavya to ye
Ladhyo na samo kinaro re.
I've traveled to every holy place of
pilgrimage on this earth. I've bathed in
every holy stream. I've kindled lamps in
every temple, but have not found my
destination.

Gnanana granthone shevya nirantara
Yogano sanga men sadhyo.

Bhakti na bhavaman bhana bhulyo to ye
marya na manana vikaro re.
I've always lived my life according to
the truth of the holy scriptures. I've practiced
yoga. I've lost my sanity in devotion to you,
yet I'm not relieved of my mind's distractions.

Mungo shun magun ne murakho shun bolun
papi kahun shun ke taro.
Kripalu karunana nidhi mane to
Guru kripano saharo re.
What can I ask, for I'm dumb?
What words can I find, for I'm illiterate? How can I
ask for enlightenment, if I'm sinful?
O Kripalu, treasure of mercy, I'm fortunate
to have the strength of Guru's grace.

GLOSSARY

Acharya: Preceptor, spiritual master, accomplished teacher.

Ahimsa: Nonviolence; doing no harm to others in thought, word, or deed.

Anahat Nad: Unstruck sound, spontaneous sounds or songs ushering forth from the heart center (Anahat chakra) during deep meditation.

Ananda: Pure joy or bliss.

Apana: That aspect of the life force controlling elimination and sexual expression, having a downward pull on the energy.

Arjuna: Famous warrior and hero of the *Bhagavad Gita*, who struggles with the dilemma of fighting others and learns about the true nature of his dharma in this spiritual epic.

Arati (also spelled Arti): offering the light to deities or to the guru, a devotional practice accompanied by song or prayer.

Asana: originally "seat," — refers to any of the countless hatha yoga postures.

Ashram: a school or sanctuary where students study and practice spiritual teachings.

Ashtanga: eight-limbed path of yoga articulated by Patanjali in the Yoga Sutras, which includes asana, pranayama, pratyahara, dharana, dhyana, meditation, and samadhi or ecstasy, and practice of the yamas and niyamas (restraints and moral observances).

Atman: Self, inner being.

Bandha: lock or holding, refers to a method of pulling up or in during yoga practice, which stimulates greater flow of prana. Key locks are mulabandha or root lock, uddiyana bandha or stomach lock and jalandhara bandha or throat lock.

Bhagavad Gita: "Song of God," — epic tale containing important teachings on yoga narrated within the *Mahabharata* as a series of dialogues between the warrior Arjuna and his charioteer Lord Krishna.

Bhakta: A person who practices love and surrender to God.

Bhakti: Devotion, love. A branch of yoga focusing on devotion to God and guru which includes ceremony, prayer, and the repetition of sacred mantra.

Brahmacharya: Behaviors bringing one closer to God, specifically moderating one's sexual energies through celibacy or sexual restraint. Also refers to purity in speech and conduct in general.

Buddha, Gautama — the historical founder of Buddhism, who lived approximately five hundred years before Christ and outlined precepts for the "middle path." As the "awakened one," Buddha also refers to anyone who has achieved enlightenment.

Buddhi: Intelligence, higher faculties of perception.

Chakra: Wheel, also refers to spiritual energy centers in the body.

Chitta: Awareness, mind-stuff, or consciousness.

Darshan: Sight or vision usually associated with being in the presence of a spiritual master.

Deha: Body; Divya-deha: Divine body — a youthful, immortal body achieved as a result of many years of focused sadhana.

Deva (Devi): God-like, goddess, having divine qualities.

Dharana: One pointedness or focused attention, one of the practices of Ashtanga or classical yoga.

Dharma: The way or path, in Hinduism considered one of the four aims of life, including the pursuit of kama (pleasure), artha (wealth), dharma (noble conduct), and moksha (liberation). Also refers to virtuous conduct or one's true mission in life.

Dhrishti: View or gaze. The focal point for one's inner gaze during yoga practice.

Dhyana: Meditative absorption, a fundamental technique of classical yoga.

Dukkha: Pain or suffering.

Gayatri Mantra: 18 syllable mantra devoted to God in the form of the sun, inspiring the awakening of higher consciousness and the removal of ignorance. This is one of the most famous, long-lived mantras in India, chanted since Vedic times.

Go (or gau): Cow, considered worthy of veneration; goshala: cow shed.

Gopi: shepherdess, devotee of Krishna.

Govinda: "Cow-herder," one of the many names for Lord Krishna.

Guna: Nature or quality, as described in the *Bhagavad Gita*, refers to the three qualities of matter or energy that make up the phenomenal world. These are sattva: purity or goodness, rajas: restlessness or passion, and tamas: inertia or ignorance. One who is liberated has transcended these qualities and remains indifferent to their appearance in his/her life.

Guru: Dispeller of darkness (Gu: darkness, Ru: light). One who through the achievement of liberation naturally transmits that state to others. Initiating worthy disciples, the guru is considered to be the only source of true progress on the path of yoga.

Guru-bhakti: Devotion to the guru. By focusing thoughts on the guru, one achieves a similar state of consciousness.

Guru Purnima: A celebration in honor of one's guru or teacher, in India traditionally held on the full moon in July.

Hatha Yoga: The primarily physical system of integrating the body and opening doors to higher consciousness, Hatha Yoga utilizes asana and pranayama to achieve balance in the body.

Hatha Yoga Pradipika: Light on Hatha Yoga, a widely used text written in the 14th century by Svatmarama Yogin, who described key hatha yoga and esoteric practices in 350-400 verses, enlarged and commented upon by other yogis and hatha yoga adepts. Bapuji's commentary on the HYP has been edited and further elaborated by Yogeshwar Muni (see suggested reading.)

Japa: The repetition of a mantra or holy name. Can be sung, chanted out loud, or repeated in silence.

Jnana: Pursuit of wisdom and knowledge, especially direct perception of reality, considered one of the paths of yoga: or jnana yoga.

Kali Yuga: This current age, characterized by an absence of moral and ethical values, lasting several hundred thousand years.

Kama: Desire or pleasure.

Karma Yoga: The yoga of action. In its ideal form, actions are to be performed without regard for their results.

Khechari Mudra: Higher practice of sahaj yoga, in which the tongue becomes elongated and gradually penetrates the upper portion of the soft palate, drawing forth a nectar-like substance. Capable of preventing disease, aging, and even death, this nectar is responsible for the gradual formation of the divine body.

Kirtan: Singing songs or hymns in praise of God.

Krishna: Incarnation of Lord Vishnu and worshipped in the Vaishnava tradition, variously known as flute player, cowherd god, Lord of the Dance. Attractive to gopis, Krishna is immortalized in the Bhagavad Gita.

Kriya: A yogic action usually undertaken for the purpose of purification; can also refer to the activities that result from the awakened kundalini energy. Many kriyas arise spontaneously after long practice of yoga.

Kumbhaka: Breath retention or holding that raises the threshold of prana within the body, leading to higher states of consciousness. Sahita kumbhaka is associated with the inhalation or exhalation and gathers the kundalini at the base of the spine, while kevala kumbhaka, an advanced form, thrusts the kundalini energy upward toward the crown.

Kundalini: Serpent power, or evolutionary energy that lies coiled like a serpent, dormant at the base of the spine, waiting to be awakened through spiritual practice. An extraordinarily powerful force, Kundalini must be systematically and carefully awakened and nurtured. The movement of this psycho-spiritual energy along the central axis of the spinal canal effects an extraordinary release of energy and transformation in consciousness, considered the supreme goal of yoga.

Lakulish: Lord or wielder of a club, the founder of the Pashupat sect, he lived and taught between 1st and 2nd centuries CE and upon his Mahasamadhi, merged into the linga while his disciples sat in meditation. That linga is now situated in the Temple of Kayavarohan where Lakulish is worshipped as an incarnation of Lord Shiva.

Laxmi (also Lakshmi): Goddess of fortune and wealth.

Laya yoga: Yoga of meditative absorption or transcendental awareness.

Linga (also lingam): A mark or sign that relates to higher powers/creativity. Tubular-shaped object of worship; can also denote the phallus or cosmic principle of creation.

Mahasamadhi: Great or highest absorption in oneness, Mahasamadhi refers to the final meditation of the saint or yogi, in which he effortlessly leaves his body and dwells in higher consciousness.

Mala: Garland or string of sacred beads used for mantra recitation.

Mandir: Temple or dwelling place.

Mantra: Sound that transcends thought; series of Sanskrit syllables offered as prayer or invocation that embody and convey the divine energies through the sounds.

Marga: (Also Marg), Path or way. Can refer to bhakti marga, path of devotion, nivritti marga (path of cessation or renunciation), etc.

Maya: Illusion or play of the Lord.

Mitahar: Moderation in diet, one of the yogic practices.

Moksha: Liberation, shift in consciousness in which one transcends duality and the mind dissolves into oneness with God.

Mudra: Seal or bodily posture that regulates the flow of prana. Also refers to gestures and hand movements activated through awakened kundalini that discharge energy or remove blockages to deeper practice.

Nada (Nad): Primordial sound that originates within and can be experienced in deep meditation. Anahat Nad: sounds (or song) arising from the heart center resulting from intense focus and inner concentration.

Nadi: Channel of energy.

Narayan: "Where man lives" one of the many names given to Lord Vishnu.

Nirbija: Seedless, refers to meditation without thought.

Nirodha: (also Narodha), cessation, restraint, control.

Niyama: Minor restraint or inner practice fostering one's spiritual focus, outlined in Patanjali's Yoga Sutras and consisting of purity, contentment, austerity, study of sacred texts, and surrender to God.

Patanjali: Yogi and author of the greatest treatise on the Eight-fold Path of yoga, entitled the *Yoga Sutras*, lived approximately 200 CE.

Prakriti: Nature, Creation, which is visible or manifest, as opposed to Purusha, which is invisible and unmanifest.

Prana: "Breath of Life," Life force, subtle energy that animates and sustains the body.

Pranam: Placing two hands together in front of the heart (or face) in a gesture of respect and love. Dandva or Full pranams: Prostration, bowing on the floor or lying outstretched with an attitude of reverence.

Pranayama: Breath control, series of breathing practices that help control one's thoughts and purify the body.

Prasad: Serenity or grace, often used in the sense of a gift, as in Guru Prasad: gift of the Guru.

Pratyahara: Withdrawal of the sense organs from their outward focus so that one concentrates inwardly; the fifth practice of Patanjali's Eight-fold Path.

Puja: Worship of one's chosen deity.

Purusha: Pure Spirit or consciousness, also referred to as the Atman.

Raja Yoga: Royal yoga: focusing the mind through meditation.

Sabij: With seed, refers to meditation focused in thought.

Sadguru: True teacher or guru, one who has attained Self-realization.

Sadhana: Spiritual path or practice that leads to union with God.

Sadhak: Spiritual practitioner or adept.

Sadhu: A saintly person who's renounced the world and wanders from place to place on holy pilgrimage.

Sahaj: Innate, natural, or spontaneous. Sahaj Yoga: Natural yoga, done spontaneously according to inner dictates arising from practice.

Samadhi: Transcendent ecstasy, in which there is total absorption in the object of meditation. Samadhi has many levels but ultimately leads to moksha or liberation.

Sanatana dharma: Eternal truth, eternal religion.

Sannyasi (also Sanyasi): One who has taken the vows of renunciation or sannyas, often referred to as "Swami."

Satsanga: In the company of truth. Often refers to an assembly or gathering with discourse, chanting of mantra, and reflection on teachings of the saints.

Satya: Truthfulness.

Seva: Selfless service.

Shakti: Power, force, divine energy.

Shaktipat: Descent of Power, the transmission of shakti or energy that occurs through contact with a guru or holy person. Often occurs in a ceremony of initiation (diksha.)

Shiva: Third deity of the Hindu triad, responsible for death, destruction, and transformation. He is seen as the destroyer of ignorance and the originator of yoga.

Shraddha: Faith.

Shuddhi: Purity or purification.

Siddha: An adept, one who has become accomplished in yoga and gained various spiritual powers or abilities.

Siddhi: Accomplishment, success. Also spiritual powers arising from yogic practice, often considered miraculous or paranormal in nature.

Sushumna (also Shushumna): Subtle nerve channel within the spinal column through which the awakened kundalini rises; it is the pathway to transcendental experience.

Swadhyaya: Self-study, important for integration of knowledge, devotion, and yoga.

Tapas: Burning or glow. Ascetic practices are said to burn up karma and impurities.

Tirtha: Pilgrimage site or center.

Urdvaretas: A spiritual process resulting from the practice of celibacy, in which the sexual fluid is reversed and flows upward, feeding the higher centers and creating an illuminated, saintly being.

Upanishads: "Sitting near," refers to key mystical teachings summarized at the end of the Vedas.

Upvas: "Sitting or dwelling near," referring to fasting. Fasting, one draws closer to God.

Vandana: Ceremony of worship, in the yogic tradition includes offering gifts of fruit, money, or other necessities to the guru in thanks for blessings, guidance received.

Vedas: Revealed wisdom. Specifically refers to the four ancient scriptures upon which Hinduism is based.

Vishnu: Second deity of the Hindu triad, Vishnu is considered the sustainer of life and is most frequently worshipped in his incarnations as Krishna or Ram.

Vritti: Activity, fluctuation of consciousness.

Yajna: Sacrifice, worship.

Yama: Restraint, spiritual discipline, as outlined in Patanjali's *Yoga Sutras* to include celibacy, non-stealing, non-grasping, non-lying (or truth telling,) and nonviolence.

Yoga: "Yoke," Union. Spiritual disciplines leading to Self-realization or enlightenment.

SUGGESTED READING

Baxter, Christopher (Devanand), *Kripalu Hatha Yoga*, Kripalu Center, 1998.

Cope, Stephen, *Yoga and the Quest for the True Self*, Bantam, NY, 2000.

Cope, Stephen, Ed., *Will Yoga and Meditation Really Change my Life? A Kripalu Book*, Storey Publishing, North Adams, MA, 2003.

Desai, Yogi Amrit, *Amrit Yoga and the Yoga Sutras*, Yoga Network International, Sumneytown, PA 2002

Desai, Yogi Amrit, *Amrit Yoga: Explore, Expand, and Experience the Spiritual Depth of Yoga*, Yoga Network, PA, 1999.

Faulds, Richard (Shobhan), *Kripalu Yoga: A Guide to Practice on and off the Mat*, Bantam, NY, 2005.

Hartranft, Chip, Ed., *The Yoga Sutras of Patanjali, A New Translation and Commentary*, Shambhala Classics, Boston, 2003.

Muktibodhananda, Swami, commentator, *Hatha Yoga Pradipika, Light on Hatha Yoga*, Yoga Publications Trust, Munger, Bihar, India, 2000.

Muni, Swami Rajarshi, *Yoga: The Ultimate Spiritual Path*, Llewellyn Publications, St. Paul, Minnesota, 2001.

Muni, Swami Rajarshi, *Infinite Grace: The Story of my Spiritual Lineage*, Life Mission Publications, Vadodara, Gujarat, India, 2001.

Muni, Yogeshwar (Charles Berner), editor and translator, *Revealing the Secret, a commentary on the Small burning Lamp of Sun-Moon Yoga (Hathayoga Pradipika)* by Yogacharya Kripalvananda, Merimbula, Australia, 2002.

Pradhan, V.G., Translator, *Jnaneshvari (Bhagavad Gita)* Vols. I and II, George Allen and Unwin, Ltd., London, 1967.

Sargeant, Winthrop, Translator, *The Bhagavad Gita*, with foreword by Christopher Chapple, State University of New York Press, Albany, 1994.

CONTACT LIST

This is a very partial list of Kripalu Yoga and sahaj yoga practitioners in Bapuji's tradition. Please consult KYTA (listed under Kripalu Center) for more extensive information on teachers and centers worldwide.

Christopher Baxter
(Devanand)
www.atmayoga.com
christopher@atmayoga.com
904-687-8482

H. C. Berner
(Yogeshwar Muni)
1/34 Imlay Street
Merimbula, NSW 2548
Australia

Leela Bruner
Power of Love Temple
22378 Mudhollow Road
Council Bluffs, IA 51503
712-545-3287
LeelaB@novia.net and/or
PowerofLoveTemple@yahoo.com

Hare Sharana (Harry) Zandler
833 Buck Lane
Haverford, PA 19041
610-642-5621

Kripalu Center
for Yoga and Health
PO Box 793
Lenox, MA 01240-0793
1-800-741-7353 (Reservations)
www.kripalu.org

For information on Kripalu Yoga
Teachers Association (KYTA) contact:
www.kripalu.com/yogateachers.html.

For Seva or study
opportunities in
India contact:
Ma Indukanta Udasin
and Sanat Shivdas
C/o Agni
Darunagar Society
Opposite Lakulish Temple
Kayavarohan, 391220
District Vadodara, India
www.jaibhagwan.com

Swami Rajarshi Muni
C/o LIFE MISSION Organization
RBG Complex
Vadodara-390018, Gujarat, India
www.lifemission.org

Yogi Amrit Desai
Amrit Yoga Institute
PO Box 5340
Salt Springs, FL 32134
352-685-3001
352-685-3002 (Fax)
www.amrityoga.org

Atma Jo Ann Levitt, MA, RN, Certified Healing Touch practitioner and Kripalu Yoga instructor, is a writer, counselor, and lecturer who compiled and edited *Pilgrim of Love*. A Senior Kripalu faculty member for thirty years, Atma designed and developed many of Kripalu's personal growth programs and helped put its transformational technologies on the map. Atma also works as an RN and Healing Touch practitioner at Canyon Ranch in the Berkshires. In addition to *Pilgrim of Love*, she has written the *Kripalu Cookbook, Sounds of the Sacred: Chants of Love and Prayer*, and with her brother and sister, *Sibling Revelry: 8 Steps to Successful Adult Sibling Relationships*.

Bapuji with water pot